D1615618

9/2208300

AN IRISH-AMERICAN ODYSSEY

An Irish-American Odyssey

THE REMARKABLE

RISE OF THE

O'SHAUGHNESSY

BROTHERS

Colum Kenny

University of Missouri Press   Columbia

Copyright © 2014 by

The Curators of the University of Missouri

University of Missouri Press, Columbia, Missouri 65201

Printed and bound in the United States of America

All rights reserved

5   4   3   2   1   18   17   16   15   14

Cataloging-in-Publication data available from the Library of Congress

ISBN 978-0-8262-2024-0

This paper meets the requirements of the

American National Standard for Permanence of Paper

for Printed Library Materials, Z39.48, 1984.

Jacket design: Kristie Lee

Design and composition: Mindy Basinger Hill

Typeface: Arno Pro

FOR MY SONS *Oisín, Conor, and Sam*

Contents

Preface

THE STORY OF THE O'SHAUGHNESSYS in Missouri, Chicago, New York, and Ireland between 1860 and 1950 is a remarkable one. They were the children of an impoverished immigrant who had fled famine and of his Irish-American wife. Their experiences illuminate the gradual assimilation of immigrants and their descendants into American society and particularly into American arts, media, and public life in the O'Shaughnessys' case.

James O'Shaughnessy of Missouri first came to my notice when I was writing a short biography of Kevin J. Kenny, who was the founder of Ireland's earliest full-service advertising agency and my grandfather. It emerged that Kevin had met James in Dublin on several occasions in the 1920s. Irish admen of the time were so impressed by the energetic and genial Irish-American that they appointed him the honorary patron of their then-new national association of advertising agencies.

Time magazine called James "the best in the business" of advertising. He had been earlier lauded as a star reporter at the *Chicago Tribune*. His brother Thomas was also highly regarded; Thomas became the leading Gaelic Revival artist in America and a promoter of Italian-American heritage. He campaigned successfully to have Columbus Day made a public holiday. Martin O'Shaughnessy was captain of the University of Notre Dame's first official basketball team, and Frank was later the first graduate of Notre Dame to be invited to deliver its annual commencement address. Among distinguished individuals who have also delivered that address has been President Barack Obama. And like Obama, both Frank and his brother John practiced as attorneys in Illinois. For his part, among his clients John represented the alleged victim in a notorious "white slave trade" case. The three O'Shaughnessy sisters led quieter lives.

James and Francis played important roles in helping to found and maintain Chicago's Irish Fellowship Club, still today a recognized part of Irish-American life, and some members of the family were active in politics.

This is a tale of dedication, hardship, struggle, and opportunities, from Keytesville through Cook County to Manhattan. It includes a striking Irish-Missouri ghost story and links this to the family's origins among the people of Kiltartan, County Galway, whose customs and language inspired both the playwright Augusta Gregory and the poet W. B. Yeats. From the medieval tower that he occupied at Ballylee, Yeats looked out across the townland in Galway from which the father of these Irish-Americans had emigrated. By a quirk of fate James O'Shaughnessy got to review for the *Chicago Tribune* Gregory's Abbey Theatre production of the controversial *Playboy of the Western World.*

The challenges of sustaining a hyphenated identity when settled in America, for so many immigrants and their children, are explored through the lens of the O'Shaughnessy family's experiences. These experiences are viewed against the backdrop of contemporary social and political developments in the United States. Included is an account of Irish premier W. T. Cosgrave's visit to the Irish Fellowship Club, Chicago, in 1928 and his meeting with the city's controversial mayor, "Big Bill" Thompson.

I hope to engage readers of any ethnic origin anywhere who have a personal or intellectual interest in the relationship between immigrants, their offspring, and their destination societies. Migration is an international phenomenon, no less so today than in earlier centuries, and the aspirations of immigrants and their children now are as worthy as those of the O'Shaughnessys in Missouri, Illinois and New York. At the outset one strives to survive, and after that to eke out at least a tolerable existence in order to create fresh opportunities. The first generation of this family of O'Shaughnessys seized its chances.

I also intend to highlight activities of members of the family that add to our understanding of the particular fields in which they worked. This is so especially in respect to Thomas O'Shaughnessy's contribution to the traditions of American and Irish art, and to James O'Shaughnessy's journalism and advertising practices, which will shed light on the early history of the American Association of Advertising Agencies.

Biography does not have to be persistently linear, and I have adopted a textured approach that moves from individual events to the collective and social contexts in order to locate the O'Shaughnessys and their achievements in a broader landscape. This allows readers who have an interest in art, advertising, journalism, Irish studies, or politics to assess more fully than would a purely chronological approach the significance of contributions made in those areas by any single O'Shaughnessy — while not losing sight of the overarching familial and other networks. And it allows people who are interested principally in the story of an immigrant family to see its members in a wider way. A focus on the collective and on its relationship to a series of events is especially suitable for a study such as this because surviving source materials relating to each person are quite limited. While the life of every O'Shaughnessy brother is seen to have had its own unique and engaging characteristics the rise of the family as a whole, emerging into public view, reflects the broader experiences of generations of immigrants in the United States.

Acknowledgments

VARIOUS ARCHIVISTS, LIBRARIANS, AND OTHERS assisted me in the course of my research, and I am indebted to them all. The State Historical Society of Missouri, Gary Cox of the archive department of the University of Missouri, and Robert Werle of the Christian Brothers of the Midwest archive helped me to piece together early details of the O'Shaughnessy family as it moved a number of times before settling in St. Joseph, Missouri, in the 1880s. In St. Joseph, James O'Shaughnessy secured his first job in the media. Thomas, it is said, had already made his first stained glass window.

Marsha Appel and Janie Hughes at the New York headquarters of the 4A's (as the American Association of Advertising Agencies has long been known) helpfully located and scanned records that were of assistance in exploring the early history of the association and its external relationships under James. These too rarely used sources include a compilation of information about the genesis of the association as well as a report prepared in 1969 by Richard Turnbull of the 4A's that refers to the early challenge of marshaling the forces of advertising in the national interest and as part of the war effort. During my preparation of this book, I had the pleasure of being invited to visit the headquarters of the 4A's on the Avenue of the Americas in Manhattan, where I gave a presentation on James O'Shaughnessy to employees of the organization of which he was the first chief executive. I also welcomed an opportunity in 2013 to deliver and discuss a paper about James O'Shaughnessy at the Joint Journalism and Media History Conference of the American Journalism Historians Association and the Association for Education in Journalism and Mass Communication, in New York City.

My faculty colleagues at Dublin City University provided useful feedback when I shared with them early research for this volume. The cost of purchasing illustrations for this book received financial support from the Faculty of Humanities and Social Sciences Book Publication Scheme at Dublin City University.

Others who have helped with research include the archivists at David M. Rubenstein Rare Book and Manuscript Library, Duke University, North Carolina, and those at the University of Illinois Urbana-Champaign, Agricultural Communications Documentation Center. The Rubenstein Library holds James O'Shaughnessy Papers relating to the period 1888-1936 as well as records of the American Association of Advertising Agencies, 1918-1998.

In addition to those mentioned above, I acknowledge the assistance of Bray Public Library, County Wicklow; the British Library, London; Chicago History Museum; Clay County Museum and Historical Society, Liberty, Missouri; the library of Dublin City University; the Episcopal Diocese of Chicago; the Irish Fellowship Club; the Irish Museum of Modern Art; the Kiltartan Gregory Museum, County Galway; the Library of Congress; the National Archives of Ireland; the National Library of Ireland; Old St. Patrick's Church, Chicago; the Roman Catholic Diocese of Springfield, Illinois; the Royal Irish Academy; the Society of King's Inns, Dublin; Trinity College Dublin. I thank, too, the Association of Advertisers in Ireland, the Institute of Advertising Practitioners in Ireland, Anne-Marie Angelo, Sharon Bladholm, Diarmuid P. Breathnach, Dr Patrick Brereton, Laura Coyle, Richard Digby-Junger, Mary de Lourdes Fahy, Terry Farmer, Prof. John Ferré of the University of Louisville, Allan Holtz, Bob Kolatorowicz, Prof. Joe Lee of Glucksman Ireland House, NYU; Michele Levandoski, Kris Lipkowski, Mike Lizonitz, Patricia Macken, Jim McLaughlin, Prof. John Nerone of the University of Illinois, David O'Callaghan, Thomas J. O'Gorman of Chicago, Brigid O'Shaughnessy and her husband, Mike Luxem, of Illinois, Marianne and her late husband, Michael O'Shaughnessy, sometime of New Mexico, Rory O'Shaughnessy of County Galway, Crystal and Leland Payton of Missouri, Anne Sears of Plano, Illinois, Colman Shaughnessy of Kiltartan, Newland Smith, Colin Smythe, Kathy Taylor, and J. H. Waters of Illinois. I am of course grateful also to Gary Kass, Sara Davis, and others at the University of Missouri Press, for their enthusiasm and encouragement. My wife, Catherine Curran, and my sons, Oisín, Conor, and Sam each deserves a special word of appreciation.

AN IRISH-AMERICAN ODYSSEY

ONE   Missouri Settlers

JAMES SHAUGHNESSY WAS AN ORPHAN when he immigrated to the United States. A boy setting foot on American soil for the first time, he had grown up in one of very many Irish rural communities devastated by a great famine during the 1840s.

James, the future father of adman and journalist James O'Shaughnessy and artist Thomas O'Shaughnessy, fled hunger and the disease that took his parents. Of all the Irish entering the United States between 1820 and 1900, "nearly one third thronged into the country in the eight short years from 1847 to 1854 — a grim tribute to the rigours of the famine."[1] Between 1845 and 1854 almost one and a half million Irish immigrants arrived in the United States, and James was among them.[2]

James Shaughnessy found shelter first in New England. His descendants believe that he worked for a farmer near Milford, Massachusetts, and in local shoe factories. Many Irish were employed around Milford, where there was a burgeoning boot- and shoe-manufacturing industry. One of these was a certain Thomas Shaughnessy, a "boot bottomer," who appears to have been the brother of James.[3] Neither James nor his brothers who followed him to America then used the Gaelic prefix "O" before their family name. Their children would later adopt it, proud of an ancient Gaelic heritage.

Settlers

It was common for Irish immigrants to stay along the eastern seaboard of the United States. But James, Thomas, and their brother John, who had been born in 1827, proved to be adventurous. They went west and made a new life for themselves as settlers in Missouri, a state that covers about twice the area of Ireland. Just how remote it was then is evident from the memoir of John Joseph Hogan, an Irish priest with whom the family became well acquainted and who appears to have been the first Catholic pastor to settle long-term in

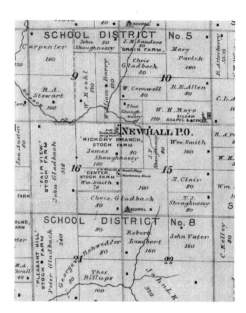

Shaughnessy and other lands around Newhall, Salt Creek, Chariton County, MO. *Plat Book of Chariton County, Missouri* (1897), p. 28 (T.55N, Salt Creek R. 19W).

northern Missouri. Hogan, when later a bishop, recalled having consulted shipping agents in Ireland in 1848, who advised him that "as the American railways had been built only as far west as the western boundaries of New York and Pennsylvania, the journey westward to St. Louis [in Missouri], about 1,000 miles, was too great to be attempted by uncertain ways, such as stagecoaches and sailing on lakes and rivers."[4] The Mississippi River, however, was navigable by steamboat, and in December 1848, Hogan spent eight days aboard such a vessel traveling from New Orleans to St. Louis.

Many Irish immigrants who went west actually fared better than the majority of those who stayed on the East Coast. By 1870 a large influx of Irish and Germans had helped to make Missouri the sixth most populated state in the Union. Its principal city of St. Louis, situated on the western bank of the Mississippi, became cosmopolitan. Travelers entered St. Louis by disembarking at the city's busy landing point, of which an inviting sketch was published back east in 1857.[5]

James Shaughnessy went west and settled in northern Missouri at this time. He subsequently opened a shoe store in Keytesville, the Chariton County seat. It was here, about 1861, that he was naturalized as a US citizen. Shortly afterward his brothers John and Thomas joined him and began

Thomas Shaughnessy,
immigrant from Newhall,
Co. Galway. Courtesy Brigid
O'Shaughnessy, Illinois.

farming tracts of land in that county, at Salt Creek Township, not far from
Keytesville. Deer were then abundant in the district.[6] The family named its
principal new homestead "Newhall," thus recalling a townland in the small
Irish district of Kiltartan in County Galway, from which these brothers
had emigrated. Their names appear on Missouri maps from 1876 onward,
designating ownership of parcels of land near Newhall.[7]

Emigrant aid societies frequently advised the Irish to leave overcrowded
eastern seaports for places where labor was more in demand. However, census data clearly demonstrate that in purchasing farmland the Shaughnessys
were an exception to the urban rule: "In 1870, for instance, only 14.6 per
cent of Irish immigrants were engaged in agricultural pursuits, compared
with 54.1 per cent of native-born Americans and nearly 23 per cent of all
foreign-born persons."[8]

Irish immigrants in the nineteenth century usually came from farming backgrounds, but most settled in towns in America. Few had money with which to buy land. Some also disliked the distances between farmhouses in the United States, which were greater than those between homes in Ireland, finding that such distances exacerbated any loneliness or sense of isolation.

Yet the fact that even the poorest immigrants were living in a society that was expanding and becoming wealthier gave them hope. Opportunities continued to beckon. In 1985, in his magisterial work *Emigrants and Exiles* that includes vivid descriptions of the experience of Irish people crossing the Atlantic to America, Kerby A. Miller, a professor of history at the University of Missouri, pointed out that "between 1840 and 1900 — while Ireland's population shrank from 8.2 million to only 4.5 million — that of the United States soared [from 17.1m] to 76 million."[9]

The Mulhollands

Another family of Irish origins, that of James and Ann Mulholland, facilitated the settlement of James Shaughnessy and his brothers in Missouri. This was not least because James married their daughter Catherine and acquired land from them. His descendants believe that he met her when going from house to house selling shoes.

About 1850, James Mulholland had been living in Indiana and was described that year in the federal census as a "Boss on Public Works." Before that he had worked on the construction of the Erie Canal in New York. But he was best known as "one of Chicago's pioneer citizens who with Ossian Guthrie helped in building the Illinois and Michigan canal."[10] Many Irish emigrants got jobs on these projects and went on to labor on the construction of railroads. Itinerant workmen who married often lived with their families in makeshift camps and huts.

Mulholland also helped to construct the railroad across northern Missouri, running two hundred miles from Hannibal on the west bank of the Mississippi River facing Illinois — via Chillicothe — to St. Joseph on the east bank of the Missouri River facing Kansas. The train replaced the uncomfortable four-horse stagecoaches that had taken forty-eight hours to make the same journey. The railroad project began in 1857 and ended in February

1859. During 1858 two rival gangs of Irish railroaders, those of contractor Mulholland and contractor Murphy, clashed. Fighting was, depending on how one viewed it, an occupational hazard or a recreational activity of the gangs building America's railroad network.[11]

Although drawn to Missouri by the Hannibal to St. Joseph Railroad project, James Mulholland began to buy tracts of land in Clark and Salt Creek Townships in Chariton County, southeast of Chillicothe. In March 1857, for example, he purchased some property from James Demsey, an Irishman who in 1841 had acquired a cabin from the first settler in Salt Creek Township and had transformed it into a country tavern "which became a favorite stopping place."[12] By 1860, then in his fifties and perhaps grown tired of managing railroad gangs, James Mulholland was described in the federal census simply as a "farmer," living in Clark Township with his wife, four children, two laborers, and a domestic servant who had three children of her own.

Pioneering Pastor

As one of a small number of Catholic families in northern Missouri, the Mulhollands soon got to know Fr. John Hogan. Hogan had come to America from Limerick in Ireland, where in his youth he heard Daniel O'Connell address great crowds. O'Connell was the foremost Irish political leader of the early to mid-nineteenth century and a champion of the oppressed. Hogan hoped to find a place where poor Catholic immigrants to the United States might settle as a community in Missouri, but he was informed when he began to look for a suitable location that government-owned land in the north of the state had all been sold, or given away to railroad companies, thus making its purchase too costly for people as impoverished as were most Catholic emigrants from Ireland. Hogan ranged far and wide in Missouri ministering to Irish women who were domestic servants and to men who worked on the railroads. In his vivid account of those years, he wrote that Irish immigrants could not find work as hired hands on farms "in competition with slave labor." He himself had prepared "poor negroes" for First Communion and was clearly shocked to see the way in which slaves were transported by river-boat in northern Missouri:

The night was very hot. Mosquitoes buzzed around in swarms, and were unrelenting in their attacks, so that sleep was impossible . . . . The darkies of whom there were about fifty on board, all athletic men, suffered many cruel hardships. Their keepers, a few armed men, held them chained together in squads, so as to hinder them from getting away at landing places. At night, formed into line, shoulder to shoulder, their faces turned one way, manacled with iron hand-cuffs man to man, they were made to lie down on their backs, on the boiler deck of the boat, without pillow, mattress, or covering — a position they could not change for one instant during the whole night, not even so much as to lie on one side. The groans of the poor fellows, as they clanked their manacled hands against the deck, or dragged and slashed in pain their booted heels on the rough boards on which they lay, were truly heart-rending. They were accused of no crime, were torn away without a minute's notice from their homes, husbands separated from wives and children, sons separated from parents, brothers and sisters. All were forced to leave dear friends and loved scenes behind them. Love of money caused it all.[13]

Hogan was based in Chillicothe, from which he traveled on demanding journeys to serve his dispersed flock. A description of another hardy pastor in Missouri recalls how, similarly, "Father James Powers had much rough pioneer work to do, being often obliged to travel great distances, his journeys being made on a little pony, and frequently he would be compelled to swim all the little streams."[14]

Hogan's fascinating account of his own early days in Missouri, recently republished, indicates what it was like for those who lived there. He discovered no land in northern Missouri that was both suitable and affordable for an Irish settlement but did begin to create such a settlement in the Ozark Mountains of southern Missouri. His efforts were ultimately frustrated, apparently in large part by the disruption of civil war. The area of natural beauty that he chose for his project in the Ozarks was to remain sparsely populated, but his ambitions are reflected in its being known even today as the "Irish Wilderness." His pioneering attempts predated those of the Irish Catholic Colonization Society of America, which from 1878 to 1891, "made a bold effort to locate the slum dwellers on the prairies of the west."[15]

Catherine Shaughnessy (née Mulholland)

One day in 1862, in northern Missouri, Hogan hurried to minister to one of his flock, Catherine Mulholland. She was the eldest daughter of Ann and James Mulholland, and the future mother of journalist and adman James O'Shaughnessy and his siblings. She was then extremely ill. Answering the sick call from Hickory Branch in Chariton County, Hogan took the train from Chillicothe for Brookfield, twenty-six miles distant. There he was met by a man on horseback who was leading a horse already saddled and bridled:

> We rode on, through the hours of the night, a journey of eighteen
> miles, in a southeasterly direction, across the several branches of Yellow
> Creek, through the timber and over the prairies, of Linn and Chariton
> counties, until we came to the Mulholland Place — the residence of
> James Mulholland — a whilom [former] railroad contractor, and at this
> time a well-to-do farmer, advantageously settled on some of the most
> productive land in fertile Missouri. Received politely and with welcome,
> I entered the elegant country mansion, and was led without delay into the
> presence of the most beloved member of the family — a young lady, faint
> and almost lifeless, over whose features and emaciated form a pallor like
> death had spread.

Hogan administered last rites to Catherine, aged just nineteen. Her mother said that their family physician, having consulted with other physicians in that part of the country, had given up hope for Catherine's recovery. But she added, pointedly, that a different kind of healer was available. What she had in mind brought Hogan face to face with the culture of an immigrant people still steeped in folklore and superstition in their "elegant country mansion." She said there was "an old man, living in this county, who has the reputation of having cured many by some charms or supernatural agency that he has, and he has sent me word, that if I would send for him he would cure my Catherine." Hogan vehemently opposed the involvement of this old man, whose significance will be considered later when discussing the family's Irish roots. Hogan dismissed him as part of "the snares and deceits of the devil." He urged the family instead to put its faith in God and persuaded them to take Catherine to see certain "eminent physicians" in St.

John Joseph Hogan, when a bishop in 1893. Cabinet card courtesy Crystal and Leland Payton, Lens & Pens Press.

Record of the marriage of James Shaughnessy and Catherine Mulholland, 12 March 1863, witnessed by Fr Hogan. From Book AB, p. 40, registers of Chariton County, Keytesville, MO.

Louis. Following a difficult journey and treatment that ostensibly included an operation, and against expectations, she recovered.[16]

Not long after this trauma, Catherine Mulholland married the immigrant James Shaughnessy, "a very worthy young man of that county" according to Hogan.[17] They wed on March 12, 1863, with Hogan performing the marriage ceremony.[18] The young couple decided to remain in Missouri, a fact that no doubt pleased Catherine's parents. In February 1864, Ann and James Mulholland sold James Shaughnessy "two hundred and forty acres more or less" for the sum of $2,000. The Mulhollands made their marks on the deed transferring this land, which suggests that they were illiterate.[19] During that same month Elizabeth, first child of Catherine and James, was born and baptized.

Fright and Alarm

Catherine became distressed after giving birth, and the family again sent for Hogan. His graphic descriptions convey not only the conditions of the time in such isolated places but also how religion and superstition continued to vie with one another even in a new world. Catherine's upset was all caused, he believed, by the remark of a friendly but "unwitted" neighboring woman, "who said to the mother after the infant's birth, its limbs were deformed, which was by no means the case":

> The young mother, from sudden fright and alarm for the safety of her
> child, lost her reason. For weeks she lay writhing in madness of the
> most violent and uncontrollable kind. Again, as on the several previous

occasions of alternating joy and sorrow, the pastor was anxiously sought. I found the dear child in one continuing paroxysm, ever requiring strong and tender hands to keep her in bed, and to prevent her from biting and lacerating her arms and shoulders, and from doing like injury to those around her. Every article of movable furniture had to be put out of the room to prevent what she had frequently attempted — jumping for and seizing whatever appurtenance she could see, wherewith to do violence to herself or those around her, who, in their sore pity had to watch at her bedside — a post of duty at which she would consentingly suffer no one but a favorite sister and her pastor. Again God's mercy was earnestly sought by the Holy Mass and prayers to restore the afflicted one to reason and health. And again, the same temptations as before had to be encountered and resisted. The Old Man, professing to have wonderful powers, but not from God, was again heard of. This time he sent word not only to loving parents, but also and especially to the sorrow-stricken husband [James Shaughnessy], to be allowed to restore the lady to health, which he promised to do if invited to make use of his profession. At this crisis I redoubled my prayers as well as my entreaties. To all I replied, that God's merciful and providential ways alone had to be followed, invoked, and confided in; and that no power but God's should be sought or admitted in the affairs and destinies of that truly Christian family.[20]

Hogan added that the family again followed his advice. Catherine recovered without benefit of "the old man." Her pastor was relieved that "the dear little infant, that had struggled for life, without the care of its mother, throughout the long storm, was received lovingly into the care and fondness of the maternal bosom." This new baby, Elizabeth, was known as "Lizzie." Catherine and James Shaughnessy went on to become the parents of seven more children by the year 1883. By a twist of fate Lizzie herself later died when giving birth. [21]

The physical difficulties of settlement in remote areas were exacerbated for the young couple by some unusual climatic and other circumstances in Chariton County. For example, following the marriage of Catherine and James Shaughnessy the winter of 1863–1864 was exceedingly cold. Much snow fell, and there was little growth in spring. Dry weather extended through the greater part of summer: "there was great drought, and vegetation became scarce. The crops of all kinds were light. During the latter part of summer and beginning of fall there was a severe form of dysentery, followed later in the season by typhoid fever."[22]

Worse than all that, however, were the ravages of civil war, which had greatly distressed parts of Missouri.

Civil War Terrors

Between 1861 and 1865 fratricidal conflict consumed the United States, and Missouri itself was bitterly divided. In 1864, less than twelve months before their first son, James, was born to Catherine and James, the county seat of Chariton County was attacked by irregular supporters of the Confederacy, and its seat of justice destroyed. This happened on September 20 that year when "the bushw[h]ackers under Todd, Threldkill and other desperate and dangerous characters.... vandals and iconoclasts" came into Keytesville and burned the courthouse, claiming that it was used as a place of rendezvous for the Union soldiers and militia. Judge Lucien Salisbury happened to be in the town and bravely intervened: "The judge prevailed upon them to permit him to take out the records. The leader of the band told him he would give him five minutes in which to get the records out of the building."[23]

Thus did the records of the marriage and first land purchases of James Shaughnessy survive. Having fled a terrible famine in Ireland, he and his brothers now found themselves embroiled in a dreadful civil war, one in which dangers came not just from the armies of both sides but from irregular gangs. Their pastor John Hogan later described the disturbances of those days, when the Shaughnessys and others found they were displaced. He wrote, "It was now the autumn of 1864, the fourth year of the war. The wildest terror overspread North Missouri. Bushwhackers and guerrillas were everywhere. Murders, robberies and burnings were of daily occurrence. And above all places, Chariton County was the theater of dark and atrocious crimes." During 1864, the Mulhollands and Shaughnessys decided to abandon their farms in Chariton County for the time being and to move to less isolated areas. Hogan kept in touch with them during their troubles, not least concerning a remarkable haunting that involved James Shaughnessy's brother John in particular. Dozens of local people claimed to have witnessed it. James himself vouched for the veracity of the ghost story. Its details are extraordinary, and it will be considered later within the context of the family's roots in rural Ireland.[24]

Birth of James Junior

On July 10, 1865, just three months after the Civil War ended, Catherine Shaughnessy gave birth to her second child and first son at St. Catharine, Missouri.[25] This boy was the future journalist and adman, James O'Shaughnessy.

To this baby's parents and uncles, poor immigrants from the west of Ireland, Missouri appeared very attractive. In 1869 the Mulhollands sold some of their land to his uncle, John, just as they had earlier sold land to his father, James. [26] At this time, Chariton County was considered to be "one of the best farming counties in the state," even if Salt Creek was not its most productive stretch.[27] It was said that "the ease with which the soil is cultivated is an important item to the farmer. One man with a team can tend from forty to sixty acres of corn. There is comparatively little wasteland in the county." Portions that were not well adapted to the cultivation and growth of wheat, corn, and other cereals were best for grazing lands. This same observer of 1883 thought that the county presented to the first settlers an easy task in subduing wild land: "The farms of Chariton county are generally large, unbroken by sloughs, but have some obstructions such as stumps and boulders, but they are excellently well cultivated." The best timber in the state was thought to be in Chariton: "Detached groves, both natural and artificial, are found at many places throughout the county, which are not only ornamental, in that they vary the monotony, but are very useful in that they have a very important bearing on the climate."[28]

Hogan may have baptized James soon after the child was born in 1865. The family's pastor certainly found himself embroiled in controversy by the autumn of that year. Missouri's Radical party wished to confer civil rights on blacks and to consolidate the Union's victory in the Civil War by passing a range of measures that included a controversial requirement that priests, ministers, and others take a loyalty oath. The Roman Catholic Church objected in principle to the Missouri Test-Oath, on the grounds that it interfered with the free exercise of religion. Among those who defied the requirement and found themselves indicted was Hogan, who had actually supported the Union and who — unlike very many on both sides in

Missouri — had long opposed slavery. For one thing, Hogan was aware that poor Irish immigrants sometimes found themselves undercut in the market for farm workers by black slave labor. For another, he had been influenced by the high ideals of the Irish political leader Daniel O'Connell, whom he had once heard speak in Ireland and who also — as President Barack Obama has pointed out more than once — inspired Frederick Douglass.[29] As regards the oath of loyalty, such oaths had long been contentious in Ireland, where they were widely regarded as a weapon of persecution used by the Protestant establishment to impose its will on a largely Catholic people.

The "enormities" of the new test in Missouri rankled lay as well as clerical Catholics. Its lay opponents included James Shields, a renowned general and judge with whom James Shaughnessy was to become well acquainted. By late 1866, Shields (1810–1879) was living in Carroll County, about forty miles from Chillicothe, and he made there a number of speeches on the political issues of his day, including the Test-Oath. Shields, a Democrat who served three states successively as their senator, had been born in County Tyrone, Ireland. In October 1866 Hogan baptized and acted as godfather to the general's son, James. In 1867 the US Supreme Court struck down the Missouri Test, and the charges against Hogan and others were dismissed.[30]

A Rural Education

With the return of peace following years of war and disorder, and despite controversy over the Missouri Test, Roman Catholics in the state resumed normal activities in the educational and religious spheres. Before the outbreak of hostilities, the De La Salle Brothers had established a school or "college" at St. Joseph. During the war soldiers occupied it as a barracks, but it reopened in 1865. In 1868 the northwestern portion of the state, from St. Joseph east to the Chariton River, was declared a separate Catholic diocese. This was notwithstanding the fact that its borders encompassed only about six hundred Catholic families, including the Shaughnessys. Hogan, friend of the Mulholland and Shaughnessy families, was thereupon consecrated as the diocesan bishop at St. Joseph. In that capacity, the following year, he sailed to Europe and attended the First Vatican Council in Rome.[31] When Hogan had set out on his mission in 1857 there were very few Catholics and not a single Catholic chapel in the whole of northern Missouri, and Catholics who lived there were loathe to attract the attention or hostility of

Protestant neighbors by building one. Twenty years later the Shaughnessys became members of the congregation of St. Joseph's Catholic Church in Salt Creek Township, Chariton County. One of a number of new chapels in Hogan's diocese, this was a frame building that had cost $1,000 to construct. By 1883 it was said to have one hundred communicants.[32]

Young James attended local parochial schools. Education was available but rudimentary, and the Shaughnessy children had to adjust to the consequences of their family moving home a number of times. Their parents retained their farm at Newhall but lived in towns not far away where their father supplemented any income from their land by selling shoes and making boots. They were resident in Keytesville when their daughter Anna was born on March 27, 1873.[33] One local paper informed its readers in 1876 that "Mr. James Shaughnessy, boot and shoe manufacturer," had removed from Howard County to the town of Moberly in Randolf.[34] If he had abandoned any notion that he might rely exclusively on farming to support him he was certainly not alone among Irish immigrants. Census figures indicate a decline by 1900 in the already relatively small proportion of Irish immigrants in the United States engaged in agriculture.[35]

During 1877 the Sisters of Loretto arrived in Moberly and founded St. Mary's Academy, a school for girls. The following year they opened a parochial school for boys in a two-room frame building. It was said later that Thomas O'Shaughnessy at the age of about fifteen made here for a local chapel his first stained glass window. If so, it was the beginning of a creative process that would reach its peak at Old St. Pat's Church in Chicago decades later. By 1880 his brother James, aged fifteen, had left school and was working as a "clerk in store" in Moberly, perhaps in the shoe shop run by his father. James later wrote that he began his career writing advertisements for his father's retail shoe store in a small town in Missouri. His brother John Patrick attended school in Moberly from 1882 to 1886. John was to become an attorney.[36]

General James Shields

If the boys received a general education in local schools, they received a political education from their father. James Shaughnessy took an active interest in civic developments, being, for example, one of the directors of

Moberly Public Schools from 1881 to 1884. He had earlier also made the acquaintanceship of General James Shields, who served Missouri as a railroad commissioner and as a member of its legislature from 1874 to 1879. In 1879 Shields was elected to represent Missouri in the US Senate. He died soon afterward.[37] James Senior played a role in Shields's funeral ceremonies at Moberly. Francis O'Shaughnessy would recall this honor, in a speech delivered thirty-five years later on behalf of the governor of Illinois at the dedication of a monument to Shields at Carrollton, Missouri. Francis then said that the acquaintanceship between his father and General Shields "grew to intimacy and it was a real, abiding affection." He added:

> One of my earliest recollections was my father's announcing in our home that General Shields had died. A few days later, when his remains were brought back from Ottawa, Iowa, which was the place of his death, to Carrollton, it became necessary to transfer them from the North Missouri Railroad to the Wabash Railroad at Moberly, where my father then lived. He was chairman of the delegation which, through the kindness of the gentlemen from Carrollton who had arrived in Moberly to escort the remains to the home of his bereaved widow, was allowed to act with them as a guard of honor. Behind the casket bearing the remains of this great jurist, statesman and soldier, my father walked along the dusty roads to the place of burial, and it is one of the recollections which is green in his memory.[38]

Moving to St. Joseph

Catherine and James Shaughnessy subsequently moved to St. Joseph, another and bigger Missouri settlement about 150 miles from Moberly. James did so "to obtain school facilities suitable to the advancing ages of his children."[39] He ran a shoe store there, too, first on Felix Street and then from 1889 on South Sixth Street — where he had "the nicest stock of Spring goods ever brought to the city," as he advertised it in the local newspaper. These advertisements also reveal that he continued not to display the Gaelic prefix "O" before his family name.[40] His sons began to find work in St. Joseph and were listed in a city directory as "sign painter" (Thomas), "clerk, Turner-Frazer Mercantile Co." (Francis, known also as "Frank"), "clerk" (James Junior) and "city salesman, Martin & Sheridan Bros." (John).[41]

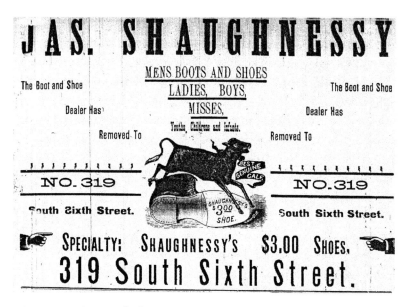

Advertisement for James [O']Shaughnessy's Shoe Store, St. Joseph, in a paper
for which his son James worked. From the *Catholic Tribune*, St. Joseph,
Missouri, 16 March 1889.

St. Joseph had been founded in 1843 on the banks of the Missouri River
in northwestern Missouri. It became a starting point for settlers moving
farther west, especially after 1859, when trains began to reach it. It was from
St. Joseph in 1860 that the famous but short-lived Pony Express commenced
its relay service to California. Another indication of the frontier nature of
the region was that on April 3, 1882, while the Shaughnessys were still living
in Moberly, the notorious outlaw Jesse James was shot dead at his family
home on Lafayette Street, St. Joseph, by one of his gang, Bob Ford.[42]

The late nineteenth century is regarded as the golden age of St. Joseph.
The city prospered and grew rapidly as a railroad center and as a leading
wholesale location for the support of expansion to places west of the Missouri River. Large proportions of its early settlers were German and Irish. It
also became a center for meatpacking. In 1886 the *Chicago Times* reported
that, "St. Joseph is a modern wonder — a city of 60,000 inhabitants, eleven
railroads, 70 passenger trains each day, 170 factories, thirteen miles of the
best paved streets, the largest stockyards west of Chicago, a wholesale trade
as large as that of Kansas City and Omaha combined. . ."[43] A regular overnight train service connected St. Joseph and Chicago.

Further Education in Missouri

The college that the De La Salle Brothers had founded at St. Joseph was from 1886 housed in an imposing, new, four-story brick building. Each pupil received moral and spiritual guidance, as well as practical training.[44] The class lists of the school for 1886–1887 include both "[Thomas] August Shaughnessey" and "Frank Shaughnessey" (sons of "James Shaughnessey" and all still without the prefix "O").[45] Throughout his life Thomas Augustin would be known sometimes as Thomas and sometimes as "Gus." The college had a good reputation for its teaching of penmanship, and in a St. Joseph city directory published in 1890, as noted already, Thomas is listed as a "sign painter." He subsequently attended the Academy of Fine Arts in Kansas City, Missouri, and worked for newspapers there and in Pueblo, Colorado, before moving to Chicago. Francis was to become a lawyer.[46]

James Junior did not continue as a clerk. He later recalled that, having worked in his father's shoe store in Moberly, he went on to spend time "teaching a country district school, back to shoe store advertising again and then studying law." An obituarist would later write that James "taught district school in St. Joseph, MO." but the words "country district" that he himself used suggest a more rural location. One may assume that the teaching involved in this temporary job was simply that of reading, writing, and arithmetic and that his return to shoe store advertising was a reference to his working again as a clerk for his father, this time in a new store when the family moved to St. Joseph.[47]

A biographical note about James that was provided on his behalf to the American Irish Historical Society in 1910 stated that James "took up the profession of teaching and then the study of law, which he abandoned to enter newspaper work." Another biographical note that he himself later provided to the *Pathfinder,* a magazine published in Washington DC that had a circulation of one million and that was preparing to publish a piece about him, recorded the fact that "Turning from the threshold of the legal profession, he went to newspaper work." There is no official record of his studying law at either the University of Missouri or the University of Notre Dame, from which respectively his brothers John and Francis graduated to become practicing attorneys. The *Pathfinder* noted that he had studied accountancy, languages, and art, but does not say where he did so. It was perhaps at the college in St. Joseph.[48]

In any event, during the 1880s, James was employed as a journalist on newspapers in St. Joseph. His work in that capacity will be considered in the next chapter.

Irish, Catholic, and Commercial

It is in records of the 1880s that one finds the first evidence of young James using the Gaelic prefix "O" before his name. Irish national sentiment had been greatly stirred in 1880 by the mission of Charles Stewart Parnell, future leader of the Irish parliamentary party at Westminster and so-called uncrowned king of Ireland, to cities up and down the United States. The biggest crowds turned out to see him in Chicago and St. Louis, and his widely publicized trip can scarcely have failed to move the Shaughnessy family to reflect on its own heritage. A small town in Missouri and a street in St. Louis were later named in his honor. The same advances in transport, mail, and communications that made Parnell's ambitious trip a political success on both sides of the Atlantic also brought news from Ireland across the United States on a continuing basis, news that was frequently and quite extensively published in many American papers that had a local Irish readership. Settled in Missouri, the Shaughnessys kept themselves informed about the old country. By the end of the nineteenth century, James Junior was to visit the land of his father's birth for the first time and to seek out a priest who was one of the leading figures in the national movement for reviving Ireland's cultural and national life. His brother Thomas ("Gus") would follow him.[49]

Both the national and religious aspects of the family's heritage featured large in the O'Shaughnessy household. James Shaughnessy Senior was president of the local St. Joseph branch (no. 203) of the Catholic Knights of America, a fraternal religious and benevolent society whose 3,500 Missouri members made regular payments into what was then a novel form of life insurance plan. This provided coverage for each member's family in the event of one's death. John, brother of Thomas and James Junior, was first vice president of the local Young Men's Sodality, another benevolent association.[50]

Meanwhile, there were bills to be paid. When in early 1889 James O'Shaughnessy's father moved the location of his shoe store from one part of St. Joseph to another he took out half-page weekly advertisements in the

Catholic Tribune, one of the papers on which his son worked in St. Joseph. The advertisements promoted his specialty, "Shaughnessy's $3.00 Shoes," and were larger and more striking than most advertisements in that paper. If his son James wrote copy for them, as is quite possible, did his son Thomas design them? At the center of the notice is a sketch of a calf leaping over a shoe. The "Condensed Local" column of the paper soon reassured readers, "The calf represented in Shaughnessy's advertisement is not a Jersey, but a good strong healthy American calf whose hide is very soft and pliant, but as tough as the tendon Achilles!" James Senior even contemplated the possibility of a partnership "with some experienced manufacturer" to build an extensive boot and shoe factory in the city.[51] His advertisements show that James Senior had not yet followed in his son James's footsteps by adopting the prefix "O" before his surname.

Heartbreak and Humiliation

Albert Johnson, a reporter working with James O'Shaughnessy in St. Joseph and a future member of nine succeeding Congresses, much later wrote that James became infatuated with a schoolteacher in the town. Johnson (1869–1957) was to recall "two tragedies, of the kind so heartbreaking to boys" that occurred while he and O'Shaughnessy were lodgers at Ogden House. One involved him and a basket of mended socks and candied jellies "and other delicacies that home-sick boys like" that was sent by his mother but opened by some callous fellow residents. They pinned all of the articles to the banisters of the stairs along with little notes that his mother had sent about them. More humiliating than this for a young man was what ostensibly happened to James O'Shaughnessy. His "heart overflowed with sentiment" according to Johnson, and he developed a secret love for the schoolteacher. "She was a gentlewoman, and very nice to everyone," wrote Johnson, adding that as Christmas approached, "Jim decided to make known in true Irish poetic style, his deep-seated love" for her. He composed an address, "half apostrophe and half poetry," and placing it in a $2 box of candy, hung it on the knob of her door when he and Johnson arrived in at 3 o'clock on Christmas morning: "Christmas dinner was at 2 o'clock that afternoon, and we had to have the dinner as our breakfast. As we entered the big dining room a ceremony was going on. Miss Montmorency was being married to a Kentucky gentleman! I thought Jim would fall dead. The lady never mentioned the poetic outburst, but the 'fine' Kentuckian told everybody in the boarding house before they started on their wedding trip."[52]

The teacher later named by Johnson as "May Montmorency" is presumably, by typographical error or by a trick of memory after a busy life, one and the same as that "May Montgomery" who forty years on was to write to James O'Shaughnessy when she saw his picture in *Liberty* magazine to ask him what had become of his brothers and of their mutual acquaintances Albert Johnson, Arthur Grubb, and "Rody."[53] In her letter of 1929, Montgomery lightly chided James for having, so long ago, "allowed an embryo serial to die of infantile paralysis because you failed to do your part and thereby closed what might have proved a brilliant career." Presumably this was a reference to some attempt by her to publish her writings in the Missouri newspapers on which he worked, perhaps inspired by the writings of local folklorist and storyteller Mary Alicia Owen who had been allowed a column in the *St. Joseph Democrat*.[54]

Bacon Montgomery

May Montgomery was a daughter of Bacon Montgomery, a man whose versatility matched the demands and opportunities of frontier life and whose life provides an insight into the balance between civilization and chaos in Missouri then. Bacon and his brother Richard had about 1860 started the *Journal* newspaper in Pettis County, Missouri. This was published at Georgetown, a small settlement on the Kansas Pacific branch of the Missouri Pacific Railway, three miles north of Sedalia. In 1861 Bacon joined the Union forces and saw action in many battles. His background in printing and journalism reportedly did not deter him from destroying a printing office in Richmond, when the editor of a local newspaper made some remarks personally offensive to him. He is also said to have compelled the editor to make a written retraction of his published statement.

As a cavalry officer when the Civil War ended, Montgomery was responsible in 1866 for the death of a notorious and very brutal bandit, one of many who terrorized Missouri then. This was Archie Clement, who liked to scalp his victims and who was a close acquaintance of Jessie James. Bacon subsequently returned to journalism, becoming the city editor of the *Sedalia*

Democrat in Pettis County, then of the *Dispatch,* and then in 1882, "when major John N. Edwards went to St. Joseph to take editorial management of the *Gazette,* he went with him as his city editor." In intervals of leave from journalism he hunted for silver, and eventually found a valuable mine. He died there in 1886 in an accident. He was survived by his daughter May, her sister, and her mother.[55]

Leaving St. Joe

Johnson wrote of James and himself: "soon after the O'Shaughnessy affair, we left, he for Chicago, and I for St. Louis, and both to better positions." He attributed his own departure not to humiliation but to a scoop that he got in September 1891 when he wangled his way under false pretenses into the cell of a condemned man, Louis Bulling, on the night before his execution. After Johnson's exclusive report appeared in the *Herald,* Joseph McCullough, editor of the *St. Louis Globe-Democrat,* invited him to join his staff.

Johnson also recalled an "odd character" at the *Herald,* a humorist and chalk-plate artist named Rodenberger, known to everyone as "Rody." He had little education "but was a rare imaginative genius" and a friend to both Johnson and O'Shaughnessy. Rody followed Johnson to St. Louis and stayed with him for a while, but "try as he would he could not hold a job. His drawings were not quite good enough for the newspapers." The two men took to writing "dime novels," Rody furnishing the plots and Johnson grinding them out when he was not working at the paper. They sold cowboy yarns and detective stories to Street & Smith in New York at two cents a word.

Another colleague and *Herald* reporter who also went to St. Louis met an even unhappier fate there. This was Arthur Grubb, a lawyer who was "well educated and brilliant in many ways," but who died in an opium den. He is said to have had a weak heart and when induced to try the drug collapsed. By a macabre coincidence, his wife was attempting to contact him at the time because their baby had taken ill and was dying.[56]

For his part, Albert Johnson later became a journalist at the *Washington Post* before moving to the state of Washington and editing there the *Grays Harbor Washingtonian.* Criticized for holding reactionary opinions on unions and race, he served as a leading Republican congressman from 1913 until 1933 and chaired the House Committee on Immigration and Nat-

uralization, steering through the "Johnson immigration law." Described by Hillier as "the most important immigration law to be enacted in the history of the country," this statute related the ethnicity of those who might in future be admitted to the United States as immigrants to percentages of existing immigrant stock and so favored northern Europeans in particular.[57]

Moving to Chicago

During 1892 James O'Shaughnessy also moved on to new pastures. From 1891 to 1892 he had acted as honorary secretary of the Officers of the Board of Trade for Buchanan County and St. Joseph. In 1892 he was also assistant

"Irish village," Columbian Exposition, Chicago 1893, with replica Blarney Castle. Contemporary postcard.

secretary of the Commercial Club but had stepped down by October that year.[58] More than thirty-five years later he would write to May Montgomery, whom he had known in St. Joseph, "I have only seen St. Joe once since I left to look for a job in Chicago." He regretted then that "I haven't kept in mind as many of my old friends as I should, I suppose because I have been working so hard all the years since I left St. Joe." He told her that he had recently had a long visit with Albert Johnson.[59]

Following the completion of the Illinois and Michigan Canal in 1848, the center of midwestern trade gradually shifted from St. Louis to Chicago.[60] The latter city was a magnet for migrants, foreign or domestic, to whom it offered opportunities to prosper. James Mulholland had worked profitably on the construction of that canal, connecting the Great Lakes and Chicago directly to the Mississippi River and thereby to the Gulf of Mexico. His grandchildren were among many who subsequently went to live in "the windy city" — as Chicago became widely known in the late nineteenth century. James and Thomas went first, before being followed by their siblings and parents.

Albert Johnson later claimed that James O'Shaughnessy was the first person to have the idea for "a Blarney stone" at the Chicago Exposition of 1893. James is said to have conceived of it being fitted in a replica of an Irish round tower, rather than in a replica of Blarney Castle as transpired to be the case: "Jim went to Chicago with his idea, which was adopted. He never received a cent although the promoters made a small fortune from it," wrote Johnson.[61]

TWO James O'Shaughnessy —
Star Reporter

DURING THE 1880S James O'Shaughnessy decided that he would not become a teacher or a lawyer, careers that had attracted him as a youth. Instead, he worked as a newspaperman. Rising levels of literacy among the public, a growing and wealthier population, improvements in print technology, and greater volumes of advertising and mass consumption meant that newspapers were flourishing. His journalism was to include dispatches from a war in Cuba, reports on the last battle between the US Army and Native Americans and a review of a controversial Irish play in Chicago.

While still a young man in St. Joseph, James began to work for the *Catholic Tribune*. The proprietors of this paper boasted on its masthead that it was "the only Catholic weekly west of New York." While the O'Shaughnessys were members of an immigrant Catholic family that played an active part in their Church's work in northern Missouri, the *Catholic Tribune* was by no means simply an organ of religion or religiosity. It published a mixture of light and local information along with American, Irish-American, and straightforward Irish news, as well as reports of developments in Catholicism. Advertisements for a range of goods and services appeared throughout it. Such a publication was a good training ground for any journalist, and it equipped James well to seek employment on general newspapers.

James was certainly not the first Irish-American or Irishman to work in the newspapers of Missouri. The Presbyterian Joseph Charless, born in County Westmeath, Ireland, is said to have published not only the first newspaper but also the first book west of the Mississippi. He owned and edited the *Missouri Gazette* in St. Louis. His son Edward, born in America, succeeded him.[1] Many other Irish immigrants and their descendants have contributed to journalism in the US since that time.[2]

The *Catholic Tribune* had been founded in 1879 in Kansas City, Missouri, but its production was moved to St. Joseph in 1880. There it became closely associated with Rev. Francis Graham. Graham had come to the United States from Ireland in 1854. He was an energetic pastor who took charge of St. Patrick's Church, St. Joseph, on New Year's Day, 1882, and at once set himself the task of remodeling, enlarging, and refurnishing it: "In 1883 he purchased the *Catholic Tribune,* of which he was both editor and proprietor until June 1889."[3]

In 1888 and 1889, Ayer's *Catalogue* lists "James O'Shaughnessy, Jr." (notably now with the prefix "O") as the managing editor and publisher of the *Catholic Tribune.* He found himself in a very competitive market. The paper then sold 3,500 copies per issue and was said four years later to have "attained a large circulation in Catholic families and was ably conducted."[4] In St. Joseph alone, a city of just 60,000 people, eleven papers were appearing daily or weekly about that time. They included one in German and two described racially as "colored." The proliferation of printed news throughout this period is striking, with one writer in 1882 reporting, "Missouri supports and maintains 471 newspapers and periodicals."[5] Anyone involved in publishing newspapers or in advertising will appreciate the hard-pressed tone of an anonymous complaint printed in 1882 that, notwithstanding the fact that St. Joseph was the third city in size in Missouri, her wholesale merchants as a rule "do little to advertise their business; some of the heaviest never putting a line of advertisements in the papers year in and year out, while many do it grudgingly, as a sort of tax which they are compelled to pay."[6]

In 1889 Michael Lawlor, the son of Irish emigrants, and Peter Nugent purchased the *Catholic Tribune* and immediately doubled its cover price. They also decided "to discard all foreign advertisements from our paper thus giving ample room to our home merchants to display their wares" (merchants who were apparently no longer as reluctant as they had once been to advertise). It is not obvious from browsing the newspaper in the months before this change of ownership that many advertisements were "foreign," unless by this word they meant "out-of-town" or "out-of-state," or to know if their decision was an implicit criticism of a strategy for which James O'Shaughnessy Junior may have been at least partly responsible.[7]

Reporter at the *Herald*

The change of ownership at the *Catholic Tribune* appears to have prompted James O'Shaughnessy to secure employment elsewhere. He moved to the St. Joseph daily *Herald*. This was then the only one of the city's newspapers to support the Republican Party. At the time he was living in the crowded "old Ogden house." Among his fellow lodgers was Albert Johnson. Johnson had arrived in Missouri from Illinois by way of Kansas with a letter of recommendation to the city editor of the *St. Joseph Herald*. He was put to work straightaway on his arrival, with less than two dollars left in his pocket to find somewhere to stay at the end of the first night's shift. Johnson would in 1934 gratefully recall what happened next: "A reporter on the paper, James O'Shaughnessy, asked me about 3 o'clock in the morning if I had made any arrangements for lodgings and invited me to go with him to the Ogden House, his boarding house. I accepted, and we struck up a close friendship which lasts to this day." Their residence hosted "at least fifty" teachers, reporters, traveling men, and their wives. Johnson was poor, and "so were most people, for times were still hard in those days'" He and O'Shaughnessy saw little of the other boarders in the house, as the two young men worked every night until three or four in the morning "and got our breakfasts about 1 o'clock, after the noon luncheons were over."[8] Had they seen even less of the boarders then they might have avoided the "two tragedies," as Johnson melodramatically termed them, that were described in the preceding chapter.

O'Shaughnessy's Waif

One cold December night the *Herald*'s city editor received word that a mother had abandoned her baby on the doorstep of a family who refused to take in the foundling. He asked the family who had notified the newspaper not to say a word to anyone else and immediately sent one of his reporters down to get the child. It seems unlikely that any editor today would make such a decision, but, according to Johnson, their editor planned to secure a "beat" or "scoop." The *Herald*'s reporter returned about midnight with the baby in a basket: "We were so busy getting the paper 'up' that we paid no attention to the infant until after 2 a.m. Then came the problem, what to do with it? We agreed to adopt it, which we did then and there. An hour later we took it to a Catholic Home. Later the baby was baptized in a Catholic church and given the name, MADONNA RODY-O'SHAUGHNESSY-JOHNSON."

If this behavior seems callous or bizarre today, it appears not to have bothered anyone then. The baby had been given a triple-barreled family name that was formed by joining those of three friends working as reporters on the *Herald*. When the story appeared, the *Herald*'s readers sent in a large number of gifts, including cribs, rings, pins, and money. Public interest was intense, Johnson recalled later that "O'Shaughnessy, himself a Catholic, was really the guardian of the child, which never recovered from exposure, and died about Easter time." James O'Shaughnessy went to Calvary Cemetery and wrote for the paper an account, headed "The Waif's Funeral," which mentioned that the unfortunate baby had been living in an institution that was named sadly the "Home of the Friendless." Only the three reporters whose names the baby bore and a female acquaintance of the three attended the funeral. There was, wrote O'Shaughnessy, "No priest, no prayer, no tear, or sound except the falling clods." This early example of O'Shaughnessy's journalism was filed away by Johnson in a scrapbook, a reminder of what may have been a troubling memory for each of the young men involved.[9]

Europe and Pawnee Bill

When he retired after serving nine terms as a member of Congress, Albert Johnson wrote a memoir of his own days in journalism. In it he mentions that his friend James O'Shaughnessy left St. Joseph for Chicago in the early 1890s. Before going, young James posed for a portrait that shows him staring straight into the camera's lens, looking young, bright, and determined.[10]

Johnson also mentioned that his friend had volunteered at least one idea for the promotion of Ireland at the great Chicago Exposition of 1893. But James did not settle down in Chicago straightaway. In an era of world fairs he worked as a syndicate correspondent in Europe in 1894, "when he was a member of the International Jury of Awards of the Antwerp Exposition." It is not known what he wrote from Europe or how he secured his appointment to the Antwerp jury. In a later application for a passport, he recorded the fact that he had lived at Antwerp, Belgium, from March 1894 until July

James O'Shaughnessy,
reporter, about 1890.
Courtesy Brigid
O'Shaughnessy.

Poster for Pawnee Bill's Wild West Show. Courtesy Library of Congress.

1894. At the same time, he also acted as an advance agent, interpreter, and press agent in Europe for "Pawnee Bill," who had earlier worked for the more famous "Buffalo Bill" Cody. "Pawnee Bill" from Illinois brought his traveling show and "Indian camp" to the world fair in Antwerp and took it on tour to the Netherlands. The show featured Native Americans, including some of the displaced Pawnee Nation, with feats of horsemanship and other attractions involving "cowboys and Indians."[11]

In a news release vaunting his later attendance at the international advertising convention in London in 1924, the Associated Advertising Clubs of the World would write about James O'Shaughnessy, "For a while he did correspondence from Europe for a syndicate of American newspapers. He acted for a season as advertising advance agent for an American wild west show touring Belgium, Holland and Germany. He concluded his European experience with a pedestrian tour of Ireland."[12] In Ireland in the 1890s, he visited a leading scholar of Gaelic studies, Fr. Eugene O'Growney, and the significance of that meeting will be considered in a later chapter.

During the 1890s James also wrote as a free-lance journalist for some New York papers.[13] By the end of the decade he had returned to Chicago. His parents and most of his siblings also moved to the city.

Chicago Journalist

Once back in Chicago, James continued to work as a journalist. Like most Irish-American reporters he was employed by general American publications rather than by ethnic Irish or other niche newspapers. There was certainly an established Irish-American press, largely printed in the English language and including the *Boston Pilot*, the *Kentucky Irish American*, and New York's *Irish World*. Such titles continued to serve their purpose, not least at times of conflict when they catered to the dual identities of immigrants as both Americans and members of a minority culture with ties to a foreign country.[14]

However, the fact that most Irish immigrants spoke English meant that they could adapt more easily than many other ethnic groups to reading general US newspapers, and the reporters upon whom these general newspapers relied for copy often included Irish-Americans such as James.

Thomas "Gus" O'Shaughnessy, too, found employment on the Chicago papers, becoming an illustrator on the *Chicago Tribune* by 1895.[15] A leading historian of the US media has written that Chicago journalism "came into its own" in the period between 1892 and 1914. The city's population was second only to that of New York, and its "papers were generally well-printed, less sensational than those of New York, and served by a group of notable journalists."[16]

The *Chronicle*

By August 1897 at the latest James had joined the *Chicago Chronicle,* which was founded in 1895 and was then the only morning paper in the city that backed the Democratic Party. It would close in 1907, its owner, John R. Walsh, having refused to endorse that party's populist presidential candidate William Jennings Bryan. Another Irish-American journalist who worked for the *Chronicle* was Richard J. Finnegan (1884/5–1955), future editor of the *Chicago Daily Times* and of the *Chicago Sun-Times* and, like James, also a future president of the Irish Fellowship Club. For his various professional and humanitarian efforts, Finnegan was paid a remarkable tribute in 1956 when the popular *This Is Your Life* television series devoted a special posthumous program to him. Among those who appeared on it was Charles Hecht, who had been trained by Finnegan and who with Charles MacArthur wrote the influential Broadway comedy and Hollywood film about journalism *The Front Page.*[17]

Writing in 1897 from the *Chronicle* offices on Washington Street, James O'Shaughnessy expressed his disappointment to Fr. Andrew Morrissey (1860–1921), president of the University of Notre Dame, for "not being able to get down to Notre Dame to report the proceedings of the Eucharistic congress." This particular congress was the second national convention of the Catholic Priests' Eucharistic League. He told the Irish-born Morrissey that he had submitted the matter to the city editor, but "several things intervened." The interventions included staffing changes at the *Chronicle,* "changes which I think the Catholic friends of the paper will not have occasion to find fault with."[18] His connection with Notre Dame was personal, for he helped to pay for the education of two of his brothers there, and his family's involvement with the university continued beyond that.

Spanish-American War of 1898

When the United States declared war on Spain in 1898, James went to Cuba to cover the action. So many journalists did so and their influence on domestic responses to the war was regarded as so decisive that it has been dubbed "the correspondents' war." However, Irish-Americans were divided on the role that the United States should play overseas. Some felt an affinity with Cubans and compared the Cubans' struggle against Spain with that of the Irish against England. They regarded US involvement as aid to that Cuban struggle rather than as expansionism. For his part, the well-known Irish-American journalist Finley Peter Dunne (1867–1936) wavered between support for the war and growing scepticism. During the 1890s Dunne assumed the persona of a fictional Irish innkeeper in Chicago's Bridgeport district, one Mr. Dooley, who kept up a running commentary on local and national matters. His innovative columns were written in a phonetic Hiberno-English dialect that gave expression to the everyday reality of ordinary Irish-Americans in that city. In the *Chicago Evening Post* and the *Chicago Journal* he satirized aspects of the Cuban adventure, and these columns proved so popular that they were sydicated nationally.[19]

Many American journalists were, at the outset, enthusiastic supporters of the war. A number not only filed reports, they actually participated in engagements. In some cases their exploits make those of today's "embedded" journalists seem positively detached by comparison. "Then everybody sailed away as if on a crusade," wrote the newspaper proprietor William Randolph Hearst. In Cuba, notes one historian of US journalism, "American commanders allowed unusual freedom to correspondents," and "as many as 500 writers, photographers, and artists, representing scores of newspapers and magazines," went to cover the war.[20] Most knew little about military affairs. Yet one of the most highly regarded, Richard Harding Davis, even led a charge and won the praise of Colonel Theodore Roosevelt. Another, James Creelman of Hearst's *New York Journal,* led an attack on a fort and seized the Spanish flag there as a trophy for his newspaper. He was shot during the engagement. But perhaps the most notable media presence of all was that of Hearst himself, who entered the war zone with a group of correspondents on what he called "the newspaper ship." After a fierce attack by the US Navy on Spanish vessels, Hearst spotted some Spanish survivors on a beach and embarked with members of his crew to capture them. These "poor Spanish sailormen — battered and bruised, half clothed, half drowned, half starved — were only too happy to be taken prisoners," he later recalled. Hearst handed them over to the crew of the USS *Harvard,* making sure to obtain in return for the twenty-nine captives a receipt, which he later had framed.[21] The extent to which Hearst and his great competitor, Joseph Pulitzer, had in the first place provoked war by means of inflammatory and unbalanced "yellow journalism" is contested.[22]

Seeing the Cuban conflict as an opportunity to further his own career, James O'Shaughnessy decided to follow many other journalists to Cuba. Only after the sinking of the USS *Maine,* in disputed circumstances in Havana harbor on February 15, 1898, had his newspaper, the *Chicago Chronicle,* eventually joined those already clamoring for war.[23] According to Gleijeses, the *Chronicle* was then "the most important Democratic daily of the Midwest." Although it had earlier criticised the US administration for not aiding Cuban rebels against Spain, it had consistently opposed war between the United States and Spain. Gleijeses observes, "It was a most uncomfortable position for a rabid Democratic paper, and it was out of step with a majority of the Democratic Party. . . . And then, abruptly, the *Chronicle*'s position changed." He notes, "The editors of the *Chronicle* never explained why they had suddenly decided that Spain was guilty, but it is difficult to resist the conclusion that partisan considerations were also behind the volte-face," and not simply the sinking of the *Maine.*[24]

Reporting from Cuba

O'Shaughnessy sailed for Cuba with the military expedition that left Tampa, Florida, on June 14, 1898, and landed at Daiquiri on June 22. He joined the men of the Fifth Army bivouacked in the little Valley of the Aguadores, just outside the town of Santiago, and reported unromantically that those who were camped farther back along the trail, scattered at intervals as far as the beach at Siboney, "were apparently more concerned about rations and such shelter as would keep off the rains than about beleaguring a city and reducing the enemy." They were short of tobacco and bacon in particular. Thus far, he reported, "scarcely more than 500 men

"HOW THE DAY WAS WON"
CHARGE OF THE TENTH CAVALRY REGIMENT U.S.A. SAN JUAN HILL, SANTIAGO, CUBA JULY 1ˢᵗ 1898

Black "Buffalo Soldiers" of 1898 celebratory print. Courtesy Library of Congress.

of the troops had fired a shot in the campaign which was then a week old on Cuban soil."[25]

O'Shaughnessy found that the trenches and blockhouses at Daiquiri and Siboney had been charged and taken without the sight of a Spaniard or the firing of a shot by the US land forces. Among those involved in the action was Theodore Roosevelt, future president of the United States, who had stepped down as assistant secretary of the navy to join the expedition. He helped to raise the 1st Volunteer Cavalry Regiment, a body mainly consisting of westerners that earned the nickname "Rough Riders" — notwithstanding the fact that most of those who fought for the regiment in Cuba fought on foot. O'Shaughnessy notes their role at Guasimas but gives no less credit for that victory to the African-American troopers of the 10th Cavalry and of other regiments who were nicknamed "Buffalo Soldiers."

O'Shaughnessy filed copy from Cuba, and witnessed the decisive victory against the Spanish at San Juan Hills on July 1, 1898. Two pieces by him were also printed in the *Chicago Tribune* on the anniversary of the war. Extracts of these are reproduced at some length in an appendix in order to provide an insight into his style of journalism. He and other correspondents discovered that they were not always welcomed with open arms by the men on the front line.[26]

O'Shaughnessy also noted a command by the Cuban rebel leader, General Calixto Garcia, that no Cubans should act as servants to Americans. The reporter remarked wryly, "The enervating climate was causing men to wish for servants who never had thought of a such a thing before in their lives."[27] When victory came it made glorious reading for people back in the United States. O'Shaughnessy wrote, "A charge was made across the flat and straight for the blockhouse. The men came up out of the sunken road, scaling the steeper side of the steep hill. The Gatling guns were raking the trenches. A white flag was waved on the hillside. It was a signal for the machine guns to stop their hail to let the infantry charge. The Spaniards were leaping from the trenches. A cheer came down the hillside."[28]

Two days later O'Shaughnessy also witnessed a controversial incident about which he was to give evidence to an official inquiry on July 7, 1899. Admiral William T. Sampson failed to rendezvous as planned with the commander of the expeditionary force, General William Rufus Shafter of the Fifth Army. The admiral had taken his flagship cruiser *New York* out of line to meet ground commanders at Siboney. In his deposition, O'Shaughnessy recalled being on the beach at Siboney where he was hoping to get for his newspaper a statement from Sampson: "I was employed as a reporter and correspondent of the Chicago *Chronicle*." He saw the *New York* approach from the direction of Morro Castle, nearer to the shore than he had ever before observed a large warship in that bight:

> A launch was let down into the water from the *New York* when it stopped; and three officers from the *New York* entered the launch. While the launch was still alongside the *New York*, I heard the report of a heavy gun coming from the direction of Morro Castle. Immediately there seemed to be a commotion among those on the decks of the *New York*. The ladder was quickly drawn up on the side of the *New York*. The officers in the launch were gesticulating to somebody on the cruiser. The firing towards the

Sold only by Griffith & Griffith
PHILADELPHIA, CHICAGO, LONDON, HAMBURG, GER. MILAN, ITALY

X/853 U.S.S. New York Admiral Sampson Flag Ship

William H. Rau Publisher,
Philadelphia, Pa.

USS *New York*, stereograph card 1898. Courtesy Library of Congress.

mouth of Santiago Harbor increased; and I could hear the heavy guns
booming at close intervals. . . . After the ladder was drawn up the *New
York* began to move. It began to swing round. . . . The launch with the
three officers in it came to the temporary dock at Siboney. I waited at the
dock for their coming, and talked with them for some time. Those officers
who were left in the launch seemed greatly chagrined when they came on
shore, and appeared as if they were at a loss to know what to do. . . later
in the day I learned of the destruction of the ships of the Spanish fleet by
those of the United States Navy. That was, then, the explanation of the
failure of Admiral Sampson to visit General Shafter after having come
to Siboney.[29]

O'Shaughnessy had been hearing in the distance an engagement that
marked a turning point in the relationship between the United States and
Europe. That day the destruction of the Spanish fleet signaled the end of
any Spanish pretension to empire and confirmed the United States on a
new course of intervention overseas wherever it would deem intervention
beneficial to its interests. Its victory in the Spanish-American War saw the

United States immediately supersede Spain as the dominant foreign power not only in Cuba and Puerto Rico but also in Guam and the Philippines.

O'Shaughnessy left Cuba with many other correspondents in mid-August on board the *Segurança*. This was the former flagship of General Shafter, who remarked that newspapermen would no longer "be in the way."[30] The *Chronicle's* man came home from war with tokens of Spain's defeat that he donated to the University of Notre Dame. He wrote, "On my return from Cuba I brought back two souvenirs of the campaign with a view to presenting them to the war museum of the university. One is the truce flag carried by the Spaniards to the treating place for the surrender of Santiago and which I took from the Spanish trenches [on] the day of the capitulation. The other is a flag of Spain which was used as a wall banner in the governor's palace in Santiago."[31] Where the journalist James Creelman is said to have seized a Spanish flag as an "emblem" or trophy for his newspaper, O'Shaughnessy donated his souvenirs to the university, where they remain. Ms Angela Kindig, archivist at the University of Notre Dame, writes, "The Truce Flag is no longer white. It's very dirty and if you look closely, you can see what appear to be blood stains."[32]

It was later claimed that nothing in O'Shaughnessy's entire career "equaled his heroic charge up San Juan Hill, in Cuba, with Teddy Roosevelt, as a foreign correspondent. . . . In the last years of his life, its memory still brought him deep personal pride. Perhaps it was the fellowship among the Rough Riders that piqued his later interest in founding the IFC [Irish Fellowship Club, Chicago]."[33] However, O'Shaughnessy's own contemporary account ("a cheer came down the hillside") does not suggest that he himself charged up the hill with any combatants, although he was undoubtedly in danger at his observation post. Nor does his or certain other contemporary accounts support any assertion that Roosevelt and his Rough Riders played a unique role in the capture of San Juan Hill that day.[34]

Indian Troubles

Later in 1898, O'Shaughnessy covered "Indian troubles" at Leech Lake in Minnesota. Angered by the loss of their land and by intrusive logging, Chippewa (Ojibwe) tribesmen engaged the military on October 5 in what is sometimes described as the last battle between the US Army and Native

Americans. Ed Conner, who was covering the Leech Lake story for the *Minneapolis Tribune*, later described O'Shaughnessy as "a wonderful reporter."[35]

In going to Cuba and Minnesota, O'Shaughnessy may have been influenced by learning of the career of another Chicago journalist with a Galway background, John F. Finerty. Finerty, the son of a former editor of the *Galway Vindicator*, had left Ireland for America in 1863. During the 1870s, as correspondent for the *Chicago Times*, he traveled with the US Army in its war against the Sioux and later reported from Mexico. Finerty subsequently launched his own successful weekly paper, the *Citizen*, which catered to Irish-Americans in Chicago.[36]

A Financial Disappointment

Some newspapers that had sent correspondents to Cuba found that the investment brought little commercial return. The war itself made potential advertisers hesitant to spend. James O'Shaughnessy's personal experience was also not entirely good; his trip to Cuba had not been as professionally advantageous as he had hoped. There was too an unpleasant side effect, as he explained to the president of Notre Dame, Rev. Andrew Morrissey, on February 27, 1899:

> Unfortunately I have been set back in my finances this year more than I expected. My Cuban trip last year was a financial disappointment to me and since returning I have lost much time and have been forced to incur much expense on account of illness resulting from exposure in the tropics. After being idle six weeks trying to get the malaria out of me I returned to work last week. I am now working for the *Chicago Tribune* in a somewhat improved position.[37]

He was not the only newspaperman menaced by innumerable forms of tropical illness while in Cuba: "Poor [Ambrose William] Lyman, one of the most conscientious of them, contracted a disease from which he afterwards died."[38] Many soldiers and journalists became unwell, and some newspapers referred to the vessels transporting them home to the United States as "horror ships."[39] The psychological effects of their experience may have lingered long after their return. In a recent study of such effects on those who report from war zones, effects that were little understood in 1898, Underwood has compared the bravado of Stephen Crane in the Spanish-American war to the indifference of one of Hearst's top writers, Ambrose Bierce, who did not bother to cover the campaign and who contemptuously referred to it as the "Yanko-Spanko War." Underwood believes that the key to their behavior was in each case traumatic experiences during earlier conflicts and that these experiences were subsequently played out in opposite ways by both men. However, the Cuban campaign was so short and generally so one-sided that most of the correspondents involved may have been spared serious psychological ill effects.[40]

"Star" at the *Tribune*

In moving to the *Chicago Tribune,* to what he had told Morrissey was "a somewhat improved position," James O'Shaughnessy was joining a newspaper that had already employed his brother Thomas as an illustrator; however, the latter seems not to have had a permanent job there. In 1899 Thomas fell on defective pavement and hurt his knee, "which confined him to bed for two months with an attendant loss of wages and a large doctor's bill."[41] During the summer of 1900 Thomas was recorded in the US census as having been unemployed for the previous five months.

James, for his part, made a name for himself as an eager and competent journalist. Half a century later the *Tribune*'s famous Washington correspondent between 1909 and the 1940s, Arthur Sears Henning, recalled, "When I came to work on the *Tribune* in [June] 1899 Dick Little and Jim O'Shaughnessy, who was to become a big-shot New York advertising executive, were the star reporters."[42] Henning's political judgment was widely respected, although he later got one important call wrong, and his error resulted in a spectacular newspaper gaffe, this being the decision by the *Tribune* to anticipate the outcome of the US presidential election of 1948 by running the front page headline "DEWEY DEFEATS TRUMAN." In fact, as it transpired later that night, Harry S. Truman had won.

Henning and James O'Shaughnessy worked at that time in an old five-story brownstone at the corner of Madison and Dearborn streets occupied by *Tribune* staff. It had been erected after the Chicago fire of 1871: "In the center of the building was a spacious wrought iron stairway ascending to the fourth floor, where the principal editorial departments were located. As a means of ascent, however, the stairway had long previously given over to an elevator, an ancient, creaking, wooden car that responded to the operator's manipulation of the vertical wire cable." Writing in May 1953, Henning also recalled,

> Reporters and other newspaper workers addicted to drink were then a
> problem. Today the newspaper is a thoroly [*sic*] sober occupation. The
> man who drinks to excess cannot hold a job in it. Things were different
> in the '80s and '90s. Then it was expected that numerous employees
> would be too drunk to work the day after payday. . . . There was a saloon
> of hallowed memory across Dearborn St from the *Tribune* known as "The
> Dizzy." It had sawdust on the floor, beer at 5 cents a glass, and four men at a
> counter opening oysters all day at 1 cent each.

Henning, who married Little's sister, described James O'Shaughnessy as "a keen newsman and facile writer who later became a big advertising agency executive in New York. We cubs sedulously studied the journalistic exploits and prose style of Little and O'Shaughnessy." In this context the adjective "facile" has none of its disparaging connotations but signifies fluency or the ability to write readily.[43]

In recalling his own arrival at the *Tribune* in 1899, Henning also wrote about Clifford S. Raymond. He noted that Raymond later became the "brilliant chief of the *Tribune* editorial page, a novelist, and a poet." The two were close friends. Henning thought that "Raymond's fixed object in life was to write fiction" and added, "I, too, had been possessed of that ambition, as what newspaper reporter had not?" Had James O'Shaughnessy also harbored such ideas? In 1900 a very short fictional tale entitled "For Love of Madelaine" was syndicated by the Daily Story Publishing Company. Among the newspapers that published it then was the *Los Angeles Times*, in a column headed "Our Daily Story." Its byline on this piece was "James O'Shaughnessy." We do not know for certain if this was the Chicago journalist of that time but the company that syndicated the piece was certainly located in Chicago.[44]

Yacht Race Coverage

While working at the *Tribune,* James used his connections at Notre Dame to help John Fay, a *Tribune* journalist and local representative of Joseph Pulitzer's *New York World,* to get in touch with Professor Jerome Green, a pioneer of wireless transmission in the United States. The managing editor of the *New York World* "wished Green to use his wireless telegraphy in reporting the big yacht race at New York." Writing to the president of Notre Dame, in July 1899, James thought that this "would be a splendid advertisement for the university."[45] One year earlier, Gugliclmo Marconi had undertaken successfully for the *Dublin Daily Express* in Ireland what is believed to have been the first live "wireless" telegraphy report of any sporting event when he sent to Dublin a stream of messages commenting on the progress of a yacht race nearby at Kingstown (now Dun Laoghaire). Marconi, whose Irish mother, Annie Jameson, was a member of the famous whiskey-distilling family, went on in October 1899 to use his technology for the same purpose in covering the America's Cup international yacht race off Sandy Hook. Thus was it that the initiative of the *New York World* was trumped, for it was at the instigation of the *New York Herald* that Marconi erected stations on Long Island and in New Jersey: "A running story, transmitted through the air to the coast, was instantly relayed by land wires to the main office of the Associated Press in New York, and thence distributed over the country." The latter operation cost over $25,000.[46]

In 1931 the assistant editor of the *Pathfinder* in Washington DC asked O'Shaughnessy for a few biographical notes to include in a short article about him. These notes refer to his spending "a period of mild experience as a newspaper correspondent in Europe" apparently sometime after his coverage of the Cuban and Indian wars, and ostensibly about 1899–1900, but nothing more is known of any such second European visit or work at that time.[47]

Hearst's *Chicago American*

James O'Shaughnessy left the *Tribune* and took a job at William Randolph Hearst's new *Chicago American,* launched on July 4, 1900. His work was greatly appreciated by its editor, Charles Edward Russell (1860–1941):

Arthur Sears Henning, a leading correspondent of the *Chicago Tribune*. He called James O'Shaughnessy a "star reporter." Courtesy Anne Sears.

Charles Edward Russell, editor *Chicago American*, co-founder NAACP. From *Review of Reviews*, 36 (1907), p. 578.

When we started *The American* . . . there was a shortage of water supply in the city. Householders were begged and implored to conserve what we had and waste none of it. And for one summer the watering of lawns was prohibited. This in a city bordering upon Lake Michigan seemed lunatic. We had on *The American* a bright and affable reporter named James O'Shaughnessy. He acquired a notion that the reason the water supply was short was because somebody was snitching it. Encouraged by the management, he obtained a permit to dig up the streets at certain intersections near the [meat-]packing houses. Then with workmen he went at night, made the excavation and discovered that the city mains had been surreptitiously tapped and certain packing houses were drawing off millions of gallons for which they paid nothing.[48]

Russell was a journalist, socialist politician, Pulitzer Prize-winning author and one of the founders of the National Association for the Advancement of Colored People (NAACP). He was proud to be one of a band of journalists that became known as "muckrakers," a term sometimes used as an insult but worn as a badge of honor by this group whom *Puck* satirized in one of its distinctive cartoons. They exposed scandal and malpractice whenever they could and counted among their friends Theodore Roosevelt in the early years of his Progressive Era presidency from 1901.[49] Hearst himself was then "making a heavy play for the support of workers, small business owners, and other ordinary people," especially those with grievances against the established order.[50]

O'Shaughnessy was to serve as more than simply a reporter for one of Hearst's newspapers. Early in 1904 he became briefly the *American*'s managing editor, in peculiar circumstances. Moses Koenigsberg later wrote, "A diverting glimpse into the inner workings of the Hearst organization early in my city editorship furnished the clue to a number of puzzles in subsequent years. The whimsicality of the incident sharpened its significance. James O'Shaughnessy became managing editor overnight. The day before, he had been a reporter on the morning edition. O'Shaughnessy was a gentleman of high character. Years later he was a popular figure in national advertising circles." Koenigsberg recalled that O'Shaughnessy had told him of his appointment as managing editor "with a sheepish grin" and added that "It was not of his choosing. In fact, it embarrassed him. He was blindly obeying instructions. The order had come from Mr. Hearst. As for his duties — he didn't know where or how to start. He would have to rely on my guidance. Noon arrived before the mystery cleared."

It emerged that a noted subeditor named Fred W. Lawrence, who was a brother of the *Chicago American*'s publisher, "Long Green Andy" Lawrence, had panicked in the face of a story from a local press association about a Catholic priest eloping with the wife of a Chicago gambler and gangster. Lawrence called Hearst personally and reminded him of their days together in California at the *San Francisco Examiner* when that newspaper had incurred the wrath of a group of Roman Catholic leaders. Lawrence persuaded Hearst that a similar storm might break when they published this latest story and so, according to Koenigsberg, Hearst "instructed that somebody of good standing as a Roman Catholic, with a distinctively Irish name, be immediately installed as managing editor of the *Chicago American*. O'Shaughnessy fit the description. His presence on the job would be the best answer to any criticism that arose." In fact, the day passed without any problem. James O'Shaughnessy avoided further personal embarrassment by taking matters into his own hands: "It was O'Shaughnessy who that night set Hearst's misgivings at rest. He welcomed relief from the humbug into which he had been thrust. O'Shaughnessy found no pride in his one-day career as a managing editor. He didn't enjoy serving as a 'stall.'"[51] For his part Fred Lawrence did not enjoy an unblemished reputation for his journalism. Hearst had sent him to Cuba to report on the Spanish-American War in 1898. It is said that his "outstanding contribution while on the island was to write a completely fictitious story about a gallant group of American volunteers who, manning a battery of Gatling guns, captured the city of Pinar del Rio from the Spaniards." While Hearst was ostensibly pleased with Lawrence's work, the reporter later confessed to the Senate Foreign Relations Committee that he had no personal knowledge of the facts and had relied on informants who were not acknowledged as sources in the story.[52]

Newspaper Wars

For a period, James O'Shaughnessy also worked as "the political editor" of the *Chicago American,* "until he abandoned editorial work to enter the field of advertising as writer and counselor."[53] A biographical note that he later wrote highlighted his work after 1900 as a "political editor and writer on business subjects." During his journalism career in Chicago he was employed by the *Journal, Tribune, News, Times-Herald, Chronicle,* and *American* "in various capacities as reporter, war correspondent, special writer, managing editor and political editor."[54] He also became president of the Western Catholic Writers' Guild.[55]

It was an exciting time. Chicago has been described as "the center of American journalism during the first three decades of the twentieth century."[56] It was also a very competitive and demanding time, and many reporters had to survive on space rates, being paid only for work that was actually published and in proportion to the column inches that this work filled. In 1900 one New York newspaperman wrote, "The making of a metropolitan daily is the fiercest, bitterest, most exhausting struggle in the world"; the writer asserted that the job of a journalist in such an environment made men old at forty.[57] James O'Shaughnessy turned forty in 1905.

Getting the story was only part of the battle; newspapers had to compete for space on crowded newsstands. Circulation wars turned physical on Chicago's streets in the early twentieth century. *Time* later wrote, "Selling newspapers in Chicago is a hard-boiled business. To the strong-arm methods of old-time Chicago circulation managers some historians trace the origin of gangsterism."[58]

Annenberg Brothers

One of Chicago's most famous circulation managers was Max Annenberg, who grew up in a tough, mostly Irish neighborhood of Chicago and who was "raised from infancy by Jesuits on Chicago's West Side district." The story goes that he endured the taunts of an Irish gang leader who stood outside the Annenberg family delicatessen and notion store and shouted, "Sheeney [contemptuous term for a Jew], get me a sausage." This bullying went on "until the day that his father put in a stock of baseball bats. Instead of a sausage, young Annenberg's tormentor received a bone-crushing blow from Max's brother, Moe, who crept up on him from the rear."[59] Max Annenberg, while still an adolescent, had worked in the publicity department of the Columbian Exposition. He was at the *Tribune* and then at Hearst's *Chicago American* when O'Shaughnessy was a journalist on those newspapers. Under the direction of Andy Lawrence at the *American,* Max and his brother, Moses, became deeply embroiled as circulation managers and "sluggers" in the violent battles and strikebreaking that eventually led to the deaths of more than twenty newspaper vendors and others, and that saw Max recruited back to the *Tribune* as that newspaper fought fire with fire in the circulation war.[60] As *Time* magazine put it,

> His confidence in himself was shared by the newsdealers, whom he made his friends by every means at his command. Once, when they were crying for newspapers to sell during a Chicago strike, he ignored death threats, put his *Tribunes* on armed trucks, saw that every newsstand was supplied. In newsdealers' tiny offices, storerooms, back-alley loafing places, the name Max Annenberg became a great name. They call him "Max," he calls them by their first names. Once when a newsdealer died and left his business to a son who knew little about circulation, Max Annenberg stepped in, said he would be responsible for the efficiency of the son's organization. Other magazine publishers, who fearing incompetence had removed their publications from the son, promptly put them back on Max Annenberg's say-so. The son prospered.[61]

If this story paints a heartwarming picture of Max Annenberg, it should also be recalled that he was put on trial for shooting an innocent bystander in the chest in 1913, during a wild expedition to an alleged gambling den to help photographers take a revealing picture for the *Tribune*. He was acquitted, a fact that led Lundberg to observe in 1936, "Annenberg was the tool of higher interests, first of Hearst and then of the McCormicks. Since they were not convicted, perhaps the jury was not as venal or stupid as might at first appear"[62] Moses Annenberg later became a wealthy media owner in his own right, fathering a son named Walter who became Richard Nixon's ambassador to the United Kingdom.

James quit full-time journalism before the circulation wars reached their violent peak in the second decade of the twentieth century. Years later he was to work closely with Max Annenberg at *Liberty* magazine.

The *Playboy* in Chicago

James left journalism to become an adman, but he could not entirely resist the lure of a good story. On February 6, 1912, he took time off from his work as an advertising agent and went to review a controversial Irish play for his former employer, the *Chicago Tribune*. The *Tribune* had recently begun to describe itself as "The World's Greatest Newspaper," a slogan that appeared on the front page of every issue between August 29, 1911, and December 31, 1976. From this Olympian height, its reviewer scoffed at the touring production rather than condemn it outright. The headline above his piece declared, "O'Shaughnessy Calls it a 'Harmless Hoax.'"

The players from Dublin's Abbey Theatre were in town to perform two works at the Grand Opera House. These were *Kathleen-ni-Houlihan* by W. B. Yeats and *The Playboy of the Western World* by John Millington Synge. The staging of the second of these two plays had caused disturbances, frequently described as "riots," in theaters in Dublin, New York, and Philadelphia.[63] Synge had offended a range of sensibilities both cultural and political. Whether or not the *Playboy*'s depiction of Irish rural life was realistic, it was certainly one that not all Irish and Irish-American people welcomed. They had struggled for social acceptance on both sides of the Atlantic, frequently contending with abiding caricatures of the Catholic Irish and with other prejudices, and within the preceding decade in America there had been a number of disruptions of plays that featured Irish characters.[64] The Ancient Order of Hibernians, a fraternal organization, had campaigned with others against the stage Irishman in US theaters generally and did not welcome now the appearance of Synge's earthy peasantry or his play's themes of lust and violence. Even Synge's language, lauded by critics as poetic, seemed vulgar to some contemporaries, as when the word *shift* is uttered instead of the more genteel *chemise* — and uttered by a man at that.

The *Playboy* is the story of Christy Mahon, a country lad who runs away from an arranged marriage and meets Pegeen Mike. She is a high-spirited girl who is about to marry a dull boy. Christy boasts that he has killed his own father, but the latter turns up very much alive. Fred O'Donovan, a pillar of the Abbey troupe, played Christy in the production, and he had earlier defended the play on the grounds of realism, telling the *New York World*, "The Irish players wanted to put on the stage the real Irishman of today — to reveal Irish conditions and real Irish character."[65] Both middle-class nationalists in Ireland and middle-class Irish-Americans who had worked hard to escape the poverty of their emigrant parents were unlikely to thank him for implying that their new status was a veneer from beneath which a "real" brutish peasant nature was liable to erupt. For the "Protestant Ethic" and the "bourgeois aspirations of a modernizing America" might be contrasted disadvantageously to any sign of indolence and irresponsibility in the Irish.[66]

Lady Augusta Gregory

Traveling with the players was Lady Augusta Gregory, one of the Abbey Theatre's two directors. The other was W. B. Yeats, who would be awarded in 1923 the Nobel Prize for Literature. The two had collaborated closely on the writing of *Kathleen-ni-Houlihan*. Staying at the hotel where the Irish Fellowship Club held its annual St. Patrick's Day banquets, Gregory was greatly concerned about the possibility of Synge's play being suppressed in Chicago, and from there she wrote about the campaign against the *Playboy*: "I see by the papers that at the La Salle Hotel, where I am staying, a meeting of Irishmen has been held at which an 'Anti-Irish Players' League' was formed, beginning with a membership of three hundred. Such a pity I couldn't have slipped in to the meeting!" She noted that a petition demanding the suppression of the play had also been circulated, and twenty thousand signatures were expected.

Gregory was underwhelmed by the quality of Chicago reporters whom she met, remarking, "Last night one of the boy interviewers–they are all boys here–came in from one of the papers. . . . A nice young interviewer; he wants to write a play around his mother's life, to show what a mother's devotion can be. Another of them is twenty-five and is going to be married next summer. He showed me his fiancée's portrait, and another went and hunted for a Don Quixote I wanted, to distract my mind from present-day things." The first "boy" showed her two statements written for the theater, one colorless and the other offering a reward of five thousand dollars to anyone who could prove the management had bribed rioters for the first night, as had been stated in the papers:

> I advised that this be put in, as people really seem to believe it is true. This young man had been to see many of the objectors. They said Synge was a "degenerate," who had lived abroad to collect a bad atmosphere, which he put round Irish characters afterwards. . . . This morning one came who is in with the Irish Clubs and had all the objections, but now seems quite friendly. . .

The interviewer wanted to know if a rehearsal could be held for the mayor so that he might judge the play, but Gregory said that the first night, under the patronage of the Anti-Cruelty Society, would give him his opportunity: "A lady interviewer then came, but I made her take her pencil and write down what I did say, which is more than the boys do. I tell them I put in my pig and it comes out sausage."

Gregory mused on the fact that she found herself defending a play that she had never much liked: "It is a strange fate that sends me into battle after my peaceful life for so many years, and especially over *Playboy*, that I have never really loved, but one has to carry through one's job." She pointed out that the players were all Irish and, with two exceptions, Roman Catholic: "I believe the play is quite honestly considered by some of my countrymen out here to be injurious to Ireland and her claim for self-government, but I know that such an assumption is wrong and that the dignity of Ireland has been very much increased by the work of the Theatre, of which the genius of Mr. Synge is a component part."[67] In the end, the mayor did not stop the play.

Among notable "society people" in the audience on the first night was Mrs. Samuel Insull, whose husband would later work closely with advertising personnel as chairman of the State Council of Defense of Illinois during World War I. Lady Gregory herself sat alone in the last row of seats. She seemed ill at ease, having been told that there would be no riot but not why the managers were so confident that there would not be: "In a crowd there are always contrary people."[68] In New York, after the disturbances on opening night, she had returned to the theater next evening in the company of former president Theodore Roosevelt:

> . . . when I said it would be a help to us, he said, "Then I will certainly
> come," and settled that to-night he will dine with me and come on. . . .
> I had asked [Finley] Peter Dunne (Mr. Dooley) but he was engaged
> to dinner at eight at the Guinnesses. He came, however, at seven and
> sat through ours. He was very amusing, and he and Roosevelt chaffed
> each other. . . . When we got to the theatre and into the box, people saw
> Roosevelt and began to clap and at last he had to get up, and he took my
> hand and dragged me on my feet too, and there was renewed clapping. . . .
> There was a scuffle now and then during *The Playboy* but nothing violent

and always great clapping when the offender was thrown out. We played with the lights up.[69]

Eugene O'Neill

Among others who also had attended the play in New York was the Irish-American Eugene O'Neill (1888–1953). Then a dissolute former student of Princeton, who some say was expelled for throwing a beer bottle through the window of its president (and future US president) Woodrow Wilson, O'Neill would later receive the Nobel Prize for Literature. He told a Boston newspaper in 1923 that the Irish players in New York "gave me a glimpse of my opportunity. I went to see everything they did. . . . They demonstrated the possibilities of naturalistic acting better than any company."[70] James O'Shaughnessy was less impressed by the Abbey's production of Synge's play than was this future great playwright.

The Chicago theater was not full for the *Playboy's* opening performance. This was, according to one reporter, "despite the considerable front-page frenzy and the efforts of the Anti-Cruelty society, which profited by the performance."[71] Perhaps some people had bought tickets solely to support the charity and had no interest in attending. Lady Gregory had earlier written in her diary that "the Anti-Cruelty Society of Chicago, at the head of which are various benevolent ladies, had asked leave to buy up the whole house for the first performance of *The Playboy of the Western World*. They meant to resell these seats at an increased price for their charity and believed it was likely to draw the largest audience. So they have taken the theater for Tuesday, February 6, and the public performance of *The Playboy* will take place the next day."[72]

James O'Shaughnessy's Review

It is clear from O'Shaughnessy's review that he had made up his mind about the play before he went to see it performed. He shrugged it off, and took a sideswipe at press agents in the process. Advertising agents did not like press agents who got publicity for their clients without paying for the services of an advertising agent.

His review is reproduced in appendix A as one example of his journalism.

He discouraged those who might wish to attend simply to see if the performance was salacious, writing, "I have seen many plays that were filthier in any one of various scenes than this play is in its whole length. In that respect it will prove perhaps a serious disappointment." He thought that, "As a piece of literature, 'The Playboy of the Western World' is a vapid hoax. Its cleverness is not sufficiently in evidence to justify it on that score. It is unpretty, but not enough so to excite anybody mentally. Even its squalor is labored and uninteresting." But he had no time for those who might disrupt the performance: "The Irish-American of any generation who would throw an egg or a dead cat over the footlights at the "Playboy" is certainly not of any class of my acquaintances."[73]

Taking a final patronizing sideswipe at the author, O'Shaughnessy observed, "The 'Playboy,' however, may do a great deal of good by calling attention to the rising school of clever young writers in Ireland, of whom Synge, who confected the 'Playboy,' could hardly be called one in spirit."[74]

Revisiting Journalism

James O'Shaughnessy moved on from journalism to become an advertising agent and chief executive of the American Association of Advertising Agencies, but his experience on newspapers informed his work in that other sector of the media, and he never forgot his professional origins. In 1925 he was a guest of the University of Missouri during its Journalism Week. The university had in 1908 led America in formal journalism education, it being described as "the first organized university school of journalism in the world offering a degree in journalism."[75] O'Shaughnessy now delivered an address on how country newspapers could get advertising to support their editorial and commercial efforts.

James O'Shaughnessy did not in old age return to journalism as a career. However, at a breakfast hosted by the AAAA he had an opportunity to relate some anecdotes from his own experiences as a reporter in Cuba. On April 22, 1926, in New York, he was one of the speakers at this event that had been organised "for the delegates from the Latin American republics" who were attending the Pan-American Congress of Journalists.[76]

In 1928, as executive secretary of the AAAA, he sent a warm message to

O'Shaughnessy reviews *The Playboy of the Western World*. From *Chicago Tribune*, 7 Feb. 1912. Ryan Walker sketches of actors, (L-R top) J.M. Kerrigan, J.A. O'Rourke, Eithne Magee, (bottom) Sara Allgood, Arthur Sinclair.

the University of Missouri's School of Journalism, which was preparing for its twentieth anniversary. In his message he expressed his belief that "Everyone in advertising must appreciate the debt that all of us owe to you, who have created more for the broadening and strengthening of the foundation structure upon which advertising operates, than any other single individual." He gave credit to the University of Missouri for teaching other colleges that journalism was not simply "a vital subject" but "that it is teachable." Recognizing the special role that Missouri has played in the process of professionalization, James wrote, "Your influence has long since outgrown the confines of Missouri; it permeates Journalism throughout the forty-eight states. The newspapers are better because you had the ability to materialize your vision and through courage and diligence to project it into a great movement."[77]

O'Shaughnessy's own experience in newspapers was to prove useful again when he later left the AAAA to become business manager of *Liberty*, a national magazine then owned by the *Chicago Tribune*.

THREE Rising Fortunes in Chicago

DURING THE 1890S NOT ONLY JAMES but also his parents and most of his siblings moved to Chicago, which is five hundred miles from St. Joseph. James and his four brothers each made a mark in the city. Their sisters lived elsewhere, one in California until her premature death, one in Arizona as a nun, and one on a farm in Missouri with her husband, William Cullen.

Chicago already had a big Irish and Irish-American population by the time that the O'Shaughnessys arrived. This ethnic community was rooted in its distinctive national past but was constructing an American future for itself that would be both socially and economically comfortable for many of the children of immigrants.

Meagher has noted, "In the 1890s, the term 'lace curtain Irish' was invented, along with other less popular adjectives like 'cut glass Irish', to describe the new phenomoenon of an emerging Irish middle class." He thought that the term was a "bit presumptuous or premature," because second-generation Irish males were still underrepresented among lawyers, agents, brokers, and bankers in 1900.[1]

Speaking Gaelic in Illinois

Irish immigrants and their children differed among themselves in their attitudes toward the politics of Ireland, with some actively backing physical force against the British and others supporting parliamentary campaigns as a better means of achieving Irish self-determination or "home rule". However, all could find common ground in celebrating distinctive Irish cultural and religious traditions. Their influence on the Catholic Church in the United States became quite obvious, but their commitment to aspects of Gaelic culture is less well remembered. Shanabruch describes how, after the defeat of the Home Rule Bill of 1892 and after the downfall of the Irish nationalist leader Charles Stewart Parnell, many Chicago Irish turned their attention to the revival of Gaelic culture:

> the Gaelic League established schools to teach the ancient Irish tongue and literature. Women met to relearn near forgotten handcraft arts. The young organised around music, dance and sport and efforts were made to have the history of Éire [a Gaelic name for "Ireland"] taught in all parochial schools in which the Irish predominated. . . . By 1909 . . . Irish history was taught in twenty-six of the territorial schools. . . . Chicago's Gaelic revival ran parallel to the same movement in Ireland and helped to finance the mother country's revival."[2]

The use of the Irish or Gaelic language by some immigrants in America is not especially surprising when one recognizes that so many had come from poor western areas of Ireland where the old tongue was heard more commonly than elsewhere on the island. Its everyday use in Ireland declined rapidly during the late nineteenthc century even as some Irish immigrants and Irish-Americans strove to teach it to their children in the United States. Nilsen has described the question of Irish-speaking immigrants in America as "long-neglected." The Irish language was still being widely used in the mid-nineteenth century around Gort, County Galway, where James Shaughnessy is likely to have spoken it fluently as a first or second language before he emigrated to the United States, and he appears to have passed it on to some of his sons. Arthur Johnson explicitly stated that his friend James Junior "spoke Gaelic" when they knew one another in Missouri about 1890.[3]

Realtor

The immigrant James Shaughnessy gave up selling shoes when he left Missouri and went to live with his sons in Chicago. By 1900 he had started working as a real estate agent in that rapidly expanding Illinois city.

That same year the US Census lists the O'Shaughnessys (all now with a prefix "O") as living in rented accommodation at 61 Lincoln Avenue, Chicago. This was a comfortable distance from the city's poorer southside districts where the Irish had long gathered. They were raising there James Berney, young son of their daughter Lizzie, who had died in childbirth. In

James O'Shaughnessy Senior at his
real estate office in Chicago.
Courtesy Marianne O'Shaughnessy.

1906 James Senior placed two identical full-page advertisements back-to-back in an Illinois directory to promote his real estate, renting, loans, and insurance business on Lincoln Avenue. He and his family subsequently moved, but not far away, and a surviving photograph shows James Senior standing in the doorway of his real estate office in Ravenswood. He was an active member of Our Lady of Lourdes Church.[4]

The O'Shaughnessys were describing an arc of social mobility that would see them firmly embedded in that middle class of Irish-Americans who came to play a formative role in the city's life for many decades. What Meagher has described as "the dramatic transformation of the political, social and economic environment of the Worcester Irish in the 1890s and 1900s" was being matched elsewhere, although its context varied from region to region. "Yankee hands" had a far weaker grip on the economy of Illinois than on New England, thus making it easier for the Irish to progress in places like Chicago.[5] The O'Shaughnessy boys were among those helping to increase the ratio of Irish-American professionals to all others. Miller has noted that "by the early twentieth century the Irish-American bourgeoisie was primarily the product of upward mobility from the laboring ranks."[6] In the case of the O'Shaughnessys that upward mobility had been greatly facilitated by their father making and selling shoes in Missouri.

University of Notre Dame

The O'Shaughnessy family's connections with the University of Notre Dame, located about ninety miles east of Chicago at South Bend, Indiana, were indicative of their rising fortunes. The gradual development of Notre Dame was a matter of pride for Irish-Americans to whom Catholicism meant so much.[7] Notre Dame had been founded by French and Irish members of the Holy Cross religious order, under the leadership of Fr. Edward Sorin (1814–1893). For some reason this Frenchman regarded the Irish as unstable and changeable and given to an excessive affection for hard liquor: "In dealing with Irishmen generally during the early years of his mission, Sorin adopted a stance toward them that was similar to one frequently encountered among high-placed ecclesiastics in Rome: listen sympathetically to complaints, counsel patience, and then discount much of what had been alleged in complaints because opposition and indignation were only matters of course with them."[8]

As large numbers of Irish-Americans began to attend Notre Dame, Sorin seems to have moderated his opinion of the Irish. In October 1885 he publicly endorsed the cause of Irish nationalism by donating one hundred dollars to an Irish parliamentary campaign fund. It was a remarkable gesture that signified the growing status of the Irish in the region. By then, most students attending Notre Dame were of Irish birth or descent.[9]

The president of Notre Dame between 1893 and 1905, when the O'Shaughnessys developed links with that university, was Fr. Andrew Morrissey (1860–1921). A leading campus religious conservative, he was known from the name of the Irish county of his birth as the "Kilkenny Chieftain." The majority of bachelor's degrees granted during his time as president were in law. During 1900, Francis O'Shaughnessy graduated with a law degree from Notre Dame. He was later said to have been a prominent campus figure while a student and was on the Notre Dame *Scholastic* staff. The *Scholastic* claims to be the oldest continuously published collegiate news magazine in the United States. As soon as Francis had his law degree, he and his brother John, who had graduated from the University of Missouri, teamed up and practiced together.[10]

The census of 1900 gives John and Francis as attorneys and their brother

James as a working reporter. The latter is also said to have studied law for a while, and a writer in Notre Dame's *Scholastic* would later refer to him as an "old student" when mentioning one of his achievements. However, there is no record at Notre Dame of James having graduated there, and he may simply have attended some lectures.[11]

The O'Shaughnessy brothers helped one another to achieve their ambitions. James and Thomas, between them, met almost all of the expenses and fees due for the education of their brothers Francis and Martin at Notre Dame, as correspondence in the university's archives confirms. This involved some hardship. In 1900 Francis wrote to President Morrissey at Notre Dame requesting an extra year to settle Martin's account, stating that he would soon be in a position to help but that "it would be impossible for us to pay that amount now without making ruinous sacrifices." He added, "If I have any success in the practice of law I will owe it to Notre Dame and our indebtedness to the institution will be paid at any sacrifice." It is said that Morrissey had an antipathy to incurring institutional debt.[12]

The athletic Martin was very active in the sports life of Notre Dame. He also signed up for a wide range of courses there between 1896 and 1900. These included Special Orthography, Grammar, Arithmetic, Latin, Engineering, Catholic Dogma, and Ancient Roman History.[13] His broad curriculum was in keeping with a Catholic tradition of classical education, but the list also serves as a reminder that the presidency of Andrew Morrissey at Notre Dame was not distinguished by an ambition for coherent academic development. As one of the university's own historians has written, "Admittedly a man of many good qualities, he [Morrissey] was nevertheless deficient in his own education and had neither appreciation of nor interest in scholarship and the intellectual life . . . he is said to have remarked: 'What we need here is a compact, tidy little boarding school. We can't compete with these other institutions that have all the money.'"[14]

Martin and Basketball

Like many of its own alumni and like the city of Chicago itself, the University of Notre Dame gradually prospered. Its sportsmen grew more confident. On November 23, 1897, the first intercollegiate football game at Notre Dame was played. In 1898 a new gymnasium was erected on the campus.

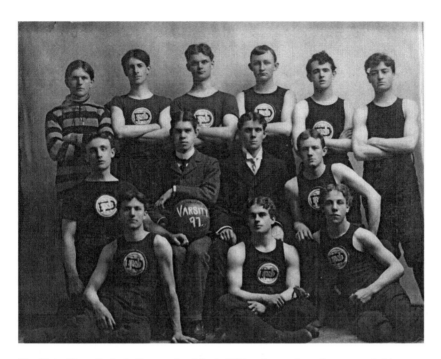

First Notre Dame Basketball team, 1897. Martin O'Shaughnessy is on the extreme left in hooped shirt. John Shillington seated at left end of front row. Coach Frank Hering center in tie without ball. Courtesy University of Notre Dame.

That same year Martin O'Shaughnessy was appointed captain of the new Notre Dame basketball team, the team having been granted formal varsity status. Coach Frank E. Hering had created the team informally during 1897, but its then-captain and leading scorer, John Shillington, had been expelled from Notre Dame when he stayed in Chicago without permission after playing a game there. Shillington thereupon joined the US Navy, and in February 1898 was killed aboard the USS *Maine* when it blew up in Havana harbor. That event precipitated the Spanish-American War and brought James O'Shaughnessy to Cuba. Martin O'Shaughnessy, the new captain, had been one of Shillington's teammates in 1897.[15]

Martin led Notre Dame's varsity basketball team to its first ever victory, beating Rush Medical 16–13 on February 16, 1898. "More significant than the first season record, however, was that competition was inaugurated that year at Notre Dame in a sport that was to find the Irish consistently in the basketball spotlight throughout the United States." So remarked Raymond J. Donovan, assistant director of publicity at Notre Dame, in the printed program for a game against Kentucky in 1946.[16] By the 1920s the sports teams of Notre Dame had acquired a collective nickname, the "Fighting Irish," which is sometimes mistakenly associated with the university's footballers alone. The process of acquiring the nickname was ostensibly given momentum in 1919 when Irish rebel leaders Éamon de Valera and Harry Boland visited the campus and were warmly welcome by its president. Eleven years earlier Notre Dame had established a chair of Irish history, said to have been the first of its kind in America. From 1920 Arch Ward deliberately fostered use of the "Fighting Irish" tag. Ward (1896–1955) was then the students' press agent and would go on to become longtime sports editor of the *Chicago Tribune*.[17]

Recalling in 1932 Notre Dame's first varsity basketball win under O'Shaughnessy a correspondent for the *Scholastic* declared, "Let those who believe that Notre Dame hasn't the right to be called the 'Fighting Irish' take one look at the list of basketball monogram men of that year. Besides O'Shaughnessy, there were also, Burns, Donahue, Fennessy, McNichols, Naughton, Powers and Steiner." In 1981 an Associated Press reporter wrote, "From these humble beginnings grew the mystique of what today has become the nation's most highly publicized college basketball team."[18] Remarkably, Burns overlooked this early basketball team in the account of organized sports in his history of Notre Dame.[19]

Martin did not graduate from Notre Dame, although it is not known if this was principally a matter of grades, personal indifference, or inability to pay. The family's sensitivity to social appearances was underlined by a comment that Francis made in his letter to Morrissey seeking an extra year in which to pay Martin's outstanding fees. He observed, "In regard to the room, we can hardly afford to pay the additional amount, and you know it would be humiliating for him to return to Brownson Hall after he had been established in Sorin Hall for a year." Sorin Hall is said to have been the first student residential facility with individual rooms ever built on an American Catholic college campus. It had opened and received its first students in January 1889, and its rooms were much sought after.[20]

Having left Notre Dame, Martin worked as a salesman for Parker Jenks haberdasher and other employers, including the Globe Iron Works. He wrote to staff of the college proposing to sell goods to students and offering the Athletic Association at Notre Dame a cut of any profits that might arise from certain sales. Although he had not graduated from Notre Dame, Martin continued to keep in touch with the university and in 1913 was elected one of the members of a new committee set up by the Alumni Association for non-alumni. He is said to have been a "successful businessman" who bore with "such resignation and patience as excited the admiration of all who saw him" the illness that led to his death in 1918 at the age of thirty-eight.[21]

St Patrick's Day

Members of the O'Shaughnessy family, as might be expected of aspirational Catholics at this time, were involved in the Knights of Columbus. Francis, Thomas, and John O'Shaughnessy all joined the organization of which their father was also a member.[22] The Knights had been formed as a fraternal association of Catholics whose members insured themselves by paying dues to that organization in case of accident or death. Local councils of the Knights proliferated in Chicago between 1896 and 1918, and one author has argued that it allowed Irish-Americans to repudiate a purely ethnic identity in favor of a strictly Catholic one that included Italians and others.[23]

However, for Irish-American Catholics, the annual commemmoration of their national saint, Patrick, was also important. Insofar as the day was celebrated in a seemly and fraternal fashion, it became a sign of their social acceptability and a vehicle for their economic advancement.

When they became founding members and, in some cases, officers of the Irish Fellowship Club, the O'Shaughnessy brothers were involved in the creation of an association that had as one of its principal objectives the marking of St. Patrick's Day. Irish emigrants throughout the world have long celebrated the feast day of their country's patron.[24] In 1902, one writer noted, "From few and rare in the middle of the eighteenth century the observances of St. Patrick's Day had become fixed institutions in most American cities and towns by the middle of the nineteenth century. From 1845 on to the present day these festal functions have spread all over the United States with the march of the Irish race." The author added, "Every urban community gives welcome and honor to the Irish anniversary, often by imposing military and civic parades, by impressive church services and eloquent pulpit utterances, by the display of flags on public and private buildings, by great banquets attended by national, state and city officials."²⁵

In Chicago, as elsewhere, the day was celebrated with a range of festivities. For example, on St. Patrick's Day 1899, Fr. Martin Murphy, a Galwayman and friend of Fr. Eugene O'Growney of Ireland's Gaelic League, had been invited to deliver an address to a gathering of some of the city's Irish.²⁶

Overland notes that the parades that became a feature of Irish communities on St. Patrick's Day managed to transcend ethnicity in their festive spirit and that, on March 17 each year, many Americans with no trace of genetic Irishness have playfully claimed an Irish identity. However, he also points out that not everyone has been amused by this fact. In an editorial on March 19, 1903, the editor of the Chicago Czech-American newspaper *Denni Hlasatel* (Daily Voice) complained, "This year, as in other years, our patriotic youth took it upon themselves to decorate their breasts with green ribbons, shamrocks, and other symbols of the Irish people on the occasion of St. Patrick's Day. Although in most cases it was done in a jocular manner, nevertheless it was a sad manifestation. . . ." The editor thought that "Our Bohemian nation with its culture, its maturity and history surpasses by far the Irish nation, and our children, American born perhaps, have no reason to be ashamed of their Bohemian origin and to try to pass themselves off as Irish."²⁷

Some of the Irish themselves were ashamed of what they witnessed at certain Irish celebrations. The upwardly mobile children of immigrants resented stage-Irish caricatures of their countrymen and frowned on those Irish who, through drunkenness or foolishness, publicly lent credibility to such caricatures. Future presidents of the Irish Fellowship Club were to recall that it was founded partly "to take the Irish off the streets," to "stop the parades that were holding up the Irish in Chicago to ridicule at that time," to "build up a spirit among the people of Irish descent here, of dignity, of cultural activities . . . . to get rid of the green hat, the clay pipe and the big stick." From its founding, the Irish Fellowship Club held its main annual celebration banquet to mark St. Patrick's Day. Just as an emerging middle-class Catholic Church in Ireland had ensured that formal devotional practices within its walls superseded the wilder popular customs that had been associated with "holy wells" and certain annual celebrations there, so the Irish-American middle classes might take ownership of St. Patrick's Day from their more unruly fellow countrymen. It was not that all parades ended, for they take place in Chicago and elsewhere even today, but they were certainly not to be the sole form of Irish-American celebration for other Americans to see.

An annual parade that used to pass St. Patrick's Church on the saint's feast day was discontinued as the twentieth century dawned. John Kelley, dean of Chicago's police reporters and unofficial historian of the city, later recalled that annual event but gave more innocent reasons for its demise than that of public disorder:

> One reason is that the "old-timer" from the Emerald Isle, who would rather go without his dinner than to miss throwing out his chest in the parade, is no longer here to celebrate. He went to his "long home" many years ago. Under the sod of Calvary, Mount Olivet, and Mount Carmel cemeteries rest thousands who, in the old days, marched gaily to the strains of "Garry Owen," "St. Patrick's Day in the Morning," or "Wearing of the Green." Another and more potent reason, however, for the discontinuance of St. Patrick's day turnout was the large number of deaths from pneumonia which usually followed among the marchers.[28]

Deaths in the Family

The fortunes of Chicago grew so rapidly that it was thought it might one day establish itself as the largest metropolis in the United States. Ultimately it remained the second city after New York, yet some of its Irish citizens evidently saw it as special. Captain Anthony Donelan, MP of Cork, told a meeting in the city in 1904 that "Chicago had come to be recognized as the capital of the Irish in the United States."[29] However, while many Irish immigrants and Irish-Americans certainly made it their home and eventually came to dominate the local administration of both the Catholic Church and the Democratic Party, there were in fact more German people than Irish in the city. Significant numbers of Poles and other Europeans also arrived.[30] There was an underlying slowdown in immigration from Ireland, but this was somewhat masked by migration to Chicago from old immigrant settlements elsewhere within the United States. By 1910 nearly two out of every three persons of Irish and German stock in the city had been born in America.[31]

A faded photograph of the extended O'Shaughnessy family, undated but clearly taken in the early twentieth century, shows the immigrant James and his wife, Catherine, surrounded by their American-born children and baby grandchildren.[32]

The O'Shaughnessy family from Missouri was just one of many that left older immigrant settlements for the expanding cities of the West and Midwest. Arriving in Chicago it bypassed the existing communities of lower-class Irish in areas such as Bridgeport on Chicago's South Side and made its home farther north.

During 1918, one year after James went to work in New York, he lost first his brother Martin and then his father. Notre Dame's internal magazine

James and Catherine O'Shaughnessy and their extended family, early 1900s. Courtesy Brigid O'Shaughnessy.

referred to Martin as having been an "efficient and successful businessman" and noted, about the cause of his death, "The disease which finally ended his life [aged 38] was a long and painful one, but he bore himself with such resignation and patience as excited the admiration of all who saw him."[33] It was feared that Martin's funeral would be impossible because of snow-drifts six and seven feet deep in some places along Winchester Avenue in Chicago, but neighbors worked until late in the night digging a trench from the O'Shaughnessy home two blocks to Robey Street where a hearse was waiting to receive his remains. This enabled pallbearers to carry the body through an aisle of snow for what the *Chicago Tribune* predicted would be an impressive funeral, at Our Lady of Lourdes Church.[34]

The O'Shaughnessy boys' father subsequently passed away. Three years earlier he had survived "a stroke of paralysis as a result of an accident." It is said that after his stroke "he devoted his time to looking after his property in Chicago and the old farm homestead at Newhall" in Missouri. He was staying at that homestead in Chariton County, superintending the building of a house on the farm of his daughter Anna, or Annie, Cullen at New Cambria, Missouri, when he died suddenly on November 8, 1918. One local paper described him as "a quiet man, very devoted to his family, and a highly respected citizen in the community." His burial and that of his youngest son, Martin, took place simultaneously and side by side at St. Joseph Cemetery, Newhall. For the preceding ten months, "the body of the son had been kept in a vault in Chicago awaiting a favorable opportunity for burial in the old home cemetery." James Junior may have been a big shot adman in New York by this time, but the *Brunswicker*, a Chariton County newspaper, entirely overlooked his existence when it stated that his late father was survived by "three sons, John P., Thomas and Francis." It also overlooked James's two surviving sisters, Anna Cullen and Mary, the latter by then Sister Mary Grace, who lived in a convent in Bisbee, Arizona. It was said at the time of his death that James Senior, from Galway, was survived by fourteen American grandchildren. His widow, Catherine, was to die in 1927.[35]

James Shaughnessy had left Ireland during a terrible famine and worked hard as an immigrant to build a secure future for his family in the United States. He saw his sons make remarkable contributions to the society in which they found themselves, rising as they did so far above the impoverished circumstances of his early life. Although no doubt dismayed by Martin's early death, he had the consolation of knowing that his other sons wielded influence in their professional fields as well as in the political and social life of Chicago.

JFK

The Irish Catholic influence in American public life was to continue to grow. It reached a high point in politics in 1960 with the election of John F. Kennedy (JFK) as president of the United States. There had been Irish-American or "Scotch/Scots-Irish" presidents before, but Kennedy remains to this day the only US president raised in a Roman Catholic family. When he was a senator from Massachusetts, JFK came to Chicago in 1956 and was the Irish Fellowship Club's guest of honour at its St. Patrick's Day banquet then, in the same year that Thomas Gus O'Shaughnessy died. Richard J. Daley became the club's president for 1957. Daley was mayor of Chicago from 1955 to 1976 and played a key role in both the nomination of JFK as the Democratic Party's presidential candidate and his election to office in 1960. The efforts of James O'Shaughnessy and his brothers in founding and supporting the Irish Fellowship Club, to which a separate chapter is devoted, may be regarded as a significant contribution to the political "greening of America."

Irish-Americans celebrated the election of Kennedy. Irish Catholic immigrants and their descendants had long met with distrust in the United States, not least during World War I because of Irish nationalist enmity toward Washington's ally Britain. Even as late as the election of JFK Protestant voters feared that Irish-Americans might owe their allegiance in matters of policy primarily to the Catholic Church and not to the United States.

FOUR Hyphenated Immigrant Loyalties

MANY OF THE IRISH IN CHICAGO, as well as their Irish-American children, felt that they had "pulled themselves up by their bootstraps" and were proud of their contribution to the United States. One such was Irish-born Richard Curran from Limerick, who had worked on a farm in Ireland before immigrating at the age of sixteen to America and there training as a plasterer. By 1912 he had his own construction business, was a member of the Knights of Columbus and of the Irish Fellowship Club, and was included in an illustrated list of "notable men" of Illinois published by the *Chicago Daily News* and based on information provided by the contributors themselves. Of the five others who identified themselves on that list as members of the club, all of whom were born in the United States, three were lawyers, one an undertaker, and one a general manager.[1] Such men of substance took a continuing interest in Irish affairs but were unlikely to wish to be closely associated with revolutionary violence in the old country.

1916

When war broke out in Europe in 1914, it tested the process of integration of immigrants into American society. As Britain fought Germany, the loyalty of German and Irish immigrants and their descendants was questioned. Could they be trusted to remain neutral or, after US forces joined the conflict from April 1917, to support the war effort? Some Irish-Americans actively opposed US participation alongside British forces, with a rebellion in Dublin in 1916 inflaming nationalist sentiment. It became imperative for leaders of opinion such as the journalist and adman James O'Shaughnessy to speak up for people like himself and his family by reminding Americans of the continuing contribution of Irish-Americans to the prosperity and welfare of the United States. During 1916 he expressed the sense of achievement and pride of the Irish in Chicago, pointing out that "Irish influence in Chicago from the beginning of its continuing history has been large" and noting that the first Fort Dearborn, constructed by 1808 on a small hill on the south bank of the Chicago River, had been built by an Irish-born soldier of the revolution. Mindful of the contribution of his maternal grandfather to the development of the city's waterways, he continued,

> The first man to till a farm and the first white family to which a child was born, as well as the first to teach a school where now Chicago stands, were all Irish. The two heroes of the Fort Dearborn massacre [of US soldiers by Native Americans in 1812] were Irish. The beginning of Chicago proper was made possible by the influence in France of an Irishman who found the money for the Illinois and Michigan Canal. The first man of prominence, influence and ability to proclaim Chicago a future great city was an Irishman. The first great builder of churches, hospitals and institutions of learning that attracted the first large influx of Irish homebuilders was an Irish bishop.

Observing that the percentage of Irish in Chicago's population had long been very large — "and so potent as to exert a marked influence on the commercial spirit, civil pride and social life of the community" — he went on to claim not just these physical achievements for the Irish in America but also the moral high ground:

> It is chiefly through Irish influence that Chicago has preserved a higher moral tone than any other very large city in history. The Irish have built more churches, hospitals and charitable institutions than all the other nationalities in Chicago, and every one of them is as free to the people of other races as to their own. Leaving out the public schools, the Irish have built more schools than all others in Chicago and the Irish chiefly maintain these schools privately, but hold them open to all.

He asserted that the Irish "give themselves to all the communities out of the love of common welfare" and ended with a flourish that perhaps betrays a note of insecurity: "All they ask of it is that they may continue as the generations before them, holding Chicago to its distinctions as the fairest, most just and kindliest — the most democratic of large cities — the most affectionately favored by Divine Providence."[2]

Woodrow Wilson and James Barry

Given the long Irish struggle for independence from Britain, it is scarcely surprising that not all Irish-Americans were enthusiastic about US forces fighting alongside the British army in World War I. Some even supported Germany.[3] This displeased President Woodrow Wilson, whose Presbyterian Irish antecedents were likely in any event to have inclined him culturally to regard recent Irish Catholic immigrants with some unease. If the future playwright Eugene O'Neill, the son of one of these, really was (as some say) expelled from Princeton for throwing a beer bottle through Wilson's window when the latter was its president and a professor there it is unlikely that Wilson's memory of that incident attenuated any such unease. Long before the US entered World War I, its president made clear his thoughts on the conflicting loyalties of immigrants when he unveiled a statue to Commodore John Barry (1745–1803). Barry was an immigrant from County Wexford, Ireland, and a naval hero of the Revolutionary War. Wilson, who on one occasion referred proudly to his own "Scotch-Irish blood," used the opportunity of the ceremony on May 16, 1914, to make an important speech that sent a very clear message to the O'Shaughnessys and other Irish-Americans. He said that

> John Barry was an Irishman, but his heart crossed the Atlantic with him. He did not leave it in Ireland. And the test of all of us — for all of us had our origins on the other side of the sea — is whether we will assist in enabling America to live her separate and independent life, retaining our ancient affections, indeed, but determining everything that we do by the interests that exist on this side of the sea. Some Americans need hyphens in their names, because only part of them has come over; but when the whole man has come over, heart and thought and all, the hyphen drops of its own weight out of his name.
>
> This man was not an Irish-American; he was an Irishman who became an American. I venture to say if he voted he voted with regard to the questions as they looked on this side of the water and not as they affected the other side; and that is my infallible test of a genuine American, that when he votes or when he acts or when he fights his heart and his thought are centered nowhere but in the emotions and the purposes and the policies of the United States.[4]

President Woodrow Wilson, May 1914, challenges Irish-America. Courtesy
Library of Congress.

The hearts and thoughts of the O'Shaughnessys were not centered exclusively in America. Their "ancient affections" mattered to them. They
cared both for Ireland and for the best interests of the United States. Their
German immigrant neighbors had a saying that might serve equally well to
express an Irish point of view: "Germania meine Mutter, Columbia meine
Braut" (Germany my mother, America my bride). A man need not forsake
his mother in order to be faithful to his bride.[5]

Apostrophe and Hyphen

By the time the O'Shaughnessys moved to Chicago from Missouri the elder
James had followed the example of his sons and added the Gaelic prefix
"O" before his family name. The letter indicates simply that one is "of" or
"from" a certain clan, and in that sense the apostrophe in their name signified their origin as much as their present identity. Nevertheless, they were

clearly proud to be Irish-American and did not regard Irish and American as mutually exclusive categories. For one thing the brothers helped to found a fellowship club that was described frankly as "Irish," not "Irish-American." At least two of them spent time in Ireland learning about the country's culture, and James himself was later to advise its advertising agents on developing Irish business internationally. Thomas dedicated one of his stained glass windows in Old St. Pat's Church in Chicago to an Irish revolutionary who died while on a hunger strike in a British jail in 1920 and whom he had earlier met during a visit to Ireland. But the O'Shaughnessys were not extreme nationalists in the manner of some Irish-Americans. Members of the family, as shall be seen, helped to organize a welcome to Chicago for the moderate Irish nationalist leader John Redmond. Redmond, a member of the United Kingdom parliament, urged Irishmen to join the British army when World War I broke out, and in Ireland many Catholics as well as Protestants did so. Redmond believed, naively, that such a demonstration of loyalty would ultimately ensure that Britain could no longer delay granting a significant level of independence ("Home Rule") to Ireland.

The Irish-American son of Lizzie, late sister of the O'Shaughnessy boys, joined the US Army when the United States entered World War I. Irish immigrants and many descendants of immigrants who enlisted included those who joined the 165th infantry regiment, better known today as the "The Fighting 69th." A prominent US poet of the time, Joyce Kilmer, died fighting for that regiment. Before his own death he had written a poem commemorating colleagues who lost their lives in action in France alongside him and their commander "Wild Bill" Donovan. Indicating clearly his regiment's Irish connections, some of its lines refer to principal saints of Ireland:

And Patrick, Brigid, Columkill
Rejoice that in veins of warriors still
The Gael's blood runs.
And up to Heaven's doorway floats,
From the wood called Rouge Bouquet,
A delicate cloud of bugle notes
That softly say:
"Farewell!
Farewell! . . ."[6]

Contention at the Club

During 1917, Chicago's Irish Fellowship Club passed a resolution urging the people of Ireland to refrain from attacking British forces and instead to join the cause of the Allies against Germany. Martin Insull, a brother of the Chicago utility magnate Samuel Insull, had pressed the club to demonstrate its loyalty to the Allied cause. The resolution was passed after a contentious debate chaired by club president James V. O'Donnell, but its adoption was consistent with members' reservations about the Easter Rebellion in Dublin in 1916. Like many Irish-Americans, most members of the club supported self-determination for Ireland but favored moderate Irish politicians such as John Redmond over more radical opponents. "Big Bill" Thompson might play the anti-British card at election times in Chicago, but Irish-Americans who had successful careers and businesses were not inclined toward supporting outright revolution. One exception was John A. McGarry, a wealthy Chicago paving contractor and the seventh president of the club. Reacting to this vote of 1917 he became the only former president ever to resign his membership. He would later return.[7] On March 18, 1918, President Wilson wrote to O'Donnell to thank the Irish Fellowship Club for its reassuring attitude.[8] During 1917 Wilson had made quiet representations to the British, pointing out that their failure to resolve their dispute in Ireland was complicating matters for the US government.[9]

De Valera and the American Irish

Éamon de Valera became the leading politician of the mid-twentieth century in Ireland. He was born in Manhattan to an Irish immigrant mother and a Spanish or Spanish-American father, and sent as an infant to be raised in Ireland. In 1916 his wife persuaded the US consul in Dublin to intervene on his behalf, on the basis of his US birth certificate, to save him from execution when the British arrested him for his role in the rebellion of that year. He subsequently visited the United States during the Irish war of independence to rally support and to raise funds for the insurgents.

Miller has written that de Valera's disillusionment with many of his Irish-American hosts in 1920 revealed how intrinsically "American" the latter had become. De Valera was particularly frustrated in Chicago in 1920 when he failed to persuade the Republican Party at its annual convention there to back Irish members of the UK parliament who had formed their own unofficial and separatist national assembly in Ireland (the Dáil), instead of taking their seats in the UK parliament at Westminster. The Republican Party only agreed to support the principle of "self-determination" for the Irish, which might stop short of complete separation from London.[10]

The Irish in America and their Irish-American children reflected a broad spectrum of political opinion. When it came to their views on Irish or other affairs, whether domestic or international, Irish-Americans shared no single stance. Most were moderate, but some were extreme. Class, religion, and other factors meant, as Kelly points out, that no all-encompassing phrase can capture their multifaceted profile.[11] The earnestness of Catholic Irish-Americans to demonstrate their loyalty was, for example, complicated by historical tensions, as noted already in relation to Woodrow Wilson. Many earlier immigrants came from a Presbyterian settler background in the northern counties of Ireland (the "Scotch-Irish" or "Scots-Irish" of Ulster). Their descendants distanced themselves socially and politically from later influxes of poverty-stricken Catholics. Moreover, no matter what President Wilson urged as regards hyphenated loyalties, some Anglo-Saxon Protestants were in no hurry in practice to see the latest Irish-Americans shake off the hyphenated nature of their identity and be accepted as full-blooded Americans. So the latter found it necessary to assert in various ways their loyalty, as is clearly demonstrated in the windows commissioned from Thomas O'Shaughnessy's studio for the Catholic cathedral in the diocese of Springfield, Illinois, in the late 1920s. One depicts Illinois troops leaving Springfield during World War I while a Catholic chaplain blesses them. Behind the troops is the state capitol and above it a gold star representing the "Gold Star Mothers" whose sons were killed during the conflict. While most of the sixteen windows feature saints, one depicts George Washington and another Abraham Lincoln. The diocesan website is frank about the motivation of Bishop James A. Griffin, who had been born in Chicago to Irish parents and who commissioned the works. It notes that "he grew up in a generation of Catholics who cherished their immigrant roots, yet identified themselves as 100 percent American. He also grew up in an at-

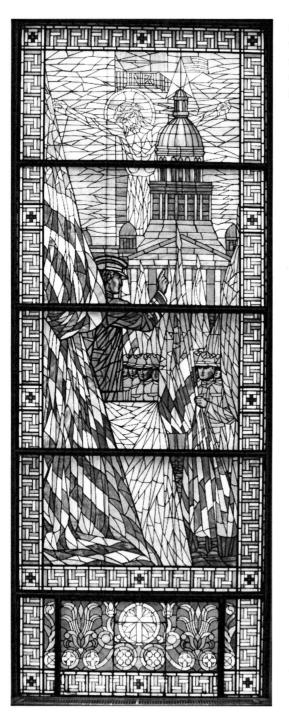

Gus O'Shaughnessy window depicting llinois troops leaving Springfield. Courtesy Diocese of Springfield, Illinois.

mosphere where Protestant Americans questioned the loyalty of Catholics because of their spiritual allegiance to the pope. The bishop wanted the cathedral church to be a statement about Catholic love of God and country and this statement is best seen in the windows." Thomas O'Shaughnessy himself stressed that the windows were "designed and made in America by Americans and of American material."[12]

Ibson observes that Joseph Kennedy, the father of the future US president John F. Kennedy, became irate when a Boston newspaper referred to him in the 1930s as an "Irish-American." This was "an invidious distinction which the betters of Boston, New York, and Palm Beach continuously pointed out." Joe Kennedy wondered, "What the hell do I have to do to be an American?"[13]

Pro-war Sentiment and James O'Shaughnessy

While some Irish-Americans rose through the ranks of the US Army and Navy, others prospered in American civilian occupations. James O'Shaughnessy was one of the latter. There was never a reason to doubt his loyalty to the United States at its time of crisis in 1917. The appointment of a person of his hyphenated background to coordinate nationally the war efforts of advertising agencies, which will be considered later, might even be seen incidentally as a means of reassuring or shaming any advertising agent of any ethic origin hesitant to participate in such efforts and, at the same time, of sending a signal to other Irish-Americans that they were valued citizens of the United States. Jackson Lears comments that "the Anglo-Saxon Protestant composition of the national advertising industry made it a fertile breeding ground for interventionist and pro-war sentiment."[14] This was perhaps all the more reason to find a chief executive for the industry's representative association who was not an Anglo-Saxon, albeit this attribute was unlikely to have been the predominant consideration in the recruitment of such a figure. In any event, for personal and professional reasons, the person whom they found for the job and brought to New York City was the Chicago adman and former journalist James O'Shaughnessy. In that capacity he was to play a prominent part in the execution of the government's information strategy during and immediately after World War I, while also creating and consolidating a national organization for US advertising agencies.

FIVE The Irish Fellowship Club
and Chicago Politics

THE IRISH FELLOWSHIP CLUB quickly became a pillar of Chicago
society and a forum for Irish-Americans and is still active today; it has been
visited by presidents and power brokers from both sides of the Atlantic.
Among its foundational and early members were James, John, Francis, and
Thomas O'Shaughnessy. Both James and Francis served terms as president
of the influential organization. The O'Shaughnessy brothers also played an
active role in party politics in Chicago.

Founding the Club

In 1951 Thomas recalled that James had with Michael Faherty "and a group of
earnest Irishmen" founded the Irish Fellowship Club half a century earlier.
Marking the club's centenary, Chicago's city council described it in 2001 as
"the brainchild of Chicago journalist James O'Shaughnessy whose grandfather, James Mulholland, designed and built the locks of the Illinois and
Michigan Canal."[1] The circle of friends who formed the club were habitués
of the very popular Vogelsang's Restaurant, located not far from city hall.
These were "men of urban significance in Chicago," "distinguished members
of the bench, the press and commerce," and "there was not a ditch digger"
or saloon keeper among them. They first organized themselves in 1901 as a
group styling itself the Red Branch Knights, in honor of an ancient Gaelic
brotherhood with its own mythology.[2] Their chosen name echoed those
of the Knights of Columbus and the Knights Templar, both organizations
that engaged in philanthropic and social activities across the United States.[3]

Members of the Red Branch Knights soon decided that the association's
name was too obscure and unsuited to their objectives and changed it to
the Irish Fellowship Club. They chose as the club's first president Edward
F. Dunne (1853–1937), a rising star of the Democratic Party in Chicago, of

whom James was an active political supporter. Paul Green has said Dunne was not typical of the Irish political machine. He was, says Green, "a reformer who, though devoutly pro-Irish and pro-Ireland, acted more like a Union League Club 'WASP' attorney than a politician from the neighbourhood." Born in Connecticut, he had in the early 1870s commenced a three-year course at Trinity College Dublin, when Oscar Wilde was a student there. However, Dunne had to leave Dublin before the completion of his studies because his father's business failed.[4]

While Dunne was the club's first president, James O'Shaughnessy took on the responsibility of being its honorary secretary under him. By 1903 the club was already assuming a leading role in Chicago's annual St. Patrick's Day festivites. Among the city's other celebrations on that day in 1903 was a solemn high mass in St. Thomas's Church (on Fifty-fifth Street and Kimbark Avenue) at which that church's pastor, Fr. John Carroll, notably gave the sermon in Gaelic, the old Irish language. He had been unanimously elected librarian of the Gaelic League of America at its most recent national convention. "Gaelic souvenirs" were distributed at this service, and the sermon was expected to attract considerable attention from "the numerous advocates of the perpetuation of the Gaelic tongue and literature in Chicago." The Irish Fellowship Club arranged to distribute to guests at its banquet in the Auditorium later that same day one thousand green sprigs of shamrock "gathered from historic spots on the Emerald Isle." About eight hundred people described as "the leading Irishmen of the city" had accepted invitations to attend. From the beginning, it is said, the club's annual St. Patrick's Day dinner was "a stunningly formal affair."[5]

In later years the club's guests of honor were to include Irish presidents and prime ministers as well as many prominent Americans.[6] Among its own presidents were to be not only James O'Shaughnessy and his brother Francis but also mayors of Chicago. Prominent politicians and their supporters from each of the main US parties have been leading members of the Irish Fellowship Club.

Hearst, Darrow and Dunne

Although the author of a biographical note on James, used when he joined the American Irish Historical Society in 1910, referred to him as a "political editor," this does not adequately indicate his proactive role both at the

Chicago American and in the Democratic Party. William Randolph Hearst deployed his newspapers to advance his political career toward winning the presidency of the United States. Koenigsberg later described the tension between political agendas and professional duties at the Hearst newspapers then as "a sour potion." Hearst ultimately failed to win the Democratic Party's nomination for president, but some of his managers worked hard for him along the way. Early in 1904 we find the *Chicago Tribune* reporting that James O'Shaughnessy, "one of the Hearst boomers," had proclaimed to it, "When I say that we are going to carry this state for him I mean it, and have facts to back up the statement."[7]

The "political editor" James O'Shaughnessy was active on behalf of both Hearst and Hearst's political ally Edward F. Dunne, until Hearst and Dunne fell out with one another and O'Shaughnessy then backed Dunne. Positioned on the "progressive" or reformist wing of the Democratic Party, Dunne was a former judge who served from 1905 to 1907 as Chicago's first Irish-American Catholic mayor and from 1913 to 1917 as the State of Illinois' first Irish-American Catholic governor. He was "the only individual to ever hold both offices," as a historian of the Irish Fellowship Club later boasted of the man who had also been the club's first president.[8] One biographer describes Dunne as "a humane liberal" and perhaps "Chicago's only truly reformist mayor" and states, "His nomination and election transcended the existing political order and were genuinely revolutionary." However, he immediately ran into trouble when he tried to give effect to his promise of taking the "street railways" or "traction" system into municipal ownership. Morton notes that "only Hearst's *American* and *Examiner* stood with the mayor," with Hearst and Dunne at that point still being allies.[9] Dunne as a circuit court judge in 1901 had dismissed proceedings for constructive contempt against Hearst's *Chicago American* in a case where "arguments closed with a brilliant speech by Clarence S. Darrow" for the newspaper. In 1903 he presided at Darrow's second marriage. Not yet widely known as a lawyer, Darrow subsequently became Dunne's special traction counsel upon the latter's election as mayor in April 1905.[10]

The alliance of Dunne and Hearst ended unhappily. On December 18, 1905, a report filed exclusively from Chicago for the *Los Angeles Times* predicted that "open warfare" between "the two would-be Progressive Democrats" Dunne and Hearst was in the offing. During a visit to Chicago, Hearst,

Edward Dunne, mayor
of Chicago and governor
of Illinois. From *Notable Men
of Illinois and Their State*
(*Chicago Daily Journal*, 1912).

who was then a New York congressman and ostensibly on the best of terms
with Dunne, "learned some things which surprised him." He had supposed
that Dunne and his people were working to aid him in his presidential
aspirations. Instead, he found out that Dunne intended to back William
Jennings Bryan for president: "The dethronement of James O'Shaughnessy, Mayor Dunne's 'next friend,' and until that time the leader of the
allied Dunne-Hearst forces, was the result of Hearst's discovery." The *Los
Angeles Times* added, "Hearst placed A. M. Lawrence, the publisher of the
Chicago Examiner, in charge of his followers, and O'Shaughnessy severed
his connection with Hearst. Since then Mayor Dunne and O'Shaughnessy
have been preparing to cut loose from Hearst and to build up a machine
of their own."[11]

O'Shaughnessy was subsequently tipped for appointment by Dunne as
Chicago's next commissioner of public works, the *Chicago Tribune* noting
in its report of city hall gossip in 1906 that O'Shaughnessy "has been one
of the most prominent of the mayor's political advisors and is just now out
of a place."[12] However, this appointment did not come to pass. Caught be-

tween competing interests, Dunne proved unable to realize his ambitions as mayor. Clarence Darrow, who was to become one of America's most famous lawyers, quit as Dunne's counsel because of Dunne's "vacillatory" nature, and the incumbent was defeated in 1907.[13]

As early as the 1890s the Irish had come to command the urban wing of the Democratic Party.[14] In Chicago they played a leading role especially in the fraught public affairs of Cooke County. And James was not the only politically connected O'Shaughnessy brother. Francis and John shared legal offices in the same suite as Dunne, and Francis later represented the Illinois governor at the unveiling of a statue in Missouri erected to the memory of that army general and Democratic senator James Shields. The latter, as seen earlier, had known the O'Shaughnessys when they lived in Missouri. Frank's Democratic Party sympathies did not prevent him on one occasion from canvassing support for an acquaintance, Joseph J. Sullivan, who in a Republican primary sought the office of municipal judge.[15]

"Gus," Charles E. Merriam, and John "Bathhouse" Coughlin

For his part, the "self-proclaimed Democrat" Thomas Gus O'Shaughnessy broke ranks on one occasion and chaired a rally of 6,000 supporters of Charles E. Merriam, who was an influential professor of political science at the University of Chicago. Merriam (1874–1953) practiced what he preached as an academic by getting himself elected as an alderman. He was a Republican, but many Democrats lent him their support when he ran for mayor in 1911 on a promise to clean up the city.[16] "Elect me mayor of Chicago," Merriam told that rally in the Auditorium Theatre, "if I accomplish nothing else during my four years' term, I will at least compel Hinky Dink and the Bathhouse to abandon their wicked partnerships with vice and crime, or I will break them." Michael "Hinky Dink" Kenna and John "Bathhouse" Coughlin had created in Chicago's First Ward what has been described as "a political machine based on graft and protection money from saloons, brothels, and gambling halls."[17] The fact that Coughlin's parents were Irish did not impress that other son of an Irish father, Thomas O'Shaughnessy. As chairman of the meeting O'Shaughnessy told the crowd that he wished to give the best service possible to the people of Chicago: "It is this conviction within me that has induced me, after twenty years of loyalty to the

Democratic Party, to cast my fortunes and lift my voice on behalf of that candidate for the mayoralty of Chicago who best voices our Democratic principles and that man is Charles E. Merriam." O'Shaughnessy made an appeal for the candidate on nonpartisan grounds.[18]

Ultimately, Merriam was narrowly defeated by the Democratic candidate for mayor, Carter Harrison Junior, whose father had bought the *Chicago Times* in 1891 before being assassinated in 1893 when he was mayor of the city. And so John "Bathhouse" Coughlin and Michael "Hinky Dink" Kenna were not broken by Merriam. Coughlin would later be among those who welcomed to Chicago W. T. Cosgrave, the first prime minister of the independent Irish state to visit America. In his recent study of organized crime in Chicago, Lombardo shifts the focus of attention from linear accounts of Italian mafia families to the more complex relationships between machine politics, vice. and urban poverty that cast a shadow over the involvement of Irish-Americans and other ethnic groups in the administration of the city of Chicago in the twentieth century.[19]

John E. Redmond MP

For his part, the lawyer John O'Shaughnessy took an interest in Irish politics. He supported moderates in the Irish struggle for an independent parliament and in 1904 was one of eight members of a committee that wrote resolutions for a meeting at the Auditorium that was convened to welcome to Chicago John E. Redmond, leader of the Irish parliamentary party at Westminster, and other Irish constitutional nationalists. Almost twenty years earlier Redmond had given a controversial speech in Chicago to a convention of about one thousand Irish and Irish-American activists from across the United States and Canada. *New World,* a weekly Catholic newspaper and the official medium of the bishops of Illinois was now strongly backing Redmond's campaign for Irish self-government, or "Home Rule," for which he was in America to raise funds.[20] He had another strong supporter in the city in the form of John F. Finerty, who was not only the editor of the Irish-American *Chicago Citizen* but also president of the United Irish League of America. Finerty told Redmond in 1903 that the *Chicago Citizen* was "the only paper west of New York that has stood in the breach against all your enemies" and urged him to come to the Irish nationalist demonstration for which John

O'Shaughnessy helped to draft the resolutions. Finerty thought that this would "certainly revive the enthusiasm that appears to have died out to a considerable extent in the country, and more particularly in the western section thereof" for a measure of self-government in Ireland. Significantly in that respect, the year 1903 was also when the militantly anti-British Patrick Ford swung his *New York Irish World* behind Redmond's constitutional gradualism because Redmond's policy seemed more likely to succeed in Ireland than might revolutionary violence.[21]

Finerty not only used his newspaper to support Redmond but himself spoke at the Chicago meeting, introducing Redmond to the crowd as the person upon whom had fallen the mantle of the great Irish nationalist leader Charles Stewart Parnell, who had toured the United States in 1880. Redmond warned the gathering of Irish emigrants and their children, "Our race is slipping from its moorings — it is dying. If we are passive and inactive Ireland will cease to be the home of the Celt. There are more old men and little children and fewer young men and women in that island than in any other country on earth." It was reported that then, with a cheer that brought passersby in from the street, resolutions were adopted declaring that the "certain, fixed, and positive demand of the Irish people is and forever shall be 'home rule for Ireland.'"[22] Redmond could not have foreseen that the aspirations enshrined in the resolutions drafted for him by the group of which John O'Shaughnessy was a member would be frustrated for years by various acrimonious divisions and delay. He was optimistic and told his supporters in Chicago, "Sectarian bitterness is dying out; never have we been in a stronger place than now."

President O'Shaughnessy and Vice President Fairbanks

When he became the fifth president of the Irish Fellowship Club, James O'Shaughnessy and his fellow officers persuaded the vice president of the United States to attend its sixth banquet on March 18, 1907, the day after St. Patrick's Day. This was a big boost for the morale of Irish-Americans in the city. Charles Fairbanks (1852–1918) used his visit to Chicago to further his efforts to become the Republican Party candidate for president in succession to Theodore Roosevelt. His train was met in the city by a delegation led by James O'Shaughnessy. The latter took Fairbanks to the Field Museum to

Menus, 1907 and 1908, designed by Thomas O'Shaughnessy and including the name of the Irish Fellowship Club translated into the Irish language. Courtesy University of Notre Dame and the O'Shaughnessy family.

inspect a display of old Irish objects on loan from Ireland: "O'Shaughnessy, it was said, spent his time filling the vice president's ear with antiquarian Irish lore."[23] The aspiring candidate may have found this lore to be less than compelling given his busy political schedule at the time.

The dinner menu at the Irish Fellowship Club that night reflected the efforts of Irish-Americans to achieve social respectability. Guests tucked into a cream of asparagus, Rachel soup to start. It was followed not by corned beef and cabbage but by a choice of chicken patties à la Reine or tenderloin of beef Provençale, with French peas and potato croquettes. This could be washed down with either claret or the Hiawatha Spring Company's sparkling water. The menu's single genuflection to Ireland was a punch called

Cailin Ban, these being two Gaelic words meaning "young fair-skinned girl" but also the title (anglicized as *Colleen Bawn*) of a melodrama by Dion Boucicault that had been popular in US theaters since first being performed in New York in 1860 and that "continued to sound a note of artistic beauty" in contrast to stage-Irish productions that many Irish-Americans found objectionable.[24]

The dinner for Fairbanks at the Auditorium was attended by "fully five hundred members of the club and half as many women." The hall was profusely decorated with the Stars and Stripes and with the green flag bearing a golden harp that is an Irish nationalist ensign. After dinner, James O'Shaughnessy rose first. He introduced Edward Dunne, who had been the club's first president and who in March 1907 was still mayor of Chicago. After Dunne spoke, it was the turn of the US vice president. Fairbanks chose to affirm the loyalty and value of an immigrant community that was not always highly regarded by its American neighbors, and over which Woodrow Wilson would place a question mark when speaking of Commodore John Barry in 1914. Fairbanks, however, acknowledged that "the Irish have been among the most potent in building up the nation" and said,

> There are no better, truer Americans than those who were either born in Ireland or who proudly trace their ancestry to that little island across the sea, the home of [Robert] Emmet and [Henry] Grattan and other orators and statesmen, who by the force of their genius, impressed themselves upon the thoughts of the civilized world. . . . Who can measure the influence of the Irish in America? American institutions and American progress are the fruit of the co-operation of many nationalities and of many mighty influences. We may say, without invidious distinction, that man for man, the Irish stand for as much in our social, commercial and national progress as do any of the sons of America, whether born in our land or beyond the seas. The influence of the Irish in America is as wide as the sphere of our national influence. They brought hither their instinctive love of liberty, their love of home and love of country.[25]

Among the speakers that night was George E. Clarke, a leading lawyer and University of Notre Dame lecturer. Clarke, who was also "one of the best known officials of the order of Knights of Columbus in Indiana" and "an influential Republican" spoke about "The Irish-American Soldier," thus pointing up the loyalty of his people to the United States.[26] The club was clearly bipartisan, as seen by its invitation to Fairbanks and by Clarke's involvement, notwithstanding a very close association between Irish-Americans and the Democratic Party in Chicago.

Sheridan and Redmond Ride Again

In addition to its annual grand banquet, the Irish Fellowship Club also had regular Saturday luncheons and engaged in occasional projects. One such project, undertaken in 1907, was the erection of a bronze statue to "Fighting Phil" Sheridan, who was described as "a nation's hero and Illinois' adopted son," and who had, through "Sheridan's ride," turned defeat into victory for Union forces at Cedar Creek, Virginia, in 1864. The club, it was reported, "holds dear the memory of the dashing cavalry leader as that of a fellow Irish-American" who lived in Chicago.[27]

During 1908 James O'Shaughnessy became one of almost ninety members of a reception committee selected by the president of the United Irish Societies of Chicago to welcome back to the city John E. Redmond MP, the Irish nationalist leader. This time, Redmond was accompanied by his English Protestant wife, Ada Beesley, and by his close political ally Joseph Devlin MP, as well as by the chairman of the council of County Roscommon in Ireland, John Fitzgibbon. Plans were put in place to take Mrs. Redmond on a tour of the downtown shopping area and otherwise entertain her while her husband attended a luncheon given for him at the Chicago Club by Medill McCormick (1877–1925). The latter was assistant editor in chief and part owner of the *Chicago Tribune*.[28]

Taft at the Club

An even more impressive seal of approval for the Irish Fellowship Club than the presence of Charles Fairbanks in 1907 was the decision of William Howard Taft (1857–1930), Republican president of the United States, to talk at its St. Patrick's Day banquet in 1910, during a one-day visit to Chicago. Thomas O'Shaughnessy designed the special banquet program, the colored cover of which he based on the ancient Book of Lindisfarne and on which he displayed both the name of the club and that of the banquet venue in

John Redmond (center) and his wife Ada Beesley visit Chicago, 1908. With them are John
Devlin MP and (right) John Fitzgibbon, chairman of Roscommon County Council, Ireland.
James O'Shaughnessy was a member of the local reception committee. Courtesy Chicago
History Museum, *Chicago Daily News* collection DN-0053494.

the Irish language only. He and his brothers Francis and John were among
150 members of the club that year who sat on its unwieldy general reception
committee, which had been appointed to make arrangements for Taft's visit.
Their brother James chaired the club's more manageable banquet committee, which had just ten members. The *New York Times* remarked on the fact
that the club had succeeded in getting Taft along to two events, one being
the banquet itself in the La Salle Hotel and the other an earlier luncheon
that followed a reception given for the US president by the Newspaper
Club of Chicago. At this luncheon he was presented with "a harp of shamrocks sent from Ireland by John E. Redmond, the Irish Nationalist leader."
Members of the club had hoped that Redmond would be able to accept an
invitation from Fr. Maurice Dorney, "without exception the most popular
pastor in the country," to return to Chicago for the dinner with Taft. But
he could not make it.[29]

The US president rode in the St. Patrick's Day parade and, all day, "he hardly saw a building or an individual that did not show the Irish color."[30] One headline declared that Taft had "Made Himself Solid with Sons of Erin." A journalist noted that Taft was due to "wander over to the La Salle Hotel, where the Irish will give him a hearty greeting. The Chief Executive will stand on Irish soil, when he addresses the banquet tonight, a piece of the 'ould sod' from County Cork having been procured for the occasion. In order that Mr. Taft may leave at 10, the banquet will be run on a close schedule. On the menu is game killed by Mr. Roosevelt [the former US president who was then on safari] and shipped from Africa for the occasion."[31]

The *Chicago Tribune* had reported the arrival of the soil from Ireland at the La Salle Hotel, its account reeking of stage-Irishry: "'Tis here — yes, glory be, 'tis here — the ould sod. Look how green it is!" James O'Shaughnessy reportedly exclaimed. "Why, 'tis as green right now as when it lay on Tara Hill," his Irish Fellowship Club colleague John Gavin purportedly added. Three crates "containing more than one hundred square feet — two tons — of real Irish sod, thickly sprinkled with the magic shamrock that thrills the heart of every true Irishman" were stored for the night in a penthouse, according to the *Tribune*. Their opening was a source of excitement: "'O, look — look,' cried O'Shaughnessy, making a dash for the box in which the real shamrock sod was packed. 'See the shillalahs [shillelaghs]!' And he drew forth the 'surprise package' containing — what do you think? Two blackthorns, 'complements' of Ed Lahiff, one of the six men who founded the Irish Fellowship Club." Lahiff, a former Chicago journalist and secretary to Mayor Carter Harrison, had retired to Youghal, County Cork. One of the blackthorn sticks that he sent had a silver band around it and was intended for presentation to Taft. The newspaper report goes on at some length to describe how the earth was conveyed to Chicago "begorrah," and mentions that one Mrs. George C. Moore intended to give Taft a sprig of ivy from the turret of Blarney Castle also.[32] Elsewhere we learn that if Mrs. Moore is to attend the banquet, she will have to leave her head uncovered:

> Women guests will not be allowed to wear their hats at the dinner, according to the mandate of the committee in charge of the affair. "I can imagine how a woman feels who has bought a $150 hat to wear on

such an occasion," said Jas. O'Shaughnessy, chairman of the committee. "It was hard for us to bring ourselves to issue the edict. But it had to be done. There is a limited amount of space in any hall. We figured it up mathematically that one woman's hat takes up the space of two and one-fourth persons. There would not be room for the waiters to get around."[33]

Taft was a heavy man, weighing then more than 300 pounds (22 stone/140 kilos). When he sat down to eat at the banquet, he occupied a very ornate chair that had been made especially for him, "the work of twelve joiners, who spent seven weeks on it under the direction of an architect."[34] The chair today is kept at the Irish American Heritage Museum in Chicago. The menu for dinner that night was an entirely Anglo-French affair, including troncon of Lake Trout with potatoes à la Hollandaise and baron of beef chasseur with French peas — there being no mention even of that redeeming Gaelic punch offered when Vice President Fairbanks visited.

The soil brought from Ireland in 1910 was the subject of a bid by Charles W. Murphy, who had abandoned his career as a newspaper editor and press agent to become instead the owner of the Chicago Cubs. He had earlier worked at the *Cincinnati Enquirer* and *Cincinnati Times-Star,* the latter owned by Charles Phelps Taft, half-brother of President Taft and the man to whom Murphy would later sell the Cubs. From 1905 on Murphy had built the Cubs into a highly successful baseball team. He offered to purchase the soil and shamrock so that he might plant them both at the baseball park where he and others who worked there, and whose ancestors came from Ireland, could cherish them. It is said that that the club instead permitted visitors to the La Salle Hotel to take home bits and pieces of the soil and shamrock as souvenirs, until it was all gone.[35]

Michael Faherty, City Builder

The president of the Irish Fellowship Club in 1910, and the man credited with getting President Taft to visit the club then, was Michael J. Faherty (1858–1950). In a personal capacity he had earlier helped to organize a campaign dinner for Taft in Chicago when the latter ran for the presidency in 1908. Welcoming Taft in 1910, Faherty reminded the assembled diners of the contribution that Irish and Irish-American fighters had made to the United States: "we gathered round the stars and stripes when it was first

Cubs v. Giants, Chicago, 30 Aug. 1908. Cubs owner Charles W. Murphy wanted Irish soil and shamrocks planted here in 1910. Courtesy Library of Congress.

thrown to the breeze, we have helped to hold it strong against all the storms and trials from that day to this."[36]

Faherty was born in Ireland. Emigrating in 1863 to the United States, he settled first in Connecticut and then moved to Chicago in 1880. He was a machinist by trade and worked in that capacity until turning to the real estate business from 1885. He was also a member of the Knights of Columbus.[37] A biographical entry in the club's official history gives no inkling of the controversies that later embroiled Faherty through his relationship with "Big Bill" Thompson, the mayor of Chicago who in 1915 appointed him president of the Board of Local Improvements. It says only that

> The Galway-born Faherty was a bulwark of the Republican Party in Chicago. Among his claims to fame was the implementation of Daniel Burnham's Chicago Plan. He oversaw the upgrading of the city's infrastructure that Burnham sought to remake as a new Paris. Faherty expedited the gracious boulevards, broad avenues and new bridges that remade Chicago. Large parcels of the Northwest quadrant of the city were developed by him and provided him much commercial success as well. The effectiveness of his Republican influence was proved with the visit of President William Howard Taft in 1910. Faherty's influence in Ireland's political life was significant. He maintained a life-long friendship and correspondence with many prominent Irish leaders.[38]

Faherty was to play a key role in persuading W. T. Cosgrave to make the first visit to America by a prime minister of the newly independent Irish state. Cosgrave would come to the Irish Fellowship Club during a period when both Faherty and Thompson were bitterly contesting a legal action by the *Chicago Tribune.* The newspaper sought the return to the city of certain monies that the two men had spent. Both Faherty and Thompson compared themselves to Baron Haussmann, who is credited with the rebuilding of Paris in the nineteenth century.[39]

Democrats and Republicans

That Faherty was a Republican again illustrates the fact that Democrats and Republicans were involved from the outset in the Irish Fellowship Club. Faherty's son Roger (1889–1967), who later became a high-ranking member of the Republican Party and the twenty-sixth president of the Irish Fellowship Club, shared a room at Yale University with President Taft's son, Robert. Other prominent Republican members of the club were its sixth president, Judge Elbridge Hanecy, and its fourteenth president, the attorney Patrick H. O'Donnell. Its twentieth president, on the other hand, was William Emmett Dever (1862–1929), a Democratic Party reformer who succeeded Thompson as mayor in 1923 — only to lose office to Thompson again in April 1927. Dever enjoyed a reputation for integrity but failed to court sufficient popularity to survive politically.[40]

SIX Gus and the Gaelic Revival

IF IT IS TRUE that nuns encouraged a young Thomas O'Shaughnessy to make his first stained glass window when he was still in Missouri, as is said, then they started him on a path that would reach an artistic summit with the decoration of Old St. Patrick's Church in Chicago. It was largely due to the quality of his work there that in 1977 the building was listed on the National Register of Historic Places.

Thomas, or "Gus," certainly did not generate by his art the kind of income for himself that James or his lawyer brothers earned from their work. He was often short of money. He also suffered successive tragedies in the premature death of a creative colleague and of his wife. But his devotion to American public art and to the Celtic or Gaelic Revival movement earned him much praise in his day.

Augustus and Augustin

The fact that Thomas O'Shaughnessy bore the second name Augustin, and was sometimes known by its abbreviated form, "Gus," may itself signify the upward mobility of Irish immigrants. Some immigrants gave their children names that were thought to be more socially advantageous than Thomas or Michael or Bridget. Catholic priests greatly admired Augustine of Hippo as one of the Church "fathers," and this saint was eminently suitable as a patron of the new Catholic middle class. Finley Peter Dunne, the Chicago journalist writing as "Mr. Dooley," had in his column on November 17, 1894, poked fun at a fictional family of Hogans who argued over the christening of their latest son, albeit in that case as Augustus rather than Augustin. The boy's grandfather had been named Michael and neither his grandmother, Bridget, nor his father saw anything wrong with the newborn also being christened Michael. Mother disagreed. She had ensured that the couple's earlier children were named Sarsfield, Lucy, Honoria, Veronica, Arthur, and even Charles Stewart Parnell:

"Whin ar-re ye goin' to christen little Mike," he says. "Little who?" says she. "Little Mike," he says, "Little Mike Hogan," he says, "th' kid." "There'll ne no little Mikes around this house, "says she, "unless they walk over my dead body." . . . "Mike is a good name," says Hogan, "'Twas me fa-ather's," he says, "an' he was as good as anny." "Don't tell me about ye'er father," says she. "Didn't I know him," she says. . . . "Ye'll be namin' no more children iv [of] mine out iv dime novels," he says. "An' ye'll name no more iv mine out of th' payroll iv th' bridge depar-rtmint," says she. Thin Hogan w[e]akened. "What ar-re ye goin' to call it?" he says. ""Augustus," says she. An be hivins [by heavens] 'twas Augustus th' priest give it. Th' poor, poor child!"[1]

Chicago 1893

Chicago continued to grow notwithstanding a national economic recession in the 1890s. Emigrants from many European countries were arriving to join people moving there from elsewhere within the United States. The city's prosperity provided an opportunity for its citizens to rise socially. As they did so they were conscious of their image in the eyes of others, and the great Columbian Exposition of 1893 gave them a chance to see themselves as others saw them — or might see them. For the O'Shaughnessys and Irish-Americans in general this was a singular moment.

Members of the O'Shaughnessy family of Missouri were among 25 million people who attended the Columbian Exposition that ran in Jackson Park for six months. Gus was particularly impressed by the examples of Irish design and workmanship that were displayed at the vast, international show. These were to be a great source of ideas for him in his later work as an artist in the Celtic or Gaelic Revival style. The University of Chicago came to house a collection of nearly two hundred facsimiles of Irish antiquities that the Dublin silver- and goldsmith Edmond Johnson made from exact plaster casts for the fair. Bowe has described these as "exquisite" and as "astonishingly accurate scale replicas."[2] Irish nationalists and many Irish-Americans were taking an interest in such traditional Irish cultural forms, as they sought to reimagine their self-identity.

Although the whole island of Ireland was still part of the United Kingdom of Great Britain and Ireland, some believed that Irish society could not be adequately represented within the main exhibition halls at the Chicago

Columbian Exposition, Chicago 1893. Contemporary Rand McNally guide.
The Midway Plaisance runs back over the horizon by the world's first Ferris Wheel.
Courtesy Library of Congress.

Exposition. Displays within these halls were dominated by imperial perspectives. Accordingly, Gaelic revivalists found their niche elsewhere. A
pair of formidable women arranged to have two substantial Irish "villages"
constructed on the "Midway Plaisance," an avenue of privately funded
exhibition areas at right angles to the main exposition. This cosmopolitian
avenue also led to the world's first Ferris wheel. Harris describes a scene
that thrilled visitors:

> The astonishing white exposition palaces were adorned by statuary and
> murals and crammed with technological marvels and art rarities. Armies of
> employees kept its fountains, canals, lagoons, plazas, and boulevards safe
> and spotless. Especially spectacular at night, by reason of newly developed

electric lights, the fairgrounds abutted a mile-long zone of privately owned rides, restaurants, exhibits, and entertainments known as the Midway Plaisance, rivaling, even outdoing the official palaces in drawing power.[3]

He remarks that, on this Midway Plaisance, "The Irish villages and their promise of economic revival through traditional crafts formed a suggestive and influential essay in cultural advertisement." There was to have been just one such village, but its two organizers, Lady Aberdeen and Alice Hart, went their separate ways. A Chicago journalist, Teresa Dean, commented stereotypically on the split, "No true Irishman, be he right or be he wrong, will be a slave to the the opinion or ruling of another, if he can help himself."[4]

The Donegal village designed and executed by Mrs. Hart stood close to the main exhibition areas and included a half-size reproduction of the ruins of Donegal Castle and a round tower. Performances of Irish music and lectures were delivered in a concert hall nearby. Lace makers, linen weavers, and both wood and marble carvers were at work. One could admire their skills and inspect "replicas of the old Celtic illuminations, engravings of the Irish carved crosses and reproductions of ancient Celtic metal work and jewelry," at least some of which were for sale. A copy of a distinctive Irish High Cross rose twenty-seven feet tall.

Another cross stood in the more remote but substantial "industries" village organized under the patronage of the Countess of Aberdeen. She was then living with her husband in Ottawa, Canada, but earlier and later was a promoter of local industry in Ireland when her husband was London's viceroy there. She had long hoped to exhibit Irish goods in Chicago. Her village now also included examples of craftwork based on old Celtic designs and initials from the famous illuminated manuscript known as the Book of Kells. For her part, she had arranged for the construction of a replica of Blarney Castle. It was two-thirds the size of the original tower in Ireland and was ostensibly fitted with a piece of the Blarney Stone, a fixture that visitors to the original edifice in County Cork kiss in the hope that it will impart to them an oral fluency known as "the gift of the gab." Some claimed that the stone in Chicago was actually a piece of local pavement lowered into an obscure position to take in the gullible.[5] As noted earlier, it was said that James O'Shaughnessy had been the first person to propose having a replica of the Blarney Stone at the fair.

Donegal Castle, part of Mrs. Hart's village, Chicago 1893. From White and Igleheart, *Columbian Exposition*, p. 567.

Lady Aberdeen's Irish village, Chicago 1893.
From White and Igleheart, *Columbian Exposition*, p. 594.

The Blarney Castle in Chicago was used to house attractive young women whom Lady Aberdeen had organized to travel from Ireland to demonstrate craft skills. That their parents worried about their exposure to the American way of life is evident from Aberdeen's subsequent assurance that the "forty Irish girls whom we brought out with us, go back the pure, true, sunny maidens that came out with us, and I know that my friends on the Board of Lady Managers will rejoice that I am able to state this without fear of challenge, but in a spirit of deep thankfulness."[6]

Aberdeen herself was a remarkable woman. A strong and imaginative person, she pushed in practical ways to help Ireland recover from the effects of dire famine and political paralysis. A friend of the liberal prime minister William Gladstone she supported parliamentary independence for Ireland and worked hard to help people to improve their living conditions. In 1893 she was elected president of the International Congress of Women, a position that she was to occupy for almost forty years. Some critics then and later have slighted her Irish village in Chicago, regarding it as romantic and false and an encouragement to patronizing tourism, but it helped to promote Irish goods, to develop at least rudimentary industries in parts of Ireland that were hemorrhaging emigrants, and to attract visitors to Ireland who would not only spend money but would bring back to America reports of Irish people and their ambitions. In an address on home industries that she gave in the Woman's Building at the Chicago Exposition in 1893, one that prefigured some of the later work of the Irish Industrial Development Authority after the foundation of an independent Irish state, she was already eager to build on the success of the Irish villages:

> we shall not be content if we are only able to open up an American market
> to our poor workers this year–that would have been but opening the
> door of hope to shut it again in their faces. No, we hope to establish a
> permanent depot for Irish goods under Mrs. Peter White's management,
> and I would like to solicit your interest–and your custom, for that. We do
> not ask you to buy for charity; we only ask you to buy what you deem to
> be good and beautiful of its kind; but in buying that, and thus benefiting
> yourselves, I will guarantee that you will bring sunshine and hope into
> many a heart and home beyond the seas.[7]

Commercially, as it transpired, the Irish villages were among the fair's most successful features. Emotionally, their impact on the families of immigrants who visited them in 1893 is likely to have been considerable. It was all very well for some contemporary critics in Ireland's predominantly industrial northeast to dismiss them as a sort of "sentimental charity," and sophisticated scholars today may complain that Irish identity was framed quaintly or offensively within a commercial enterprise, but visitors to the fair who had been prompted or forced by circumstances to abandon Ireland, many of whom could not easily afford to return, encountered inspiring reminders of their origins. Given the tendency of immigrants in general to equate an emancipated homeland with their own nation's respectability in the United States, an international showcase of their national art and crafts bolstered their self-esteem regardless of what a minority of cultural or political critics said of the particular Irish villages at the Chicago Exposition.[8]

Debates about how Ireland ought to be represented or "branded" on the world's stage continue today, and authenticity is still an issue. It has been observed, for example, that "Americans are sometimes surprised to learn, Michael Flatley of Riverdance fame is not Irish, but an American born and raised in Chicago, and that the show itself is *faux* Irish and a classic example of hijacking country of origin image." By comparison with that summary judgment of a stage show that grew out of a televison filler during the annual Eurovision Song Contest, Bowe's 1994 description of Thomas O'Shaughnessy as "eccentric" in his later guise as a Celtic Revival artist seems relatively restrained.[9]

Earning His Living

During the 1890s, Gus used his budding artistic skills to find employment as an illustrator on Chicago newspapers, including on the *Tribune*. About the turn of the century he paid an extended visit to Ireland where he studied the Book of Kells and other works of Irish art. On his return to America he found employment at the *Chicago Daily News* where his work from 1902 to 1905 included comic strips. Such strips still appeared only irregularly in most daily papers, and one of his, headed "Point of View" was distinctive because its main figure seems to be a self-caricature of O'Shaughnessy himself. A leading comic strip historian has described his comic work as "elegant and sophisticated."[10]

He also drew sketches for the *Daily News,* including one of the aftermath of the fire at the city's new Iroquois Theater in 1903. More than six hundred people died in that disaster. His sketch was widely reproduced.[11] In 1904 he presented to the Chicago Historical Society a watercolor of the former church at Cahokia, said to be the oldest building in Illinois. He attended courses at the Chicago Art Institute and later lectured in Roman Art at the Palette and Chisel Academy.[12]

Irish and Italian

The great world's fair at Chicago was named in honor of Christopher Columbus, born in Genoa, whose voyage of 1492 across the Atlantic in the *Santa Maria* had led to the settlement of the Americas by Europeans.[13] Columbus visited Galway at least once, "most probably in 1477" writes Quinn, and until recently it had been thought that the first Irishman to reach America since the days of St. Brendan was possibly one William of Galway ("Guillermo Ires, natural de Galney") on board the *Santa Maria.* Although scholars now believe that William may not in fact have been on board, it is certain that many other Galwaymen later sailed west, for mortality rates during the Great Famine were especially high in Connaught, and most immigrants to America between 1876 and 1914 emanated from western Ireland.[14]

Thomas O'Shaughnessy, the son of one of those immigrants was very interested in Columbus. He rescued for Chicago replicas of the *Santa Maria* and other ships associated with the explorer that had been constructed for the world's fair, and organized a pageant in honor of Columbus's arrival in the Americas. O'Shaughnessy is credited, as shall be seen, with persuading authorities to declare Columbus Day a public holiday.

Another Irish-American mark of respect for the Italian explorer was the foundation of the Knights of Columbus by Fr. Michael McGivney, himself the son of immigrants from Ireland. This fraternal organization provided an alternative to secret societies of which the Catholic Church did not approve, and it came to count among its many members James Shaughnessy of Ireland and Missouri as well as some of his sons in Chicago.

POINT OF VIEW.

Comic strip by Thomas
O'Shaughnessy, *Chicago
Daily News*, 1901.
Courtesy Allan Holtz.

Pentwister (the comic artist) - "Say, I've done it this time! Gee! 'Slipshod'; ain't that a screamer? Fellow slips on a banana peel! He, he! Ha, ha, ho!"

"Mister, if you can see any fun in a man's misfortunes you have no sense of humor.

"That's the proper place for such a fool joke! Didn't know I could be such a donkey!"

"Now for the editor and a big price for my skit. I can hear 'his nibs' roar with laughter now!

"Who left that measly banana skin on our steps? Help! Help!

In 1905 Thomas was a founding member of the Ravenswood Council of the Knights of Columbus, which particular council his lawyer brother Francis also joined.[15] On one occasion, in 1908, Thomas and these knights became embroiled with some citizens in a dispute over the removal of the Drake Fountain and its statue of Columbus from downtown Chicago to South Chicago: "This incident will serve to turn the Italian vote against the Republicans," claimed Thomas. He and his family had bypassed South Side when they moved to the city from Missouri, but the district had long been home to many poor families from Ireland and elsewhere. The way in which Thomas referred to the neighborhood suggests a social gap that was attitudinal as well as economic, for he claimed, "It was an insult to the name of Columbus to send the statue to South Chicago." Unsurprisingly, as the *Chicago Tribune* subsequently reported, "The citizens of South Chicago are beginning to grow restive about the remarks of the Knights concerning their quarter of the city," and we learn from the newspaper that "Mr. O'Shaughnessy headed a committee which was somewhat coldly received by Public Works Commissioner Hanberg, who is a South Chicagoan." Commissioner John J. Hanberg had been instrumental in having the fountain transported to his part of the city.[16]

The social divisions between "ginteel" Irish-Americans and their less wealthy compatriots were explored about this time by the local writer Clara E. Laughlin in her single foray into realistic fiction. This was her 1910 novel, *Just Folks*. Laughlin was the daughter of Irish immigrants who had come to Chicago from Milwaukee. A journalist, she became an editor at *McClure's Magazine* in the 1890s.[17]

A Pageant for Columbus

Gus grew concerned not only about the statue of Columbus. He also became alarmed when he learned that replicas of the three Spanish caravels in which Christopher Columbus and his entourage sailed to America in 1492 were to be scuttled. Spain had made a gift of replicas of the *Nina*, the *Pinta*, and the *Santa Maria* to the Columbian Exposition of 1893, and they remained moored in Chicago. South Park board accepted his offer to oversee the vessels, and he began to spend time on board them. His "self-assigned hours on these boats stimulated his imagination. His sense of color, theme and drama was challenged."[18]

Thomas worked closely with a Jewish lawyer to have Columbus Day offically honored, and Italian-Americans welcomed his initiative. Irish and Italian Catholics frequently encountered one another at events organized by the Knights of Columbus.

His efforts led to his directing a gala "Columbian Water Pageant of Landing Day" on October 12, 1911. According to a contemporary estimate, 50,000 people assembled in Jackson Park, 100,000 in Grant Park, and another 100,000 along the shoreline to observe the pageant: "With prodding the next day from a Chicago *Daily Tribune* editorial that exalted the water pageant, Mayor Carter Harrison was inspired to proclaim Columbus Day a legal holiday for Chicago. The rest was history. Similar parades sprung up in places like Columbus, Ohio." Columbus Day became a national holiday in 1937, and is today celebrated each year on the second Monday in October.[19]

It was later reported of O'Shaughnessy's pageant, "The spectacle was of such historic authenticity and beauty that it was chosen for filming by the Selig Polyscope company, and became the first multi-reeled motion picture ever made." This was *The Coming of Columbus* (1912), which the movie company described as its "masterpiece." The "authenticity" of the pageant itself could not of course include its setting because Columbus never sailed anywhere near the Great Lakes. Such a detail did not deter the city council from praising Thomas at length and also claiming that "the City of Chicago by reason of situation and historic possessions, and by reason of the lively scene of gratitude in the hearts of its people is the fittest place on the western hemisphere for the celebration of the immortal achievement of Christopher Columbus upon the recurrence of its anniversary."[20]

The pageant was repeated the following year. Thomas received then a telegram from Theodore Roosevelt, who was a presidential candidate at the time, telling him that Roosevelt was withdrawing from his planned participation in the event in the face of objections that his presence would be politically contentious.[21] When in 1913 the caravels left for Detroit, in an incongruous attempt to transport them ultimately to San Francisco, Thomas and others successfully campaigned to have them returned and they were back in time for yet another pageant in 1914. The replicas that he had ensured were saved for the city were later lost to fire.[22]

In 1937, the Illinois lodge of the Order Sons of Italy, a leading Italian-American organization, acknowledged that Thomas O'Shaughnessy had

Thomas "Gus" O'Shaughnessy
at work, 1914. Courtesy Chicago
History Museum, *Chicago Daily
News* collection (26 May 1914)
DN-DN-0062780.

been "instrumental in having Columbus Day declared a legal holiday."[23] In 1992 the *Chicago Tribune* reported that Joe O'Shaughnessy, son of Thomas, had told it that recent controversy about Columbus and his representation as an oppressor of Native Americans "would hurt my dad to the bottom core. There's been too much Columbus-bashing."[24]

Old St. Pat's, Chicago

Thomas was impressed by Italian exhibits at the great Chicago Exposition of 1893. He liked even more what he saw at the two Irish villages that formed part of it, and that included many Irish artifacts and replicas of ancient Celtic treasures.[25] For some time a cultural movement known as the "Celtic Revival" or the "Gaelic Revival" had been gathering pace, mainly in Ireland but also among Irish-Americans, with its participants finding inspiration in old art forms and stories. O'Shaughnessy gave formal expression to that movement in Chicago. He drew on it in 1907 and 1908, for example, when designing banquet menus for the Irish Fellowship Club or, as he also termed it in Irish on those menus, the "Cumann cómhluchda Éireannach i Chicago."

He was afforded his greatest opportunity to express the Gaelic Revival style at St. Patrick's, a church that has been a pillar of Irish-American social and religious life in Chicago for over 160 years. Founded in 1846 and standing at the intersection of Adams and Des Plaines, it was one of the few structures that had survived the city's great fire of 1871 and is said today to be Chicago's oldest public building. For more than forty years after its foundation the parish was one of the largest and most prosperous in Chicago. Then the nearby business district expanded, and the congregation of the church declined. Early in the twentieth century it was decided to revitalize "Old St. Pat's," as the church has come to be commonly known. Stained glass and painted windows were added, and its interior redecorated with striking stencils in Celtic Revival style. These additions and renovations were the work of Thomas O'Shaughnessy.

O'Shaughnessy had become an active member of Chicago's civic life, being "involved in everything from promoting the observance of Columbus Day to speaking on the nature of the skyscraper as a member of the Municipal Art Commission." From 1911 onward he began to ornament Old St. Pat's with patterns inspired by the Book of Kells, Ireland's most renowned illuminated manuscript.[26] His glass work at Old St. Pat's is frequently admired, including one window in memory of an Irish political martyr Terence MacSwiney that will be considered later. Entering the church in 1928, the same year in which Irish prime minister W. T. Cosgrave also visited it, John Drury and his female companion were delighted by what they found in what J. J. Walsh had described a little earlier as "one of grimiest, busiest parts of the city." Drury wrote, "Anne was captivated by the walls and leaded windows, which reflected Gaelic designs and motifs, and by the general tone of soft green throughout the place." He told her that every year, on St. Patrick's Day, "thousands of Irish-Americans scattered over the city form a pilgrimage to this historic edifice to attend the masses. Among them are notables of the political and business world who as youngsters were reared in this parish. Furthermore, because of its beautiful Irish art work, the church has become a shrine to many artists and lovers of the beautiful."[27]

It took Thomas O'Shaughnessy more than a decade to complete his work at Old St. Pat's, but it is now a monument to Irish-America, and Barton has sung its praises at some length. Chicago historian Ellen Skerrett writes, "Restored to their original beauty in 1996, O'Shaughnessy's designs continue to

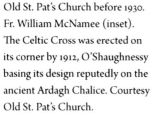

Old St. Pat's Church before 1930.
Fr. William McNamee (inset).
The Celtic Cross was erected on
its corner by 1912, O'Shaughnessy
basing its design reputedly on the
ancient Ardagh Chalice. Courtesy
Old St. Pat's Church.

O'Shaughnessy's glass on display
before being mounted in a window
of Old St. Pat's, 1920. Courtesy Old
St. Pat's Church.

challenge conventional notions of Irish identity and sacred space." She also
describes Old St. Pat's as being "the best-known example of Celtic Revival
Art in America."[28] The building today features in the National Register of
Historic Places. On St. Patrick's Day 2012, Ireland's prime minister ("Taoiseach") Enda Kenny attended mass there, having spoken the evening before
at the Irish Fellowship Club.[29]

   Not long after Thomas began his work for Old St. Pat's he was commissioned by the Old-Time Printers' Association of Chicago to design a
window in memory of Henry Olendorf Shepard. The association, orga-

nized in 1885, comprised individuals in both the printing and publishing businesses. The stained glass window that it commissioned was presented to the Chicago Board of Education in 1914 and was installed in the Shepard Public School at South Francisco and Fillmore to commemorate Shepard as president and publisher of *The Inland Printer* and founder of the Inland Printer Technical School. It was said at the time to be the first example of a process of manufacturing art glass being used uniquely by O'Shaughnessy.[30]

Madness

Thomas had good relations not only with Italians and Jews but also with people from other immigrant communities. He studied briefly under the fashionable Professor Alphonse Mucha of Prague, Bohemia, who gave a series of lectures at the Chicago Art Institute before 1910, and who himself completed some commissions for the Bohemian Catholic Church in America.[31] Thomas also worked closely with Henry Wilson Barnetz, with whom he is said to have rediscovered an ancient way of making stained glass. In 1916 the two began to construct twelve "art glass" windows for the Catholic abbey of St. Procopius at Lisle, Illinois, using copper and tin instead of lead for binding. The designs were reportedly based on windows in the European abbey of Emmaus (Emauzy) in Prague, which was later badly damaged by US bombing during World War II.[32]

In May of that year Thomas married Brigid McGuire, who had been born in Ireland and whose mother's brother was Fr. William McNamee of Old St. Pat's Church. Brigid was managing editor of the *Chicago Citizen*.[33] Unfortunately, the year ended less happily for Thomas when the demands of the Lisle commission completely overwhelmed Barnetz. In a graphic report of what happened, the *Chicago Daily Tribune* informed its readers that

> Months of ceaseless toil . . . resulted in incurable insanity, and Henry Wilson Barnetz, artist, died in the state insane asylum, leaving his widow and nine children in meager circumstances in the little Swedenborgian art colony at Glenview, Illinois.
>
> The designs took months to complete and then began the most intricate and delicate work of all, the painting of the faces and hands and feet of the figures on the white glass which was pieced into the designs.

In O'Shaughnessy's studio on the twenty-first floor of the Stewart
building the two artists worked early and late painting. Brushes so fine that
they consisted of one and two hairs were used in the shading. Two weeks
ago O'Shaughnessy arrived at the office one morning to find Barnetz
walking back and forth across the floor, his figure draped with sheets and
his feet bound with sandals which had been used by the models.

When taken to his home in Glenview he became violent and a week
ago the family accompanied him to Elgin. There his hallucination that he
was a model never left him and he pleaded with O'Shaughnessy, with tears
streaming down his face, to hurry and paint him.[34]

The headline on this *Tribune* report declared, "Artist Martyr To 12 Windows: Henry W. Barnetz Leaves Widow and Nine Children Little But Fame."
In fact, not even fame would be theirs in this context. Barnetz's role was all
but forgotten, and Thomas O'Shaughnessy alone in future years was to get
sole credit for their work. For example, decades later Father Michael Ko-
mechak of the Benedictine community at Lisle told the *Tribune* about these
windows: "They're interesting from the point of view that at that time the
monastery was serving the Czech and Slavic immigrants, and here you have
the monks hiring an Irish artist." The death of Barnetz no doubt heightened
O'Shaughnessy's aversion to the use of paint on windows, an established
practice to which he had already developed strong aesthetic objections but
which involved less expense for those commissioning windows than did
the process of staining glass.[35] The windows that were completed for Lisle
include depictions of Christ carrying the cross and stages in the life of St.
Benedict. They were installed in the chapel of Benedictine Hall.[36]

Thomas met further and greater misfortune in January 1919 when the
woman whom he had married less than three years earlier died of pneumo-
nia, leaving him alone with two small children, Attracta Mary and Joseph,
to rear. It is said that the faces of the Irish Saint Brigid that he subsequently
completed in stained glass at Old St. Pat's and at the cathedral in Springfield,
Illinois, resemble that of his late wife's sister, Rose.[37]

It may have made him feel a little better later in 1919 to see himself described as someone who had long "devoted a great part of his time to patriotic services in the field of art." It was noted, "He personally organised and
directed the first historic pageants, which were given in Chicago free to the

public, and has contributed materially to the development and expression of American spirit in American art."[38]

Playing the Piano

As Irish-Americans became more prosperous they acquired the tokens of middle-class respectability and pleasure, of which one was the piano. The O'Shaughnessys appreciated its importance as an instrument of both pleasure and social status. Mass production of pianos during the nineteenth century meant that many families could now enjoy owning one, with their daughters taking music lessons and with guests gathering at house parties to sing songs and to dance. This stimulated to a certain amount of snobbery on the part of people who previously had exclusive access to piano enter-tainments, and resentment on the part of those who could not afford the instrument. Gay has written, "The bourgeois piano proved an especially savoury target, giving rise to spiteful remarks." Finley Dunne described it as "the one sure and visible symbol of social ambition" and used its absence to define the gap in fortunes between Chicago families. It was a great blow to have to sell it: "Hope goes out with the piano," he wrote in 1899. Its place in Irish middle-class life was well understood by James Joyce, who played it himself and who refers frequently to pianos in his collection of short stories entitled *Dubliners*.[39]

For men separated from their families by conflict, piano music was a reminder of home or of the local tavern. The development of mechanized player pianos, using perforated paper or metallic rolls, faciliated the instru-ment's popularity in the days before recordings had become widespread as an established alternative. When in 1917 the United States entered World War I, the Knights of Columbus selected one hundred Steger player pianos for use in recreation centers at various military and naval camps. When the war ended, Steger drew attention to this patronage by means of full-page ad-vertisements published in 1919. The company's advertising manager, Charles E. Byrne, said, "The order was prepared by Thomas O'Shaughnessy, who for many years has been the foremost exponent of Celtic Art in America." In a report headed "Advertisement by Noted Artist," the *Music Trade Review* boasted, "In simplicity of design, artistic beauty and the forceful manner in which they drive home the Steger story, these advertisements set a high

Steger advertisement designed by Thomas "Gus" O'Shaughnessy.
From the *Music Trade Review*, 18 Oct. 1919.

standard."[40] James was clearly not the only O'Shaughnessy to make money by working for advertisers.

Thomas was active in the early 1920s in events commemorating the 250th anniversary of the arrival of the Jesuit missionary Jacques (James) Marquette in the Chicago area. In doing so he secured the cooperation of the Chicago Lodge of the Order of Elks and helped to organize a historical reenactment. He also designed a souvenir program. He had long been interested in this priest, and with his grandfather Mulholland's acquaintance Ossian Guthrie and others had determined the former location of a hut in which Marquette was said to have stayed by the river. From 1907 this site at the lower end of Robey Street (later Damen Avenue) was marked with a tall mahogany cross that he designed, and that at his request the Willy Lumber Company manufactured and later replaced when it was maliciously destroyed. Between 1924 and 1930 it was removed to make way for a bridge, and was subsequently lost.[41]

In 1925, in Paris, Gus acted as spokesman for the US delegation at the international Exposition of Modern and Industrial Art, and he wrote later that he "was accorded the highest honor given an American artist" there: he was made a member of the French academy.[42] A jury of the Chicago Art Institute gave him an award for ecclesiastical art connected to a special exhibition marking the Eucharistic Congress held in Chicago in June 1926. His winning poster among hundreds of designs submitted showed the Chicago skyline behind a monstrance and other religious images. One of the purposes of the exhibition, "according to Thomas A. O'Shaughnessy, chairman of the committee in charge," was to "combat some of the bolshevist tendencies" in contemporary art and "to counteract the voluptuous materialism increasingly manifested by artists." He added, "The exposition will also serve, we hope, to draw the mind of the artist to religion as a theme for his creations and prove the church as an institution which can make admirable use of artistic productions."[43]

Illinois and Beyond

Among Thomas O'Shaughnessy's glass works were windows for St. Catherine's Church, Spring Lake, New Jersey. His commissions were not confined to Catholic institutions and included, for example, one for the Methodist

Board of Education in Chicago and great mosaic windows for the Elks' Temple, New Orleans. Perhaps his windows' most distinctive ingredient was glacial silt found near Ottawa, Illinois.

Living in Illinois, he benefited from the expansive building program of Bishop James A. Griffin, whose Cathedral of the Immaculate Conception at Springfield was dedicated in 1928. This features more than a dozen stained glass windows from the O'Shaughnessy, Kugal Studios in Chicago. As noted earlier when discussng the hypenated nature of immigrant identity, Griffin deliberately wanted some of the windows to underscore the loyalty of Catholics to the United States. So eight of them on the north side tell the story of the spread of Christianity, including scenes of Irish missionaries at the court of Charlemagne and the king of Poland giving thanks for his victory over the Turks at Vienna, while eight on the south side deal with facets of the Church's contribution to American society, including St. Brendan preaching to native Americans and Columbus later landing in the New World.[44]

Thomas O'Shaughnessy wrote that a unique feature of his windows was their not being "leaded" as are "the church windows of the old school." Instead, he used copper and tin as the metal binders of the countless bits of colored glass forming the mosaic pictures, and this, he believed, made them much stronger. Another unique feature, he declared, was that at night the windows showed the pictures and ornaments "in full color and detail." This was because they were made of finely cut translucent glass "akin to the translucent glass known to the ancients." He wrote that American chemists had rediscovered the secret of making translucent glass and claimed that this let in much more light than did older forms of transparent colored glass.[45]

During 1931 the Artists' Guild collaborated with Thomas O'Shaughnessy at his then-fourth-floor studio on West Superior Street to design a stained glass window for the Episcopal church of St. Stephen's in the outer Chicago suburbs. Known as "the little church at the end of the road," and festooned with many works of art, this had become a shrine for creative souls. Its pastor, Irwin St. Tucker, was a Christian socialist who for seven years had worked as a reporter in the Midwest and South before becoming a minister, and who continued to earn his living during the week as a copyreader and religious editor at the *Herald and Examiner* in Chicago. In 1931 a brick chancel was added to the old wooden building at St. Stephens to provide

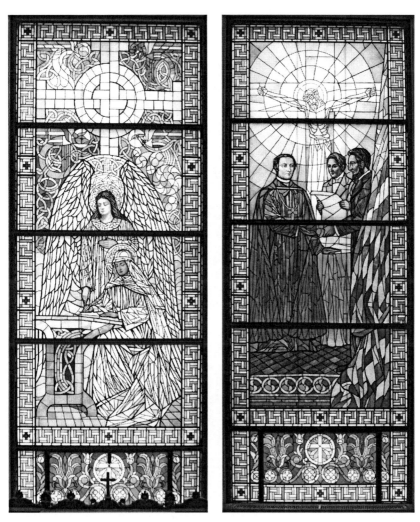

O'Shaughnessy windows from the Cathedral of the
Immaculate Conception, Springfield, Illinois: (left) St. Bride;
(right) Lincoln. Courtesy Diocese of Springfield, Illinois.
©Terry Farmer Photography

Window by Thomas O'Shaughnessy and the Artists' Guild,
St. Stephen's Episcopal Church ("the little church at the end of
the road"). Courtesy of the Episcopal Diocese of Chicago.

settings for both the Artists' Guild window and another window that a famous actress named Lotta Crabtree had commissioned in memory of her mother — but that had lain in storage for forty-two years after the church at which her mother used to worship in New York rejected it "on the ground that the donor was an actress."[46]

The Artists' Guild window was designed by a dozen people meeting at O'Shaughnessy's studio, and it was installed during a single evening at the church while a choir sang. The artists numbered parts of each panel "according to the colors of glass in O'Shaughnessy's huge collection." While they enjoyed a banquet in the church basement, where a soup kitchen was usually located, workmen cut out the many fragments of pot-metal glass in accordance with their instructions and placed these in a big, bronze frame. The cross and circle that dominated the design evoked old Celtic crosses and were said to mean "Christ is the light of the world." A lower panel displayed the seal of the Artists' Guild, being a winged horse ridden by a warrior with a palette for a shield and a paintbrush for a spear.[47]

The Illinois Chamber of Commerce later observed that in 1934 the Artists' Guild window from St. Stephen's Church was given a place of honor in the Hall of Religion at Chicago's World's Fair, or "A Century of Progress" as the celebration of the centenary of Chicago's incorporation was also known. O'Shaughnessy there contributed to the Illinois Host building, too. But he did more than make glass for the event, being appointed the artistic director of the fair's Irish village: "A central attraction of the village was O'Shaughnessy's huge Celtic-inspired Tara Hall, a half-timbered building embellished with applied banks of insular interlace and fanciful scroll work and displaying national symbols such as the Irish harp." No doubt he recalled visiting the Irish villages at the Chicago Exposition forty years earlier.[48]

Ralph Adams Cram

Thomas O'Shaughnessy was also an occasional visitor to the University of Notre Dame. He kept Matthew Walsh, president of the university from 1922 to 1928, informed about his work on glass windows. Walsh himself used to visit the O'Shaughnessys in Chicago, noting on one occasion that he had dropped in on them and found that "Frank, John and Gus were all in the office at the same time so we had an interesting half hour."[49] In 1925, Walsh attempted to set Gus up with a stream of work from the prominent American architect Ralph Adams Cram, who today is remembered especially for his work at Princeton. Cram was to feature on the cover of *Time* magazine the following year, and designed the South Dining Hall on the Notre Dame campus at South Bend. A campus guidebook describes this structure, which opened in 1927, as the "undisputed apogee of collegiate Gothic architecture at Notre Dame" and "one of the finest examples of the genre in the United States."[50] In December 1925 Walsh wrote to Francis O'Shaughnessy,

> When Dr. Cram was here in connection with the designing of our new mess hall, I had an hour or two with him after we had finished our business talk. In the course of his conversation he told me that the big problem right now was in getting hold of some one who could handle the work in the windows of his churches under construction. He complained that although there were several good men, there was no one that he knew of who combined artistic skill with spiritual sence [*sic*]. At this point in the conversation, I began to expatiate on what your brother was doing, and Mr. Cram was very much interested, and expressed a keen desire to see some of his work. I promised him that I would get in touch with Gus immediately. Just as we had finished our conversation, who should come along but your brother Jim, and his daughter. It really seemed as if the whole thing had been planned. [I] told Jim what I had been relating to Dr. Cram, and again the Dr. urged that Gus get in touch with him without delay . . . I really believe it would mean something big to convince Dr. Cram of what Gus can do.[51]

James was probably back in Chicago at that time to visit his brothers for Christmas. No doubt both he and Frank conveyed this good news to Thomas, but little or nothing seems to have come of the opportunity. Thomas found it hard to make a living as an artist. Notwithstanding Walsh's intervention on his behalf and the commissions by Fr. McNamee at Old St. Pat's and by Bishop Griffin at the Cathedral of the Immaculate Conception in Springfield, he became embittered by what he saw as the failure of the Catholic Church institutionally to appreciate or to support his work. In 1934 he wrote to Notre Dame, asking one of its former presidents if he realized that "in the thirty-four years I have given to bringing the beautiful art of

Ireland back to the service of the church no Catholic organisation has in any way given me cooperation." He complained, "I am permitted to starve and must see my children homeless paupers." Fr. John W. Cavanaugh responded by having a "Memorandum for Superiors" typed up for Thomas in which he pointed out that the latter had designed the Diamond Jubilee cover for the Notre Dame *Scholastic* "in beautiful Celtic spirit and motif" and that Thomas was "probably the best exponent of the beautiful old Catholic Celtic Art now living." Thomas had included with his first letter a copy of notes prepared for the Illinois Chamber of Commerce that referred to the fact that the window of American glass that was given a place of honor in the Hall of Religion at the Century of Progress fair had been built in his studios and was a "pot metal window," being of a type that is free from paint and so "beautiful by night as by day." In his opinion, this type of stained glass was superior to windows that were painted and afterward burned, but many church commissions opted for the latter, less expensive type. He regretted the fact that even his most famous work had been marred by bad taste: "I was permitted to put one unpainted window in St. Patrick's Church [Chicago]; all the other windows were spoiled by using painted faces. In Springfield (Illinois) Cathedral, the architect was permitted to specify painted faces."[52] Nevertheless, it may have been a consolation to him that in 1936 he was admitted as an honorary officer to the French Academy of Arts for his work in stained glass. This further award by the French was presented by the consul of France at the downtown college of DePaul University at a meeting of the DePaul Art League of which Thomas was a co-founder.[53]

Relative Obscurity

Old St. Pat's Church has a photograph of Thomas O'Shaughnessy working on an image of "Naomh Firgil" (Gaelic for "Saint Fergal"). The photo is dated 1943, which is the year that Thomas decided to retire from glass production and to donate to the University of Notre Dame 10,000 mirrors of varied sizes, ten to fifteen tons of colored glass in sheet form, "and all the equipment necessary to transform these sheets of glass into masterful mosaic works and beautiful windows." Described then by the Notre Dame student paper as "well known as a lecturer on art and Celtic culture," he went on to reprise his design of the Irish Fellowship Club's banquet programme

Thomas O'Shaughnessy at work in the 1940s. Courtesy Old St. Pat's Church.

of 1910 for its half-centenary banquet in 1951. But he did not take part in those festivities "due to the recent death of my brother James."[54]

He died on February 11, 1956, "in relative obscurity" writes Barton. Yet in his article celebrating the artistry of Thomas O'Shaughnessy, as manifested in particular at Old St. Pat's, Barton recalls, "At the turn of the century, he had been one of Chicago's most celebrated artists, a tireless promoter of Irish culture."[55] The *Chicago Tribune* reported briefly the passing of this "stained glass [and] mural artist, noted for his work [and] credited with initiating Columbus Day."[56] The children whom Thomas had feared would become "homeless paupers" lived long lives. Attracta later married and died only in 2005. Joseph O'Shaughnessy worked at the *Chicago Sun-Times* for forty-nine years, retiring eventually as its advertising director.

Some artists today have continued to draw inspiration from O'Shaughnessy's legacy, not least Sharon Bladholm of Chicago who once worked on the restoration of his doors at Old St. Pat's. There were bits missing from glass in the doors that matched an exact green in a stock of glass pieces and sheets that had belonged to Thomas, and that "by a lucky chance" she had been able to purchase. She used these pieces to repair the doors.[57] However, the doors were later deemed no longer serviceable and have been replaced.

When the renowned Conrad Schmitt Studios of Wisconsin were undertaking work at Old St. Pat's Church in the late twentieth century, they wrote, "Of all the stained glass conservation/restoration projects we have executed not one artist from our country or abroad exhibits the gift of genius as does Thomas O'Shaughnessy." They remarked that he was "brilliant in using translucent and opalescent glass" and explained in detail how his craftmanship matched his creativity.[58]

A discrete study of Thomas O'Shaughnessy and his studio is overdue. The full range of his work merits closer attention by art historians.[59]

SEVEN James at the Helm of US Advertising

JAMES O'SHAUGHNESSY CAME TO PLAY a major role in the development of modern US advertising. As a youth in Missouri, he had turned his hand to promoting his father's footwear business by writing advertisements for it. As managing editor of a newspaper in St. Joseph, Missouri, he subsequently saw at close quarters the relationship between advertising and journalism. The latter depended on the former in almost every case to keep the presses rolling. Advertising agencies in the modern sense were then only beginning to emerge in their own right as a sector of the media economy, and the line between journalism and copywriting was a fluid one. Settled in Chicago as a journalist, James O'Shaughnessy crossed that line and founded his own agency. He embarked on a journey that was to see him acknowledged as a leading force in the sector, particularly in his capacity as chief executive of the new American Association of Advertising Agencies (AAAA or the 4A's).

It was later said of James O'Shaughnessy, "He was conducting his own advertising agency in Chicago when along came the movement for organizing and harmonizing the advertising interests. This was just the meat for the easy-going but thorough, smiling, Irish-Missourian who talks and thinks advertising in plain, simple and understandable language as a business. 'Jim' set out to sell confidence in advertising agencies."[1] When he took up his job at the helm of the 4A's, he took charge of an organization that was helping to transform the image and behavior of admen. If advertising was publicly scorned as a professional activity in the years leading up to his appointment, it was being publicly praised by US presidents by the time that he quit the association.

Advertising Manager

O'Shaughnessy's first significant foray into advertising after leaving St. Joseph and subsequently parting company with Pawnee Bill, for whose wild west show he had undertaken promotional work in Europe, was within the Hearst group of newspapers. Referring to him in 1924, the Associated Advertising Clubs of the World recalled that he had worked as a journalist in Chicago on the *Journal, Tribune, News, Times-Herald, Chronicle,* and *American* but that he also became advertising manager of the *Chicago Examiner.*[2] Both the *American* and the *Examiner* were owned by Hearst, whose arrival in Illinois shook the *Chicago Tribune.* Medill McCormick, its assistant editor in chief and part owner who later became a US senator from Illinois, "decided that the *Tribune* could no longer disdain advertising solicitors, as it had done," and he reorganized its business and advertising departments. Sole "solicitors" had sold space directly for newspapers, as did Leopold Bloom, James Joyce's fictional Dubliner in *Ulysses,* and their solitary function was already being superseded by the modern full-service advertising agency.[3]

E. W. Scripps attempted to buck the advertising beast by running a newspaper that did not depend on advertisements. His tabloid-size *Day Book,* launched in Chicago in 1911, was ultimately unsuccessful. This polemical newspaper catered to the working person but was unable to sustain its critique on the basis of subscriptions alone and, for this and other reasons, closed down during World War I.[4] James O'Shaughnessy had no such fundamental objections to the role of advertising. On the contrary, and perhaps defensively in response to criticism from cultural, political, and religious sources, he was to assert its virtues as a force for economic and social good.

A biographical note that he furnished to the *Pathfinder* in 1931 highlights his work after 1900 as "political editor and writer on business subjects." It also states that between his acting as advertising manager for a Chicago newspaper and becoming an advertising agent himself, James O'Shaughnessy worked as the advertising manager for "one of the minor magazines," but does not identify this title.[5]

Marriage and Children

During the early years of the twentieth century James became president of the Western Catholic Writers' Guild.[6] His honorary office allowed him give expression to his faith in a practical and vocational way. At the same time he pursued more personal interests. If while in Missouri he had been publicly humiliated as a young man contemplating marriage, as Albert Johnson claimed, in Chicago he found a way to tie the knot. In 1907, when he was forty-two years old, James O'Shaughnessy married a woman considerably younger. This was Mary Hynes "of the Hynes family of Galway," born to an Irish immigrant father in St. Louis in 1884. The couple intended to have children. Indeed, as Catholics, they were expected if not morally required to do so.[7] Perhaps partly because of this commitment James decided to take his career in a more lucrative direction. It led to his founding his own advertising agency.[8] A growth in demand for advertising helped him to succeed.

Total advertising in US newspapers and periodicals multiplied three and a half times between 1892 and 1914: "This tremendous increase, at a ratio more than ten times that of the increase in the number of daily papers, meant greater profits in newspaper publishing than had ever been known before."[9] Where four books on advertising appeared in the United States between 1895 and 1900, at least seventy-five were published between 1900 and 1910 — "and these books were especially rich in original ideas." Even before the turn of the century an expanding advertising community in Chicago had entertained pioneering ideas about the relevance of scientific research and training to their business, including the application of psychological insights.[10] Between 1905 and 1920 the number of firms or individuals listed as "General Advertising Agents" in Chicago increased from about 30, handling around $15 million in advertising, to 108, placing $75 million in advertising.[11] The boom both facilitated and benefited from a growth in consumption that new technologies accelerated.[12]

His Own Agency

Starting out on his new career as an advertising agent, James joined the Gundlach Advertising Company in Chicago.[13] In 1911, as an employee of Gundlach, he traveled to Cedar Rapids, Iowa, to give what was described as "a snappy talk" to the Ad Club there. By 1911, while still at Gundlach's, he had become a director of the Chicago Advertising Association and chairman of its trade extension committee.[14]

Within a year of his trip to Cedar Rapids, James founded his own agency, the O'Shaughnessy Advertising Company. It was located in the landmark Heyworth Building, on Madison Street, Chicago, between State Street and Wabash Avenue. He was described during 1912 as "a man of exceptional ability" who was "very well known as an expert in mail-order promotion, a keen analyst of merchandising problems, and a fluent, forceful, public speaker." That same year, his employees formed a team to compete in the Chicago Advertising Baseball League. The O'Shaughnessy Advertising Company's clients included a large music house that retained him specifically to advertise its harps, as well as the Leap Resilient Wheel Company that produced "a radically new wheel for automobiles."[15]

In 1912, in a small periodical devoted to the relationship between adver-

Heyworth Building, Madison Street, Chicago, 1912. Its occupants then included the O'Shaughnessy Advertising Company. Contemporary postcard.

JAMES O'SHAUGHNESSY

President and General Manager of the O'Shaughnessy Advertising Company, Chicago. Mr. O'Shaughnessy is a man of exceptional ability. He is very well known as an expert in mail-order promotion, a keen analyst of merchandising problems, and a fluent, forceful, public speaker. His success as an advertising agent has been remarkable.

James O'Shaughnessy, 1912.
From *Advertising and Printing*, Nov. 1912.

tising and printing, he waxed eloquent about printing and described it as being, among other things, "the chief medium of advertising expression" and "near enough to be called the mother of modern advertising." The caption under an accompanying photograph included the observation that already, "His success as an advertising agent has been remarkable."[16]

Truth in Advertising

In 1912, James O'Shaughnessy reviewed for the *Chicago Tribune* Synge's *Playboy of the Western World.* His review of the Irish play, considered earlier, was dismissive. In 1913, by contrast, he "expressed hearty approval" of a declaration of a joint committee of the Associated Advertising Clubs of America that had been meeting in Baltimore, Maryland. The committee advocated radical revision of the methods of verifying the circulation claims of newspapers, finding then-current methods confusing and inadequate. The committee now "advocated truth as the foundation of all dealings," and James agreed with its proposition. He was eager to promote professional standards among both publishers and advertisers. A former *Tribune* journalist, he praised what he regarded as that newspaper's honest approach to business and proclaimed, "This crusade for honest advertising which the *Tribune* is leading may be more fully appreciated when we contemplate that advertising is today the greatest educative force of civilization. The least of its evils is conspicuous. It should be without spot or flaw."[17] Already James was displaying the kind of rationalizing hyperbole that he would deploy later when working for the American Association of Advertising Agencies. Not all of his contemporaries thought that advertising was "the greatest educative force of civilization."

He was but one of a number of admen campaigning for Truth in Advertising, and also for truthful claims relating to the circulation of particular newspapers. If the sector did not take steps to distance itself from patently dishonest practices then others might impose unwelcome restrictions. Already New York and Massachusetts had passed laws against fake advertising. Prompted by Samuel C. Dobbs of Coca-Cola, the Associated Advertising Clubs of the World had adopted "truth" as their slogan at their 1911 convention.[18] One historian in 1998 wrote skeptically of such efforts by advertising practitioners, "Since the 1910s, they have developed mechanisms to recommend and to pressure members to conform to standards in ethics, but they have rarely been able to enforce them."[19]

Business Expands

From 1914 to 1915 James O'Shaughnessy served as secretary-treasurer of the regional Western Advertising Agents' Association, which had been founded in May 1911 and of which he was also a director.[20]

Agricultural advertising is said to have more than doubled in the United States during the second decade of the twentieth century. James O'Shaughnessy was later to express his great respect for farming papers and he capitalized on the opportunities that they presented. In 1915 *Printers' Ink* reported in New York, "Copy is being sent farm papers by the O'Shaughnessy Advertising Company, Chicago, for the National Dairy Machine Company, Silica Products Company and Indiana Spring Company. This agency is also advertising Moxley's Butterine and Kneipp Malt Food in daily papers."[21] As his business grew he looked for new opportunities. During 1915, he was one of the incorporators and promoters of the Hibernia Fire Insurance Company, which took its name from the Latin name for Ireland. This was a business "as safe, as necessary and as profitable as the banking business itself," at least according to its promoters' advertisement headed "A Big Opportunity." Its campaign was aimed at anyone with even as little as $20 to invest.[22]

During 1916 O'Shaughnessy participated at long distance in an event organized to demonstrate the value of new technology to business. The occasion was a dinner of the New York Association of Advertising Agents, in this instance "an unusually elaborate and featured affair" organized by a telephone company that "arranged so that everybody present held a receiver and was able to enjoy the novelty of hearing people converse with New York at numerous points as far away as San Francisco and vice versa as clearly as if they were using a local telephone connection." Among conversations on the transcontinental line was one between George C. Sherman in New York and James O'Shaughnessy, by now acting as vice chairman of the Western Advertising Agents' Association, in Chicago. Later that evening, motion pictures of both San Francisco Bay and the Seal Rocks were projected in New York for the "very large attendance" at the dinner, "while the roar of the

waves, pictured on the screen, was actually heard." This was made possible
by placing a telephone transmitter on the Seal Rocks and connecting it to
the transcontinental line![23]

O'Shaughnessy's career also benefited from the rapid urban development
of Chicago, and particularly from the public relations problems of paving
contractors there. *Printers' Ink* noted, "Ever since municipalities undertook
the letting of paving contracts, taxpayers have viewed the work with suspicion. No matter how well the job was done there was always someone
to raise the cry of 'graft,' 'skimping,' and 'politics.'" There had been such an
outcry in Chicago about the quality of paving that, the magazine was pleased
to note, twenty "progressive" contractors had now turned to advertising as
a solution, at the suggestion of James O'Shaughnessy. He was "familiar with
the part advertising had played in settling the Chicago car strike; he had
seen what it had done in 'selling' the Torrens method of title registration
to Chicago real estate owners, and he believed that advertising could also
be made to solve the problem of the paving contractors." Large space was
taken in seven Chicago papers, pointing out some facts about how street
paving contracts were managed. Coupons were included for a booklet
that O'Shaughnessy designed to educate taxpayers about pavements and
paving — and to which he assigned the copyright date of St. Patrick's Day
1917. *Printers' Ink* reported a "flood" of requests for the booklet.[24]

As he tried new methods of persuasion, his business expanded. Sometime before May 13, 1916, according to Chicago's *Broad Ax* on that day,
O'Shaughnessy's advertising agency moved to "extensive quarters" in the
Westminster Building at 110 South Dearborn Street. This pro-Democrat,
black newspaper added that James "is proving himself to be one of the best
and keenest business men in Chicago."

Red Cross Campaign

The involvement of US forces in World War I had immediate consequences
for many families, including the O'Shaughnessys. Young James Berney, the
son of James O'Shaughnessy's deceased sister, Lizzie, had been reared by his
grandparents in Chicago and was living there. In 1914 he played the part of
Columbus in a pageant for children mounted by his uncle Thomas and the
Knights of Columbus at the Columbus replica caravels.[25] He also worked

at the O'Shaughnessy Advertising Company. But in 1917, when the United States went to war, he enlisted and sailed for France where he served as a machine-gunner with the 149th Field Artillery.[26]

The war also had consequences for James O'Shaughnessy. In April 1917 the Western Advertising Agency Association pledged support to the Red Cross, which was about to campaign for the recruitment of 150,000 new members. The association made James head of its publicity and advertising committee for this purpose and told the Red Cross that it would obtain space for twenty-two full-page advertisements urging Chicagoans to "wake up and enroll." Theodore Roosevelt had been persuaded already to "devote at least five minutes of his speech on Saturday to asking citizens to enroll in the Red Cross."[27] The Red Cross campaign prefigured some of the work that James would undertake in the near future when he became the first chief executive of the American Association of Advertising Agencies. His knowledge of the media, gained over decades in journalism and in advertising, and his involvement as head of the Red Cross committee meant that he was well placed to be judged the best man for that job when it was created.

Not least as a director of the Western Advertising Agents' Association, who had also served as its secretary-treasurer, O'Shaughnessy favored the coordination of advertising practices across state lines. It made commercial sense to him.

Precedents

At least six successive efforts had been made to organize the agency business nationally before the AAAA was formed. As early as 1888 there had been an association of General Newspaper Advertising Agents, and in 1890 an American Advertising Agents Association met at the Waldorf-Astoria Hotel in New York City.[28] James O'Shaughnessy thought that the Affiliated Association of Advertising Agents, formed in Philadelphia in 1916, had successfully "pioneered the idea for a national organization." *Printers' Ink* later credited him with having made sustained efforts in this respect before 1917.[29] Among others involved in attempts to start up a lasting organization had been Newcomb Cleveland of the Erickson Advertising Agency, Frank Presbrey who later wrote a definitive study of early advertising, and Patrick F. O'Keefe from Boston who is credited with coining for florists that enduring slogan

"Say it with flowers."[30] They wished to eliminate what Lee has described as "chaotic conditions in the advertising agency field" at that time.[31]

Four independent regional organizations of advertising agencies had also been founded and continued to exist. There was one each in New York, Boston and Philadelphia, and another in Chicago, the Western Advertising Agents' Association of which James O'Shaughnessy was an honorary officer, for agents in the Midwest and West. Turnbull has remarked that these four regional or local organizations "do not appear to have been weak associations hoping to combine for survival, but healthy and vigorous arms of what soon was to become a strong body."[32]

George Creel and his Campaigns

The immediate catalyst for the creation of the successful organization that finally emerged and became known as the American Association of Advertising Agencies was President Woodrow Wilson's decision to utilize the goodwill and experience of advertising agencies when the United States entered World War I in April 1917. George Creel, who was then appointed Chairman of the Committee on Public Information, later explained that the president wished to make known "to every corner of the civilized globe . . . the full message of America's idealism, unselfishness, and indomitable purpose." He recalled, "We fought prejudice, indifference, and disaffection at home and we fought ignorance and falsehood abroad. We strove for the maintenance of our own morale and the Allied morale by every process of stimulation. . . . Our effort was educational and informative throughout, for we had such confidence in our case as to feel that no other argument was needed than the simple, straightforward presentation of facts."[33] Studies of the committee and of contemporary propaganda efforts suggest that the newspaperman Walter Lippman had helped to persuade President Wilson that it was better to educate public opinion than simply to suppress the truth or merely whip up hatred of the enemy.[34]

Creel was born in Missouri, just two counties away from that in which James O'Shaughnessy first saw the light of day. Like James, Creel had worked as an investigative journalist. He now wanted admen to help him to achieve the president's objectives. He later recalled, "The work of the Committee [on Public Information] was so distinctly in the nature of an advertising

George Creel at
the White House.
Courtesy Library
of Congress.

campaign, though shot through and through with an evangelical quality, that we turned almost instinctively to the advertising profession for advice and assistance."[35] Yet if he sought "advice and assistance" he had no intention of surrendering his control of the government's publicity strategy to agencies. Some admen were taken aback by the extent of the powers being assumed by Creel, whom *Printers' Ink* described frankly in April 1917 as "Uncle Sam's newly-appointed press-censor and publicity promoter." Creel told its special Washington correspondent that the chairman's job "gave him control not merely of publicity and advertising for the State, War and Navy Departments, but for the entire Governmental organization and all its branches." This news elicited immediate clarification: "When the *Printers' Ink* representative, fearing that he must have misunderstood the new publicity chief, asked if he construed his responsibilities to include the supplanting, for instance, of the extensive Office of Information which has been maintained for years past by the Department of Agriculture, Mr. Creel stated that it was not his idea that the new institution would supplant such established institutions, but that it would have supervision over the whole field." *Printers' Ink,* unimpressed by this distinction, headed its report "Creel expects to 'clear' any government advertising done: the exact definition of his powers is yet in doubt." Its correspondent worried, unduly, as it was to transpire, that "advertising is evidently an afterthought with Mr. Creel." He reported the latter as saying, in respect to army recruiting, that if the president had his way about compulsory military service "there will be no need for advertising." Creel was simply indicating that not everyone in Washington agreed that admen had an important role to play in the government's forthcoming campaigns and implying that this fact required him to manage their involvement. *Printers' Ink* expressed concern about his advisors: "Most of the men who have thus far been appointed to assist Mr. Creel are known as newspaper writers, and have had no advertising experience, whereas such limited advertising as the War and Navy Departments have done in the past, having, for the most part, been placed through agencies, there is no person on the regular staff of either department who manifestly qualifies for advertising execution."[36]

Liberty Loan Discord

Facing this national challenge, admen needed to respond effectively. But Creel later recalled that "there was a sad lack of accord in the initial contacts between the government and the advertising experts." When the First Liberty Loan was announced in May 1917 a committee of admen headed by Herbert Houston, William H. Rankin, and O.C. Harn went to Washington to urge a campaign based upon the outright purchase of advertising space in newspapers and other mediums. They found themselves contending with the opinion that the job of communicating whatever was necessary could be paid for out of donations and appear in print without the service of agents. Creel attributed this idea to "the first days of war enthusiasm" and "a definite repugnance to any suggestion that savored of profit." He wrote that "voluntary" was the magic word, and "even though it took five dollars to secure the gift of a dime, there was a glamour about the donation that blinded every one to the economic waste." Advertising was regarded as a business, not a profession, and Creel thought that "the majority looked upon the advertising agent with suspicion, even when he was not viewed frankly as a plausible pirate belonging to the same school of endeavor as the edition-de-luxe book canvasser."[37]

In the event, "the advertising experts withdrew from Washington, feeling somewhat as though casualties had been sustained." However, "instead of sulking they proceeded to prove themselves and their theories by actual demonstration." Rankin, who was a leading force in US advertising, evolved what came to be known as the "Chicago Plan," this being the purchase of space in the press by individuals or groups, and the donation of such space to the uses of government. The plan was inspired by the Red Cross drive in Chicago, of which Rankin was general director and in which James O'Shaughnessy was also involved. That drive had induced businessmen to stand the cost of thirty-five full-page advertisements in the daily papers, with the result that every dollar membership was reportedly secured at an expense of two and a half cents as opposed to an expense of twenty-three cents per member in New York, where all effort was "voluntary." According to Creel, the "Chicago Plan" was applied to the First Liberty Loan by almost every advertising club and agent in the country, and "fully one million dollars were contributed to the campaign. . . . In Muncie, Indiana, where full dependence was placed upon the Rankin idea, not a single [advertising] solicitor being used to sell bonds, the city more than doubled its quota in record time." He added, "The Second Liberty Loan saw much the same achievements on the part of the advertising fraternity, and the showing gave me opportunity, even as it afforded justification, for recognition of advertising as a real profession, and to include it as an honorable and integral part of the war-machinery of government."[38]

Although admen were concerned about Creel's powers, they soon consoled themselves by noting his abandonment of early efforts to secure free publicity for government enterprises through random public relations initiatives that sought to persuade publishers to print favorable feature stories and other editorial items prepared by persons of some reputation as magazine writers. One observer was pleased that "super-press-agentry has been found wanting in results."[39]

American Association of Advertising Agencies

As admen engaged in dialogue with Creel, they became increasingly convinced of the benefits of coordinating their own position on professional matters. The American Association of Advertising Agencies was founded on June 4, 1917, at a meeting held in the mayor's office at city hall, St. Louis. Advertising agents had assembled in that Missouri city, along with advertisers and publishers, for a convention of the Associated Advertising Clubs of the World. According to *Printers' Ink,* the note struck at this convention was, in general, one of "war time service." The agents decided to consolidate the four existing organizations of agencies at New York, Boston, Philadelphia and Chicago, and to manage paid staff to carry out plans contemplated for the new AAAA. They chose William H. Johns of the George Batten agency in New York to be their first president. He was a former chairman of the New York agents' association, while his company's eponymous founder had himself chaired the American Advertising Agents Association that met in 1900 but then faltered and failed. Both William H. Rankin and James O'Shaughnessy were among those who now became members of the executive board of the new AAAA.[40]

The founders identified their "first important task" as the establishment for the association of offices, the duties of which would include taking over the work then being done by volunteer committees. There was a certain sense of urgency about what needed to be done. Among pressing tasks contemplated for these offices, which were to be located in New York, was work on such matters as the gathering of information on which to base official recognition, uniform cost systems for agencies; uniform order blanks, and the collection of data useful to agents; in general, they sought to give a definite point of contact with the American Newspaper Publishers Association, the Association of National Advertisers, the Periodical Publishers Association, the Farm Press Association and other bodies. "In all the contemplated plans," they declared, "the underlying idea is to raise the standards of agency practice, and to make for better relations between agents, clients, and space sellers all round."[41]

The newly founded AAAA needed to employ a chief executive whom it could trust to coordinate its work both quickly and effectively. James O'Shaughnessy, who already sat on its governing council, was that person. At its first quarterly meeting, held at Cleveland on September 25, 1917, the board of the AAAA appointed him as its first executive secretary and agreed to establish its headquarters in Manhattan. James immediately resigned as a member of the board and took up his duties as an employee on October 1 that year. It would be claimed when he stepped down from this position

twelve years later that he had taken it "at considerable personal sacrifice."
On November 15, 1917, the AAAA opened its offices at the Metropolitan Life
Insurance Company Tower overlooking Madison Square.[42]

James Goes to New York

In 1870 Galway-born Patrick Ford had come to New York and founded his
populist and successful *Irish World,* which by the turn of the century had become the preeminent Irish-American newspaper. He had worked earlier on
American papers in Boston and Charleston.[43] From 1895 Mickey Duggan of
Hogan's Alley also made his appearance in the New York press. Commonly
referred to as the "Yellow Kid," this comic Irish-American character by R. H.
Outcault was depicted in a large yellow nightshirt. A child of the tenements,
he turned up in both Pulitzer and Hearst newspapers, where his strip was
frequently used as a vehicle for trenchant editorial opinions. This is said to
have inspired the coining of "Yellow Journalism" as a term of disapproval
for the sensational coverage of events by these two press groups.[44]

By the time James O'Shaughnessy came to New York in 1917 he had abandoned his career in journalism, where he had been employed by Hearst and
others, and settled instead on one in advertising and media consultancy. He
was to play a central role in attempting to transform the image of admen
and their profession.

A Note of Patriotism

The new association was distracted from more formal or normal professional concerns by the immediate need to be seen to support the war effort.
It launched into a campaign to have all advertisements carry a patriotic
message.

O'Shaughnessy sent a bulletin to members of the AAAA informing them
that the association was being asked to cooperate in a nationwide movement
to aid the government in its broad purposes. The request was being passed
along "with our earnest approval," having been proposed to the government
by Miss Eula McClary, "the well known magazine writer." O'Shaughnessy
explained that the general purpose of the idea was "to awaken the people of

The Metropolitan Tower and Flatiron Building, Madison Square, Manhattan. Contemporary postcard 1913.

the United States to a more lively sense of greater service to all of the aims and purposes of the Government." While advertisers might choose their own wording, "All expressions in this connection should be inspiriting to faith in President Wilson and devotion to the cause of the Government and loyal and unwavering support to its every undertaking to bring victory to the standard of democracy." The executive secretary of the AAAA made it clear that while the initiative depended on voluntary effort, everyone was expected to take part, for Washington desired that "every display ad[vertisement] of every possible description appearing anywhere and everywhere in the United States in the month of March should sound a patriotic and helpful note — something inspiring to those who are carrying the burdens of grave responsibility for us — something encouraging to those who are offering their lives for us — something helpful to those whom we are helping and who are helping us." He was "certain" that its members would "gladly seize this opportunity to render a patriotic service."[45]

US Division of Advertising

Acting on a recommendation from George Creel, President Woodrow Wilson formalized the cooperation between his government and the agencies by issuing an executive order on January 20, 1918: "I hereby create, under the jurisdiction of the Committee on Public Information, heretofore established by executive order of April 14, 1917, a Division of Advertising for the purpose of receiving through the proper channels the generous offers of the advertising forces of the nation to support the effort of the government to inform public opinion properly and adequately."[46]

William H. Johns, president of George Batten Company and president of the new American Association of Advertising Agencies was appointed to chair the board of control of the new division. Others invited to participate in the government's initiative included the president of the Associated Advertising Clubs of the World (AACW), representing 180 clubs with a combined membership of 17,000. Primarily advertisers constituted these clubs, and the inclusion of the AACW's president thus complemented that of the agencies' representative. The purposes of the new Division of Advertising were said to be to relieve publishers of indiscriminate and duplicated requests for space, and to make the donations of space yield the very highest results, "by having them administered by one office, which would be informed on everything that was being done, and where copy for the purpose could best be prepared."[47] Creel wrote, "By this one stroke of President Wilson's pen every advertising man in the United States was enrolled in America's second line, and from the very moment of their enrolment we could feel the quickening of effort, the intensification of endeavor. Offices were taken in the Metropolitan Tower in New York, a skilled force assembled, and from these headquarters the generals directed the energies of an army of experts. . . . Never was there a machinery that operated with such automatic efficiency."[48]

Creel's fellow Missourian James O'Shaughnessy described the division as "essentially a part of our own national Headquarters." This was not least because the rooms of the division adjoined the offices of the AAAA in the Metropolitan Tower on Madison Square.[49]

It has been said that, during 1917, "The administration commenced American participation in the war with a campaign to agitate the deepest levels

Liberty Bond
advertisement.
Courtesy Library
of Congress.

of the popular psyche, employing all the techniques of persuasion and manipulation that the infant industries of advertising and mass entertainment could provide."[50] On Christmas Eve that year O'Shaughnessy wrote to members of the AAAA that "since the advertising agencies have been specially honored by the Government in the selection of the President of our Association [Johns] to a position which in effect is that of Federal Director of Advertising [i.e., chair of the board of control of the US Division of Advertising], and since much of the work of this division will necessarily fall upon the agencies, it is of grave importance that every member of the Association make ready to stand by to do his big share in a worthy manner."[51] This division took on army and navy recruiting and the sale of Liberty Bonds, as well as the final Victory Loan. The US government issued Liberty Bonds from April 1917 onward as a way of financing its war effort, with the public encouraged to buy them as a patriotic duty. A bond could later be redeemed for its purchase price with interest.

Limits of Patriotism

However, patriotism had its limits, as one advertising agency was no doubt surprised to discover when in 1918 it notified the AAAA that it had waived its commission on that part of its client's advertising space that had been contributed by the client for government purposes through the Division of Advertising. Chairman Johns advised the agent, "You will probably be disappointed to learn that your splendid generosity in waiving your commissions on the advertising, donated by your client, is contrary to the ruling which I made as chairman of the Division of Advertising." Johns acknowledged, "The spirit which prompted your action is certainly most commendable but, on the other hand, there is no reason that I can see why advertising agencies in their generosity should be called upon to give away both cash and service as a result of the Division of Advertising." Just in case his point might somehow be missed, he added, "If commissions are waived by advertising agencies then they should be paid for the great amount of time and service which they are rendering through their executives and through their copy and art departments. There is no reason why they should give both." O'Shaughnessy copied this policy to other agencies in a letter on June 28, 1918.[52]

Creel's Committee on Public Information in Washington separately harnessed the work of the "Four Minute Men," a voluntary organization that originated early in 1917 in Chicago but that soon became national in its range. About 75,000 speakers made themselves available to it for the purpose of making patriotic speeches, mostly in cinemas during intermissions of approximately four minutes when the screening of movies was halted. Among those in Chicago who "rendered valuable assistance to the organization" was James O'Shaughnessy's brother Francis.[53]

On October 8, 1918, William H. Johns, as president of the AAAA and chairman of the Division of Advertising, reported to the association's executive board that while some of the heads of departments and bureaus in Washington were at first disposed to disregard its work and that while some of them had undertaken to handle their own advertising, "finally all of them had recognized the outstanding value of the Division and were now favorable to the use of its facilities and advantages." The substance of his report was in effect that the division's efforts had resulted in educating "official Washington" very largely to the value and use of advertising, "and also to the advantage of using organized, skillful direction in advertising." Johns thought that the division had also served advertising itself insofar as it had "removed much of the prejudice against it which had been at our entrance into the war — one of the things so much deplored in official Washington." Success was breeding success, with the two largest agencies in "the western territory" that had declined to join at first now inquiring about the requirements for membership.[54]

War Ends

The Division of Advertising of the Committee on Public Information was dissolved on December 15, 1918, the war having ended on November 11 of that year. A testimonial to the effectiveness of the work done by the AAAA and its members through the division came in the form of a letter from Major General Enoch Crowder, provost marshal general, stating, "The concentrated power of your Association has been revealed in a striking fashion; and I wish to congratulate its members upon their readiness to contribute their special skill to the effective work of raising the Army. It has been a very direct contribution."[55]

Yet even as the Division of Advertising was being wrapped up, the government found it useful to continue working with advertising agents in a coordinated fashion. For example, the Department of Labor secured the cooperation of the AAAA and its members in persuading advertisers to insert prepared messages in their advertising. The purpose of this initiative was "to minimize labor unrest during readjustment following the war." In December 1918 O'Shaughnessy, for the AAAA, circulated to agencies some slogans suggested by the Department of Labor. They included, "Let's all keep Industry humming by working together, employers and employees, in harmonious co-operation."[56]

In January 1919 the chairman of the Federal Trade Commission complimented the AAAA on the united effort of agencies that the association had coordinated during the war, saying, "It is largely due to this effort that there are 27,000,000 Liberty Bond owners in this country and that there is a war saving stamp in every home."[57]

Creel in Ireland

Although George Creel's Division of Advertising was wrapped up and would no longer be working with James O'Shaughnessy, Creel himself had not finished dealing with Irish-Americans. Facing renewed Irish-American demands that the US government support calls for the creation of an independent Ireland, and recognizing how Irish politics continued to complicate relations between Washington and London, Wilson sent Creel to Dublin in 1919 as his emissary. There he met Michael Collins and other leaders of the insurrection against British occupation of the island.[58]

An Irish-American group styling itself "The American Commission on Irish Independence" had been campaigning for President Wilson to support efforts by Irish nationalists to have Ireland admitted in its own right to the Paris Peace Conference of 1919 that preceded the establishment of a League of Nations. Edward Dunne, the first president of Chicago's Irish Fellowship Club, was a leading member of this group. Its public posturing complicated what turned out to be an unsuccessful campaign.[59]

In 1920 Creel published *Ireland's Fight for Freedom*. This book was a passionate and detailed argument in favor of an independent Irish state, in which he noted that there were "over 15,000,000 people of Irish birth or descent" in the United States and that "America has always been first with the Irish-American. Men of Ireland gave heart and strength to Washington, they died by thousands that the Union might endure, and of the army raised to crush German absolutism fully 15 per cent were of Irish birth or descent."[60] With World War I behind it, Washington clearly felt free to acclaim rather than to demand the continuing loyalty of its citizens of hyphenated identity.

Suspicion of the New

O'Shaughnessy later wrote, "None of the older advertising associations had a welcoming committee on the platform when the 4A's came to town."[61] Born partly out of necessity during war, the American Association of Advertising Agencies faced continuing resistance from some admen, particularly at the regional level. It fell to O'Shaughnessy to put the new association on a firm footing after the war, but not everyone thought that he was wise to have become its first executive secretary. He explained that some of his personal friends among publishers and agencies told him they were sorry for him when he sold his agency in the Midwest and moved to New York in October 1917: "They added in sympathetic confidence that if the real purpose of the Association were to bring the agencies into working cooperation for the common good, it was a handsome dream that couldn't come true. They assured me the agents were too individualistic to be harnessed into team work."[62]

Publishers as well as some admen regarded the new association with suspicion. O'Shaughnessy wrote that "it found itself surrounded by questions, doubts, resentments and innocent curiosity. Its objects were set out broadly in terms so generous that it was suspected by some of concealing ulterior motives." He added, "More than one important medium owner questioned the propriety of any sort of an organisation of agents. Some of them seemed to look on it as a union that would start trouble; perhaps a fight for a closed shop."[63] One "conspicuous" agency opposed the very idea of an association as "intermeddling in private affairs." Another agent complained that joining would "cramp his style." Several feared that "an association concerning itself with ethics would have a leveling effect on a creative profession and impair individual distinctions."[64] While many leading agencies backed the AAAA, some highly paid men such as Albert Lasker suspected that the leveling effect might not only be moral but financial, leading to reduced fees. He remained aloof. Others resented rubbing shoulders with much smaller outfits.[65] James subsequently concluded that "practically all of the criticism was well intended" and noted wryly that "most of the keener critics joined later."[66]

Advertising Agencies Corporation

In the summer of 1919 the US Navy asked the AAAA to select an agency to handle a big campaign for new recruits that was said to involve "the largest list of publications ever used on a single schedule of advertising." The campaign involved placing advertisements in about 8,000 publications. Members of the AAAA responded to this continuing government business by forming a new composite agency of advertising agencies on the basis that the Division of Advertising had proven the idea practicable. This composite agency was the Advertising Agencies Corporation, which was incorporated at New York on September 15, 1919. O'Shaughnessy said, "It was impossible to differentiate the Association from the Corporation in many things." All members of the AAAA were members of the corporation. Employees of each body shared the same premises. James O'Shaughnessy of the AAAA was also the corporation's "general manager."[67] The committee that had developed this idea included one of America's most famous admen, Stanley Resor of J. Walter Thompson. Described as a "pillar of unbending rectitude" both within the AAAA and in respect of his own professional behavior, he is said nevertheless to have allowed some of his subordinates to engage in "unbuttoned tactics."[68]

When the navy had sailed, the army marched. At "the first representative national gathering" of the AAAA, held in Boston in October 1919, the question of the expenditure of $300,000 entrusted to the American Association of Advertising Agencies by the government to be used in putting across the "Join-the-Army" campaign was reportedly settled.[69] Unsurprisingly in such lucrative circumstances, the AAAA organized its office so that there might be no reason why O'Shaughnessy could not "devote fifty per cent of his time to the work of the Advertising Agencies Corporation and fifty per cent to Association work, and have neither suffer."[70] And O'Shaughnessy, on behalf of the Advertising Agencies Corporation, was among those present in New York in 1920 at a meeting with Admiral William Benson to plan for the disposal of nearly 1,800 ships as well as salvage and surplus supplies.[71] The following February, he briefed admen in Atlanta about the "the gigantic advertising program" that the government had outlined for the US Shipping Board.[72] But this arrangement suited to wartime did not last long after peace came. An undated brochure that the Advertising Agencies Corporation produced about 1921 failed to convince other government bodies to do business through it. The corporation was finally wound up in March 1928.[73]

Achievements at the AAAA

James was by no means the only adman to move from Chicago to New York. In 1920, it was reported, "In New York City, as a living tribute to Chicago's fame in the advertising world, there are almost a hundred men originally from the western metropolis who have made notable successes in advertising." Among the two dozen men who were named (and they *were* all men) was James O'Shaughnessy, as executive secretary of the American Association of Advertising Agencies.[74] That same year, on March 27, *Editor & Publisher* identified some of the continuing abuses in advertising and urged agencies to cooperate and to standardize their practices.

In his role in New York from 1917, James had certain priorities: "The earliest concern of the 4-A's was to efface the memories of the free-for-all days when knocking the other fellow was almost a social requirement."[75] John Benson, president of the AAAA when James later retired, was to recall then that O'Shaughnessy as its first executive secretary "did much of the pioneer work in organizing the Four A's and in its early growth. His wide acquaintanceship with publishers and advertising agents was a big asset to the Association."[76] O'Shaughnessy was to promote his association's objectives at many meetings of agents and businessmen across the United States, sailing on board the *Buckeye State* from Baltimore via the Panama Canal to Los Angeles in 1921 or addressing more than one thousand leading publishers, advertisers, and advertising agents at the annual convention of the Audit Bureau of Circulation in Chicago in 1926, for example.[77]

Self-interest

One motivation for the creation of the AAAA was, of course, self-interest. It was believed that when membership of the new association became recognized as an industry standard it would reduce competition from those who were not members. Moreover, agencies that combined were able to ensure a standardized discount rate that was consistent and, from their perspective, realistic. They soon negotiated this rate so that it stood at a level that was a couple of percentage points higher than the previous norm. One of the association's first presidents noted that the AAAA "was formed with the frank purpose of protecting the agency business and the agency franchise."[78] Self-interest on the part of agents in some instances could also benefit the media in general, as practices were adopted that helped to streamline operations.

When he spoke at the fifth quarterly meeting of the association, one year after his appointment, O'Shaughnessy noted, "The headquarters in New York have grown as you might have expected, until now we have ten persons regularly employed there." He talked about the remarkable level of commitment by members of the association and added, "Evidence comes to me constantly from publishers that they are astounded at the work we are doing, that they did not believe that in their lifetime they would see the agencies united as they are in this Association."[79] One of its practical achievements was the acceptance by newspapers, publishers, and agencies of a standard order form. This task of convincing all to use a single form was said to have required "serious attention and a large amount of time."[80]

Lies and Press Agents

Meanwhile, just as some Irish-Americans who had risen socially were annoyed by the appearance of Synge's Irish *Playboy* on the American stage, so certain advertising agents were not amused by what they regarded as the stereotypes and caricatures of Aaron Hoffman's *Nothing but Lies* that opened at the Longacre Theater in New York on October 8, 1918, and ran for four months. The play's title was a satirical riposte to the Truth-in-Advertising movement that O'Shaughnessy had publicly supported. If the latter did not actually write the anonymous review of the play that appeared in *Printers'
Ink,* he no doubt agreed with the reviewer's sentiments. Its author finds that the playwright has depicted all advertising men as liars and most of them as crooks. Having scornfully dismissed Hoffman's representation of "life as it is not lived in an advertising agency," the reviewer criticizes the producers for their decision to "allow a play to go on the boards which so grossly libels a serious and important profession, and one which has well proven its value to the community by — to take a single example — its war efforts of the past eighteen months." The reviewer, referring to press agents in a way that is reminiscent of a comment in O'Shaughnessy's earlier review of *Playboy of the Western World,* notes that the author of the new play has had considerable experience as a writer for the theater and wonders if he unwisely drew his ideas of advertising people and practices from theatrical advertising "and from the customs and standards of the press agent." If so, the playwright should in all fairness state that fact in a boldface announcement on the program, for "If your only acquaintance in the flock is the black sheep, you are hardly apt to give a fair description of the condition of snowy pulchritude of the rest of the brethren."[81]

As it happened, like O'Shaughnessy, Hoffman (1880–1924) had been born in Missouri and lived in Chicago before migrating to New York City. The reviewer draws a distinction between Hoffman's play and an earlier one by Roi Cooper Megrue and Walter C. Hackett, *It Pays to Advertise*. The latter had been staged first in 1914 and also revolves around the idea of advertising. In that case at least, the reviewer of *Nothing but Lies* now concedes, "the unjust idea of advertising" which *It Pays to Advertise* gave "was perhaps necessary in the working out of the plot." Yet if so, this fact had not prevented one agency from judging the depiction of advertising in *It Pays to Advertise* to be so odious that it provoked that agency to run in the press a series of advertisements criticizing it.[82] The agency was Sherman and Bryan, where the painter Edward Hopper then occasionally appeared looking for work.[83]

During 1917 and 1918, as the AAAA set about its work, *Printers' Ink* ("A Journal for Advertisers" as its masthead proclaimed) frequently pointed out various factors that made press agentry an "evil" for both public and private business corporations. The journal encouraged the employment of professional agencies and said that depending for public relations on in-house or individual press agents who by grace or favor managed to get free coverage in newspapers and magazines was compromising and inefficient.

In March 1918, the advertising sector was relieved to learn that N. W. Ayer would be handling the million-dollar campaign of certain Brazilian coffee growers. A rumor had gone around publication circles that the Brazilian money "would all be used in 'publicity' or press-agent work, instead of straight advertising." It was said that this was the first extensive campaign of its kind for coffee and that it would benefit from the retention of an agency not least because the work planned to precede its launch was to include "a thorough inquiry to determine just where coffee stands in the diet of the American people and a thorough commercial research to determine the best possible means of advancing the sale of coffee through the various branches of trade and ultimately to the consumer."[84]

Greed, Fear, and Progress

There are few old photographs in the archives of the 4A's, but one survives of eleven of the top admen in the United States attending the AAAA annual meeting in Boston in October 1919. They include Stanley Resor of

AAAA Annual Meeting, Boston, October 1919. *Front Row* (L-R). H. H. Charles (Charles
Advertising Service, New York), Harry Dwight Smith (Fuller & Smith, Cleveland),
W. R. McLain (McLain-Hadden-Simpers, Philadelphia), Newcomb Cleveland (Erickson,
New York). *Back Row* (L-R) James O'Shaughnessy (AAAA, New York), William H. Johns
(George Batten, New York), Thomas E. Basham (Basham's, Louisville), Jesse F. Matteson
(Matteson-Fogarty-Jordan, Chicago), O. H. Blackman (Blackman-Ross, New York),
J. W. Barber (Barber's, Boston), Stanley Resor (J. Walter Thompson, New York).
Courtesy the 4A's.

J. Walter Thompson and Newcomb Cleveland of Erickson's. Each of the
eleven wears a hat, in the fashion of the time, with James O'Shaughnessy
sporting a bowler.

In a fit of enthusiasm O'Shaughessy told the convention that "Boston will
be the biggest city in the world if New England manufacturers will begin
advertising on a normal percentage and will maintain that pace for 25 years
in growing ratio." He noted, "Boston has more newspapers than any other
city in the country compared with its population."[85]

O'Shaughnessy's characteristically easy-going style of public speaking, a
mixture of affability and reassurance — some might say "Blarney" — was also
evident on the night of a celebratory dinner in New York in 1921. Following
a string of jokey addresses by leading admen who recalled notable moments
in the history of their local organization, originally independent but now a
council of the AAAA, O'Shaughnessy was called upon to speak. He told the
admen that the "truly national organization" to which they belonged was
"the most remarkable organization that business men ever builded. There is
no friction, no jealousy, there are no sectional differences." He claimed that

those who founded it "have made for themselves immortality in their wisdom, because this profession of ours will survive when all other professions have gone to decay." He predicted that future challenges "will lift us in the Social School until we stand in the forefront of those who serve their fellows well.... There is no profession which can invite the younger man to a better future than ours. Every day shows that we are more and more magnificent."[86] One need not be a socialist to harbor reservations about O'Shaughnessy's benign view of advertising. However, while his rhapsodic opinions may seem naive today, they were of their time and would partly be echoed in 1931 by as hardened a politician as Franklin D. Roosevelt.

When O'Shaughnessy returned once more to Boston in 1923, it was to address several hundred members of the Chamber of Commerce. New technologies were being developed and his speech was broadcast by radio through the Shepard Stores station, "and for the first time in New England the permanently installed public-address system was used." Having reviewed the great growth of advertising in the United States, he told his audience, "It should not be inferred that greed and fear are the great incentives to advertising. Such motives alone could never have brought about the magnificent advertising structure of today." He claimed that "pride of achievement and joy of good will are the great sources of this towering activity."[87]

There were more than twenty committees of the AAAA, as its president John Benson wrote in 1923. It was formed, he stated then, "with the frank purpose of protecting the agency business and the agency franchise." But the only way to protect business permanently was "to make it useful to advertiser and publisher, to make it strictly honest, financially sound, professionally capable, businesslike in all its relations." Benson summed up the work of the AAAA in this context by the one word "standardization," including in this the creation of a standard order blank and standard rate card and the setting of standards of admission to the association.[88]

Sybarites

During his speech in Boston in 1923, O'Shaughnessy said of advertising in the United Statets: "The activity has grown so large it has given to America an atmosphere of advertising that nurtures its progress." Such a pervasive commercial atmosphere was not to everyone's liking, but O'Shaughnessy remained a persistent advocate for the sector and at times bordered on the fanciful in his claims for it. In April 1924, he praised an editor who had recognized the importance of outdoor advertising, and he criticized as "sybarites" (effeminate persons devoted to luxury or sensual pleasure) those who wished to see its growth limited. As a frank and uncritical statement of the purported benefits of unregulated advertising his speech on that occasion would be hard to beat. He thought that the progress of business in general in the United States had been due to a very large extent to advertising efforts, of which outdoor media were a significant part. To stop the growth or the use of outdoor media would be to weaken the progress of business. Suggesting in effect that there was something wrong with a person who opposed outdoor advertising, James showed that his easy-going personality had a sharp edge: "It is true, there are people in this country who are too delicately refined for commercial effort or for sympathy with it. These sybarites are offended by many forms of business, all of which are essential to the general welfare." He thought, "Good outdoor advertising, as for instance that which is handled by the National Outdoor Advertising Bureau, is produced in good art, and handled in good taste. It is not offensive to the most refined normal person. On the contrary, it is pleasing to those who are capable of appreciating art, and who are not offended by the mere fact that art is serving industry." Claiming that if outdoor advertising were suddenly abolished, the energy withdrawn from business promotion by that act would affect the commerce of the country, even "perhaps to the point of producing a panic," he recalled a time when all forms of advertising were "highly objectionable to the super few" and remarked that the same sort of objection still held sway in some countries, with "mummifying effect." He went so far as to claim that advertising "is the most effective educational force, next to the church and the school." He deployed sarcasm in its defense, remarking, "It is true, it does cause more rumbling of wheels in factories, more noisy commercial trucks in the highways, longer freight trains and more smoky factory chimneys. These objectionable features of our progress as a people and of our work in industrial life are indissolubly linked with outdoor and other forms of advertising." He promised that "the builders in advertising service" such as the AAAA could and would remove every cause for just faultfinding.[89]

In 1924, the AAAA established a research department that was to carry out various qualitative studies of newspaper and magazine circulation, as distinct from the audit bureau's quantitative analyses. Furthering its commitment to research, it published in 1927 *Papers of the American Association of Advertising Agencies*. In 1937 Lee acknowledged the role played by James O'Shaughnessy in fostering a coordinated and genuinely objective or scientific approach to research in this field.[90]

On a personal level, O'Shaughnessy found his fortunes improving to match his reputation. His home was located in a pleasant area outside Manhattan. In 1924 James and Mary and their children were living with their Polish servant Agnes Grzenia on McKinlay Street in Tuckahoe, Westchester, New York, where James would later be elected president of the village board and be known as "mayor."[91]

Visits to London and Dublin

The growth of advertising globally was evident in July 1924 when an International Advertising Convention took place at Wembley in London. It met mainly in the Palace of Industry of the British Empire Exhibition and, for an event of its nature, was unprecedented in scale. A very large contingent of us advertisers and agents sailed for England to participate in it. O'Shaughnessy spoke at one of its fourteen parallel sessions, that of the press representation department, on the topic of "Magazine Advertising in America." His session was at the same time as that of the advertising agents' department at which Newcomb Cleveland of the Erickson agency was speaking about "Agency Association Progress in the U.S.A."[92] So he could not have been present to hear the tribute that Cleveland paid to him when the latter told the London meeting that at the AAAA, "We have been particularly fortunate in our executive secretary, whom I wish to mention at this time and who is known to many of you — James O'Shaughnessy, who gives his whole time to the association. Mr O'Shaughnessy has been with us from the start. He has been indefatigable in the work. It is close to his heart. The association is greatly indebted to him."[93]

If James O'Shaughnessy was not there to hear Cleveland sing his praises, he was able to read a glowing "news story" that the Associated Advertising Clubs of the World sent from their New York headquarters to editors "for immediate use." This singled him out as "conspicuous among the advertising men who are coming from the United States to the advertising convention in London." It claimed that "Mr. O'Shaughnessy is the most widely known figure in advertising" and that "he is accredited with knowing more people in advertising and publishing than any other individual." Indeed, it added, *everybody* in advertising in the United States and Canada, or who has been in the United States, "will probably tell you he knows Jim O'Shaughnessy." The writer believed that this was partly accounted for by the fact that James O'Shaughnessy had spent his earlier years in newspaper work, "as reporter, editor, war correspondent, special writer and advertising manager for various newspapers, chiefly in Chicago."[94]

This same statement noted that the American Association of Advertising Agencies was already "universally known as the Four A's" and had written ethics for the guidance of advertising agencies. It had endeavored to foster the spirit of brotherhood among advertising agencies throughout the world, and "it is practically true that almost every advertising man and publisher who comes to New York from either side of the world becomes a caller at the Four A Headquarters." O'Shaughnessy had arranged to open temporary offices for the Four A's in Bush House, London. This building was to become a British landmark and home to the BBC World Service from 1941 to 2012, being a prestigious American construction project in the course of completion at the time of the convention.

From London, James O'Shaughnessy traveled with a party of advertising agents to Ireland. For some this was merely a social excursion, but for others, including James, the visit had personal and professional dimensions. He visited his ancestral home county in Ireland. At an official function in Dublin he met the first prime minister of the newly independent state, W. T. Cosgrave, whom he would arrange to accompany in 1928 on train journeys from New York to Chicago and Washington. He also found himself giving advice to Irish advertising agents and agreeing to become the patron of their new national association.

Smelling of Roses

O'Shaughnessy celebrated his early achievements when he later noted that the AAAA had cooperated with publishers to save millions for all parties by reducing the number of motions required in getting an advertisement published. His association also "urged upon publishers the standardization of column widths and pages sizes, and they have cooperated with us to the end that still other millions of dollars have been saved in the advertising transactions." He added, "In a less spectacular way, perhaps, we have secured the constructive cooperation of typographers, engravers, plate makers, and paper makers. Also, of various departments of the Government."[95]

So successful was O'Shaughnessy's association in creating good working relations between agencies and the media that, in 1925, it found itself in court alongside the American Press Association and the Southern Newspaper Publishing Group. The three faced a complaint of unfair competition by allegedly combining and conspiring to compel national advertisers to employ advertising agents in placing advertisements in newspapers throughout the United States in instances where advertisers wished to benefit from certain reduced rates or charges. This Federal Trade Commission complaint was finally dismissed after trial in 1930. During 1927 James testified before the commission, and while doing so likened advertising copy to a wonderful rose that depends for its splendor on many other factors. *Printers' Ink* was quite taken by his rosy simile's value as a means of demonstrating that "Copy is no longer a matter of pure inspiration."[96]

The Farmer and the Adman Should Be Friends

O'Shaughnessy's speeches as executive secretary of the AAAA were frequently a bland mixture of coaxing and praise, asserting the benefits to society at large — and to agencies in particular — of the work of his association. He was jollying people along, building up membership and consolidating the relationships that the association had established with the media and others. He avoided controversy in public.[97] From time to time, however, blandness yielded to apostolic fervor. Thus, addressing the Agricultural Publishers Association in Chicago in 1925, this Catholic man born on a farm in Missouri who made his living working in Manhattan for admen, posited an almost mystical union between both sectors. The farm press and the adman should be friends. He told them:

> . . . the best news you print is the advertising, because that is instructive, informative, and kindly. You are free from the criticism that lodges against some other forms of publications in a very high sense because

you print almost entirely things that are of the same spiritual character as advertising.

There is nothing sordid in a farm publication, there is nothing hurtful, nothing scandalous. You have none of these moral things to answer for that appear in certain other forms of publications. So the advertising you carry runs nearer to your total operations than it does in a daily paper, and we belong, if it is all true, more intimately to publications of your character than we do to publications of the daily press.[98]

It is clear from such sentiments that he had a low opinion of some publications, but he regarded advertising itself as benign. It was a form of objective information and a public service, rather than a type of emotional or psychological manipulation that could corrupt society as some of its detractors thought. His elevation of it to a moral level equivalent to that of churches and schools was at one with the outlook of the author of a popular and remarkable book entitled *The Man Nobody Knows.* That author was Bruce Barton (1886–1967) of the Barton, Durstine & Osborn advertising agency and his book was published in 1925. Barton represented Jesus as an archtypal businessman and successful salesman, manly and self-confident, and his book drew on examples from advertising. It has been described as "a prime example of the materialism and 'glorified Rotarianism' of the Protestant churches in the 1920s."[99]

Mindful of Missouri

While James O'Shaughnessy was critical of some newspapers, he gave credit where it was due to those members of his former profession of journalism who were committed to high standards. He was also, of course, more than willing to help publishers to generate advertising revenue. So it was that in 1925 he visited the journalism school of the University of Missouri. He was there to participate as an adman in its celebrated Journalism Week, consisting annually of a round of public addresses, conferences, and gatherings of journalists that attracted editors, publishers, artists, authors and advertisers from across the United States and abroad. Drawing partly on his own experiences on newspapers in St. Joseph, Missouri, O'Shaughnessy delivered an address on "Getting National Advertising for the Country Newspaper," telling his Missouri audience that "to be a truly national advertiser one must use country papers." He pointed out that national campaigns were now the work of advertising agencies: "It was once an advertising agent. There are many publishers at this convention who remember that time. Later it grew into more than one man's work." Agencies had developed to meet the demand of clients for a full range of services under one roof: "Those who write have only one of the many skills assembled to make the roundness of the modern advertising agency organization. Some of the others are in research analysis, market measuring, planning, media, accountancy, transportation, and of course, art in several of its expressions."

He complimented Missouri, along with Kansas and Washington, for leading the way in grouping country newspapers as "a definite class," because to use them in national campaigns meant that they must make a national picture. He said, "We Missourians ask others to show us what they are trying to sell to us. Pay the other fellows the compliment of thinking of them as if they were Missourians. Show what you have to sell to the national advertisers, explain all its values and virtues and keep explaining until they not only know but appreciate. Then the sale will follow."[100]

Almost a Prophet

Just two years before the Great Crash of 1929, with the US economy booming, James O'Shaughnessy was tempted to make a remarkably bullish prediction about the future. However, he wisely hedged his forecast by using the word "almost." In the article that he wrote for the *Los Angeles Times*. he stated, "There is almost enough advertising being properly done in the United States now to protect business against an unmerited recession." And, he said, the AAAA had inaugurated particular national research directed at making the investment of advertising a "still more exact" affair.[101]

In 1928, he was invited to speak at the Georgia Press Institute in Macon about the relationship between advertising agents and editors. The *Atlanta Constitution* remarked that this was "a subject upon which his views have become authoritative." It reported, "Advertising men state that Mr O'Shaughnessy knows more agents and more publishers than any man in the country and his talks on the relationships between the two groups are sought by conventions and similar gatherings throughout the United States."

It declared him also to be "thoroughly acquainted with the sectional field, due to his contact with southern advertising men."[102]

Coolidge and Hoover

It was a sign of the success of advertising agents and their association in establishing their sector as a recognized part of the mainstream economy that American presidents began to praise it. Calvin Coolidge paid a warm tribute to agents in an address before members of the AAAA in Washington, DC, on October 27, 1926. O'Shaughnessy's association had "scored a coup": "The normally taciturn Vermonter provided a lengthy and stirring endorsement of advertising." Coolidge remarked, "It seems to me probable that of all our economic life the element on which we are inclined to place too low an estimate is advertising." He described the function of advertising in terms of its ostensible educational value, in that it informs its readers of the existence and nature of commodities by explaining the advantages to be derived from their use and creates for them a wider demand: "It makes new thoughts, new desires, and new actions. By changing the attitude of mind it changes the material condition of the people." Coolidge was touching on the nature of a consumer society where producers not merely vie to meet the need of the public but where advertising is deployed to create a demand for commodities that people previously did not realize that they wanted:

> Advertising creates and changes this foundation of all popular action, public sentiment, or public opinion. It is the most potent influence in adopting and changing the habits and modes of life, affecting what we eat, what we wear, and the work and play of the whole Nation. Formerly it was an axiom that competition was the life of trade. Under the methods of the present day it would seem to be more appropriate to say that advertising is the life of trade.[103]

While critics might argue that the communication of information about products and services was neither inherently neutral and objective nor devoid of deceit or of hidden persuasion related to emotion and desire, such a presidential endorsement of its economic benefit vindicated O'Shaughnessy's work on behalf of the association of which he was the executive secretary. Members of the Pacific Coast chapter of the AAAA were so pleased that they had 273 copies of the presidential address printed, with one on vellum specially bound for Coolidge himself. Three years later Herbert Hoover sent a message for inclusion in the English-language booklet of the International Advertising Convention in Berlin, of which convention's transportation committee James O'Shaughnessy was general chairman. In his message the US president asserted, "The economic, social and international values of advertising are now so generally understood that I need not enlarge upon them." He added, "The noteworthy advance in the ethics of business, easily perceptible in the last twenty years, is in no small measure due to the self-examination cheerfully exacted of themselves by business men in their practice of the art of advertising."[104]

FDR on Advertising

In 1931, when governor of New York, Franklin D. Roosevelt expressed views on advertising that were at least as optimistic and uncritical as the rosy rhetoric of James O'Shaughnessy and the warm endorsements of Coolidge and Hoover. He did so in the pages of a trade publication unseen by the general public, but his views stand as a monument to the progress toward social respectability that had been made by admen during the years when James O'Shaughnessy was at the helm of their national association. Roosevelt went so far as to attribute to the practice of advertising recent advances in civilization:

> If I were starting life over again, I am inclined to think that I would go into the advertising business in preference to almost any other. This is because advertising has come to cover the whole range of human needs and also because it combines real imagination with a deep study of human psychology. Because it brings to the greatest number of people actual knowledge concerning useful things, it is essentially a form of education. . . . It has risen with ever-growing rapidity to the dignity of an art. It is constantly paving new paths. . . . The general raising of the standards of modern civilization among all groups of people during the past half century would have been impossible without the spreading of the knowledge of higher standards by means of advertising.[105]

Messinger explains these views of 1931 as being consistent with FDR's general interest in the media and in persuading people rather than dictating to them.[106]

EIGHT

Two Midwestern Attorneys

WHILE THOMAS MADE A PRECARIOUS LIVING as an artist, and James prospered in advertising, their brothers John and Francis worked as lawyers in Chicago. Francis, in particular, was a stalwart of the Irish-American community in that city, but it was John who played a role in a sensational scandal that highlighted the alleged trafficking of young immigrant women into prostitution.

John Patrick O'Shaughnessy

John Patrick O'Shaughnessy (1868–1948) had graduated in 1895 from the law school of the University of Missouri, where he was a tribune of the Phi Delta Phi legal fraternity. He appears to have gone east for a while, but the 1900 census describes him and his brother Francis as lawyers in Chicago. Francis had that year graduated from the recently revamped law course at the University of Notre Dame. The two immediately went into practice together.[1]

In 1904 John helped to write the resolutions for a meeting welcoming the Irish parliamentary leader John E. Redmond to Chicago. In 1909 he became associated with Irish crafts, but in circumstances very different from those with which his artistic brother Gus was familiar. John was retained in a notorious case that involved allegations of a "white slave trade" in women. A young Presbyterian lace maker from northern Ireland, Ella Gingles, had been accused of theft. She claimed that the accusations were false and arose from her refusal to become involved in prostitution. She had been found unconscious in a hotel bathroom and told police that she was "almost forced into a life of shame by women who pretended to be her friends" and that she had been drugged, gagged, and abused.[2]

John O'Shaughnessy, attorney.
Courtesy Brigid O'Shaughnessy.

Helping Ella Gingles

Gingles later recalled that the Irish Fellowship Club employed attorney John Patrick "O'Shaughnessey" to take up her case and to investigate it, and that he was also involved in her defense:

> I was taken to the office of Mr. O'Shaughnessey [*sic*] and was told that he, as well as Mr. [Patrick H.] O'Donnell [Attorney], would be my friend. Mr. O'Shaughnessey was rather cross to me at first and seemed to doubt whether or not I could make any lace. He seemed to fear that I was a common thief, and not a real lace-maker. He said to me, 'Can you make lace?' I told him, 'Yes, I can make lace of any ordinary pattern known as Irish lace.' He said to me, 'You sit right down there in that chair and make some lace, if you can make lace.' I replied that I had no thread.
>
> Mr. O'Shaughnessey then sent out and got some thread of the kinds which I told him to get, and I sat down and worked with the thread for several hours making lace. At the end of the time I was able to show Mr. O'Shaughnessey a piece of the grapevine pattern, which is well known in

Ireland, and which is the pattern which I used when I won my prizes in my native home of Larne for lace-making. It was the same kind of lace which I had made on one or two occasions for Miss Barrett at the Wellington hotel. The pattern agreed with some of the pieces of lace which I was accused of having stolen from the Wellington hotel.

This exhibition of my powers to make lace convinced Mr. O'Shaughnessey that I was not a fraud, and that I could do what I had claimed that I could do. From that time forward he became my active friend and fought hard for me.[3]

O'Donnell, who subsequently became the fourteenth president of the Irish Fellowship Club and who was a well-known Republican, conducted her examination in court while O'Shaughnessy dealt with other aspects of the case. Gingles claimed that the woman who "tried to force her into a life of shame" had in a compromising way mentioned to her Tom Taggart, a former national chairman of the Democratic Party. At one point, John O'Shaughnessy was interrupted in an attack on Tom Taggart's French Lick Springs resort in Indiana by a statement of Judge Brentano "to the effect that respectable people go there." The *Chicago Daily Socialist* alleged that city officials were trying to protect the "white slavers" of whom Gingles was the alleged victim.[4]

The language used by lawyers at that time can on occasion seem today to have been as quaint in its own context as some of that used by John's brother James to sing the praises of advertising when he worked at the AAAA. In his closing address to the jury in the Gingles case, for example, O'Donnell declared that "one of the sweetest of God's creatures is this peasant girl of Ireland." He added, "I come of a sturdy race, but I learned courage from Ella Gingles." He is said to have reduced an engineer on the jury to tears, and left other jurors moist-eyed. However, the assistant state's attorney claimed cynically that much of this emotional peroration was simply taken from a speech that O'Donnell had delivered seven years earlier and that had "dealt with an experience of the attorney's father after he arrived at New Orleans as an immigrant from Ireland and awoke from the delirium of yellow fever to find a white haired slave bending over him."[5]

Nevertheless, the jury acquitted Ella Gingles, and she immediately made arrangements to return to Ireland. Her case had attracted attention across the United States, with the *New York Times,* for example, reporting that the court was jammed with woman, "several of whom obtained entrance through trickery and forgery of passes, it is said." It was noted that "among the organizations that have taken up the girl's side" were the Woman's Christian Temperance Union, the Daughters of the Confederacy, the Socialist Women of the United States, and the Irish Choral Society.[6] It is difficult to think of another cause that might have united such groups, but there was continuing public concern about the vulnerability of young immigrants such as Gingles, who herself had gone first to Montreal from Ireland before moving to Chicago. Thomas Gus O'Shaughnessy supported Charles Merriam's bid to clean up Chicago given persistent accounts of women being forced or seduced into prostitution. But some denounced Gingles as a hysteric, and it was alleged that she had faked the incident. The fact that certain organizations were so eager to take up her case has been depicted recently as an example of continuing attempts to infantilize women by denying that they might freely choose to work in the sex industry.[7]

Francis O'Shaughnessy

John's brother Francis enjoyed campus life at the University of Notre Dame and was a prominent student figure there. It was noted earlier that he worked on the staff of its *Scholastic* magazine. As soon as he had graduated in law, he and John went into practice together as O'Shaughnessy and O'Shaughnessy.

He made a point of attending thereafter every annual commencement ceremony at Notre Dame and held a number of offices in the university's alumni association, being its president in 1910 and 1911; he also became a member of the university's board of trustees.[8]

Francis kept well in with the Democratic Party machine in Illinois and represented the state's governor, Edward Dunne, on at least one official occasion, the unveiling of a statue of General James Shields, his father's late acquaintance. Both Dunne and Francis O'Shaughnessy served as presidents of the Irish Fellowship Club.

Francis O'Shaughnessy took particular pride in his work as the attorney for the commissioners of Lincoln Park, a sprawling green area of Chicago adjacent to Lake Michigan. In a report for Governor Dunne and the com-

Attorney Francis O'Shaughnessy.
From Thompson, *Knights of
Columbus in Illinois*, p. 313.

missioners of that park he wrote that he "tried at all times to treat the work connected with Lincoln Park as a matter of first importance, and gave it precedence over my private practice." There was much to be done in this connection, as the secretary to the commissioners pointed out when he wrote that "possibly more legal questions of great import have come to the attention of the Commissioners of Lincoln Park for disposition during the period 1913 to 1916 than in any similar period in the history of the Park." O'Shaughnessy's work here included a claim for damages growing out of the death of "a boy who was in the employ of the Commissioners" and a case for the condemnation of property to enlarge the municipal bathing beach at Clarendon Avenue. More striking is his reference to a suit by one "John Williams, et al.," which was then pending in the US Supreme Court and which he helped to present. Williams, notwithstanding his British-sounding name, was chief of the Pokagon Band of the Potawatomi People who had taken action against the commissioners of Lincoln Park and others: "The Indians claim title to submerged lands along the shore of Lake Michigan, and all lands which have been reclaimed from the bed of the lake." O'Shaughnessy expected Williams and the others to lose the case, which they did.[9]

President of the Irish Fellowship Club

Francis used both his professional skills and his connections to help Notre Dame from time to time. In 1923, when he was president of the Irish Fellowship Club, he arranged for Matthew Walsh, president of the university from 1922 to 1928, to talk at the annual St. Patrick's Day dinner on the subject of "Irish fellowship." The club's publicity committee requested some details of Walsh's activities as a chaplain at the front during World War I, but O'Shaughnessy was careful: "This will be used advisedly so that nothing will be said in the press that would retard your ecclesiastical ascent." At the same time O'Shaughnessy arranged that Notre Dame would display at the club three items from its prized sword collection and that these would be guarded by two young men in military uniforms. The swords had belonged to Irish-born General James Shields, General Thomas Francis Meagher, and Colonel James Mulligan.[10] Shields, as seen earlier, had been an acquaintance of the O'Shaughnessys in Missouri. Meagher (1823–1867) was a revolutionary leader in Ireland who made his way to the United States, where he studied law and worked as a journalist and lecturer before joining the US Army and leading Irish recruits on the Union side when civil war broke out. Mulligan (1829–1864) raised the Illinois "Irish Brigade" and commanded federal forces at the first Battle of Lexington in Missouri. He is famously said to have told some of his men when they tried to carry him fatally wounded from battle, "Lay me down boys, and save the flag."[11] These three occupied a special place in the pantheon of Irish-Americans in Chicago, as had been reflected in one of Finley Peter Dunne's "Mr. Dooley" columns almost thirty years earlier. During 1894 the Dooley character refers to an incident on Archer Avenue in the heart of Bridgeport on Chicago's South Side, this being a "free fight up an' down Archey road because Dan Dorgan said Shur'-dan [Sheridan] was a better gin'ral thin Thomas Francis Meagher. Thim was th' only two after Mulligan was kilt that th' Ar-rchey road cared f'r."[12]

Commencement Address

In January 1928 Francis O'Shaughnessy successfully endorsed a proposal that Edward J. Kelly (1876–1950) be awarded an honorary doctorate at Notre Dame. This was notwithstanding what appear to have been reservations on the part of the university's president, who raised "many restrictions which we have to take into account in picking a limited number of candidates for such honors" and who proposed discussing the matter over lunch rather than handling it by correspondence. Kelly, the son of a Galway father and German mother, was chief engineer of the sanitary district of Chicago and president of the South Park Commission, and would in 1929 succeed Roger Faherty as president of the Irish Fellowship Club. He was to become mayor of Chicago from 1933 to 1947, and he played a central role in the creation of an abiding Democratic Party machine in that city. Not alone did Notre Dame agree to honor Kelly, but it surprised Francis O'Shaughnessy by also offering Francis himself an honorary doctorate.[13]

As well as being offered this doctorate in 1928, Francis was paid the further compliment of being invited then, albeit at short notice and as a substitute for us Assistant Attorney General William Donovan, the opportunity to deliver the annual commencement address at the university. He accepted the invitation. "Wild Bill" Donovan, as he was known, was a former commander of the famous "Fighting 69th," the New York infantry regiment closely associated with Irish-Americans that was mentioned earlier in the context of its activities in World War I. During 1928 he invited the Irish prime minister W. T. Cosgrave to lunch during the latter's visit to Washington. Donovan later became the founding director of the us Office of Strategic Services, the forerunner of today's cia. He was to give the commencement address at Notre Dame in 1929, one year after Francis O'Shaughnessy did so.

Although he agreed to deliver the commencement address in 1928, Francis O'Shaughnessy at first demurred in respect of the award of an honorary doctorate. He wrote to Notre Dame, "I have not yet reached heights as a lawyer or a public man to merit a Doctor's Degree." He thought that the university's president, Matthew Walsh, would be criticized for choosing him out of the great body of the alumni. However, Walsh prevailed upon him to change his mind, noting that his humble refusal had been "just the kind of thing that in my personal opinion makes you deserving of recognition on the part of your Alma Mater."[14] Recording the award, *The Notre Dame Alumnus* noted his qualities as a lawyer as well the fact that he had become "eminent for his Christian manhood, his public spirit in the service of his state and city, and his service to his Alma Mater in the organization of the Notre Dame Alumni Association."[15]

O'Shaughnessy was the first Notre Dame alumnus to be invited to deliver a commencement address at the university. His words on the occasion were cautionary and conservative, no doubt reflecting the concerns of many Catholic parents of his generation and presumably indicating one of the reasons why he had been invited: "We are engulfed with corruption in politics; the home is falling under the wreckage of divorce." He urged the graduating students to walk a path of moral rectitude, and condemned divorce and birth control as twin evils to the state that should be outlawed. Described by a local newspaper as "a prominent practicing attorney of Chicago" and by the Notre Dame *Scholastic* as "a distinguished Chicago lawyer" and "a remarkable orator," Francis O'Shaughnessy identified the key to success or failure not as a college education but as common sense, energy, and the avoidance of "dissolute habits."[16] Miscamble omits his speech in a recent volume of "memorable" commencement addresses delivered at Notre Dame. However, shortly after its delivery, President Walsh informed O'Shaughnessy that the latter had understood the purpose of the occasion better than anyone who had spoken to graduates during Walsh's time at Notre Dame. Walsh added, "I would not say it aloud but I am happy at the thought that Colonel Donovan was called to Europe on his government mission."[17]

Later commencement speakers at Notre Dame have included Joe Kennedy, his son John, Ignatius Aloysius O'Shaughnessy, J. Edgar Hoover, and President Barack Obama. Minnesota-born I.A. O'Shaughnessy (1885–1973) was not merely a namesake of the O'Shaughnessys of Missouri. He was an oil millionaire whose parents came from Ireland and who are said to have settled first, as apparently did the father of Francis and his siblings, in or near Milford, Massachusetts. It is not known if the two families were distantly related. I.A. O'Shaughnessy became the largest single benefactor of US Catholic education of his day. A trustee of Notre Dame, in 1953 he and his wife, Lillian Gertrude Smith (1886–1959), funded the construction there of O'Shaughnessy Hall. This became known to students as "O'Shag." As it happened, their daughter Eileen (1913–1997) married John J. O'Shaughnessy (1912–1971), who was the son of that John who went into legal practice with Francis in Chicago.[18]

A Fine Funeral

In 1930 Francis O'Shaughnessy died in Chicago. During the funeral at Notre Dame on August 1 Charles O'Donnell, president of the university, gave a sermon. O'Donnell told the congregation, "At Notre Dame it is the rule that whenever a member of the [Holy Cross] Order dies, each priest offers the holy sacrifice of the Mass and each brother offers up the rosary, the Way of the Cross, and Holy Communion for the repose of the soul of the departed." The religious order's superiors had requested the same treatment for Francis O'Shaughnessy. O'Donnell now said, "So far as I can learn, this is the first time in the history of our community that this has ever been done. . . . Notre Dame's love for him was not less than his love for Notre Dame." His brother James subsequently made arrangements for the printing of this sermon.[19]

John and Francis were part of the fabric of the Irish-American community in Chicago. Like Gus and James they supported the Irish Fellowship Club from its foundation. As members of the Catholic middle class and as Illinois lawyers, the two achieved a social status in Chicago that their father could scarcely have imagined for any future children of his when he first came to America.

It is not known if their father ever returned to Ireland after he left it for America, but as the O'Shaughnessy children rose in the world some of them certainly sailed east to the country of their ancestors.

NINE Irish Roots

JAMES AND GUS O'SHAUGHNESSY and their siblings were the grand-children of John Shaughnessy and Ann Gallagher, who lived and died in Ireland. James Shaughnessy, who crossed first the Atlantic and then half a continent and settled in Missouri, had been born to John and Ann between 1838 and 1842.[1] His family had at some point dispensed with the Gaelic prefix "O" (meaning "of") before its name, but by the beginning of the twentieth century he and his children had restored it.

During a period of great famine in Ireland in the mid-nineteenth century, large numbers of Irish people immigrated to America, especially from the impoverished and overpopulated west of Ireland. James Shaughnessy was among them.[2] According to a brief obituary of him published in a local Missouri newspaper in 1918, his parents had died before he left Ireland.[3] If so, he was certainly not the only young Irish boy who crossed the ocean as an orphan during those terrible years.

His son James, the journalist and advertising executive, returned to the land of his ancestors at least three times, touring part of it on foot and giving advice to Irish advertising agents. Another of his sons, Thomas, copied parts of the Book of Kells when he came to Dublin.

Newhall and Kiltartan, County Galway

James Shaughnessy and his brothers, who also immigrated to the United States, named their new homestead in Missouri "Newhall," thus recalling a very small rural area (or "townland") in the Irish barony of Kiltartan, County Galway that was also known as Newhall. There had been five houses in Newhall in Ireland in 1841, with a total of twenty-five people living in them. By 1861, after years of famine, the remaining thirteen inhabitants occupied only three dwellings.[4]

This part of Galway, including Kiltartan and Coole, had long been home

Newhall, County Galway, today and the road taken by
James Shaughnessy when emigrating.

to part of the extended O'Shaughnessy clan. Family members were the he-
reditary custodians of St. Colman's girdle and crozier, which were medieval
religious relics. Thus it is probably no coincidence that James O'Shaughnessy, son of the emigrant James, christened his own son Colman. As it
happens, an elderly man named Colman Shaughnessy today lives less than
a mile from the old Shaughnessy homestead in Newhall, County Galway.
He believes that his great-great-grandfather and the father of James Shaughnessy who immigrated to Missouri "came out of the same house" and were
brothers or near cousins, although no records exist to confirm this.[5] With
or without the prefix, people in this part of Galway pronounce the name
"shock-nessy" and not "shaun-essy" as some do elsewhere.

In the course of centuries of conflict between Catholic Ireland and Protestant England, ownership of the lands of the O'Shaughnessy lordship had
been transferred to persons who were Protestant and loyal to the king in
London. Catholics who lost their lands clung to their religion. There was at
Newhall a large dry hole about fifteen meters long and eight meters wide that

became known in Gaelic as "Poll an Aifrinn" ("The Mass Hole"), a name that suggests that priests discreetly celebrated mass for local people there during the penal persecution of Catholics in Ireland.[6] Religion was very much part of one's personal identity in the area, and the three brothers from Newhall who settled in Missouri brought with them their loyalty to the Catholic Church.

By the nineteenth century many of the O'Shaughnessys or Shaughnessys of Kiltartan and elsewhere had become simply tenants of their former lands. In 1803 one Richard Staunton was landlord of Newhall. Living in a thatched house, he was in 1820 visited by members of the secret agrarian society known as "Ribbonmen" who relieved him of two long guns and a case of pistols but did not harm him. By 1826 these and other lands at Gort were owned by the Gregory family and remained in its possession into the twentieth century. The Gregorys' home was at Coole Park near Kiltartan crossroads, about three miles by road from Newhall and Ballylee.[7]

One "John Shaughnessy" is registered as living in Coole Village in the Tithe Applotment Books of 1826. A man of that name also gave information about Newhall to John O'Donovan when the latter compiled his greatly admired Ordnance Survey Name Books in the 1830s. It is not known if these references to John Shaughnessy were to one and the same person, or if either or both are to the husband of Ann Gallagher and father of that James Shaughnessy who settled in Missouri. The paucity of records for the period and the turmoil of the times make it difficult to trace reliably the ancestry of particular families. Fahy has described the impact of the Great Famine on Gort, and that impact was considerable.[8]

Thackery, Robert Gregory, and Famine

In 1842, the English novelist William Makepeace Thackery visited Ireland. Already unhappy due to personal circumstances that included a difficult relationship with his Irish mother-in-law, he was not cheered by encountering widespread evidence of starvation throughout the south and west of Ireland. As he traveled up to Gort and on by Kiltartan toward Galway City he was cast down. He wrote,

> Then we passed the plantations of Lord Gort's Castle of Loughcooter,
> and presently came to the town which bears his name, or vice versa. It is

a regularly-built little place, with a square and street: but it looked as if it wondered how the deuce it got into the midst of such a desolate country, and seemed to bore itself there considerably. It had nothing to do, and no society. . . . Between Gort and that place [Oranmore] we passed through little but the most woeful country."[9]

The local landlord Robert Gregory (1790–1847) was taking steps at Gort to alleviate the worsening effects of famine when he died, ostensibly of an illness contracted from those whom he was trying to help. His son William (1817–1892) was a member of parliament for Dublin City who opposed famine-relief measures that he thought were an unjustifiable imposition on landlords. His name is associated to this day with a particular amendment to the Poor Law Act of 1847. This "Gregory Clause" prohibited the relief from poor rates of anyone who occupied more than a quarter-acre of land and also (until 1848) of their dependents. While broadly supported in parliament and ostensibly intended to prevent the government in London placing an unreasonable and unrealistic burden on Irish landlords, the measure came to be regarded as a cruel and crude means of encouraging people to emigrate and of helping landlords who wished to take advantage of famine by clearing their congested estates. The measure's infamy was enshrined in a ballad of 1849 called "Gregory's Quarter Acre" that includes the lines,

When ruthless tyrants work so sure,
To swamp with famine breaker,
The death surge tumbles o'er the poor,
In Gregory's Quarter Acre.[10]

William Gregory had not been living at Gort, and local tenants had little reason to expect that their lot would improve under him. However, notwithstanding his posturing in parliament, he appears to have been moved by the reality of suffering that he now encountered on taking up residence in succession to his father at Gort, and he subsequently came to be regarded locally as a generous man. He would later recall the events of 1847, events that propelled so many across the Atlantic, claiming that he did all that he could to alleviate dreadful distress and sickness in the neighborhood:

I well remember poor wretches being housed up against my demesne wall in wigwams of fir branches. There was no place to which they could be removed. The workhouse infirmary and sheds were crowded. Fortunately these patients did better in the pure open air than those who were packed together within four walls. There was nothing that I ever saw so horrible as the appearance of those who were suffering from starvation. The skin seemed drawn tight like a drum to the face, which became covered with small light-colored hairs like a gooseberry. This, and their hollow voices, I can never forget, and yet they behaved with the greatest propriety. I believe a few sheep were stolen, but in my neighbourhood at least there was a total absence of crime. There seemed to be a general race to get out of the country at all hazards; farms were abandoned, even where no rent was asked, fences were broken down, houses unroofed; in short, if an army of Huns and Vandals had swept over the country they would hardly have created greater terror, desolation, and despair, and yet within two years all this gloom had passed away and Ireland seemed brighter, richer, and more hopeful than before. But the disastrous perversity of the Government in throwing the feeding of a starving population on private enterprise to be exercised for the first time to any such extent, has never been forgotten or forgiven by those who remained at home, and of those that went in those days the Times wrote: "The Irish are pouring out of Ireland with a vengeance."[11]

Thirty years after the famine, in 1880, William married Augusta Persse (1852–1932); as Lady Gregory she became a renowned folklorist and playwright and one of the founders of the Abbey Theatre, Dublin. The words that she put into the mouths of characters in her own plays were written mainly in the Kiltartan dialect of English, being that spoken by James Shaughnessy when he went to America. Augusta Gregory became a close friend and patron of the poet and playwright W. B. Yeats, who stayed with her at Kiltartan and who himself in 1917 purchased a medieval tower at Ballylee that overlooked Newhall townland and its deserted fields. Here he would write, for example, "I pace upon the battlements and stare/On the foundations of a house." From those battlements he could see where James Shaughnessy had lived. Sometime before 1918 Augusta Gregory's son Robert sketched the tower with Newhall and other townlands in the background.[12]

In her collection of local lore entitled *The Kiltartan History Book,* Lady Gregory included an account by a resident of Kiltartan who remembered the terrible poverty that James Shaughnessy and his brothers had fled. Gregory is known to have visited homes in Newhall, and at least one woman living there when she was collecting stories between 1898 and 1900 was old enough to have had vivid memories of the 1840s:

> The Famine; there's a long telling in that, it is a thing will be remembered always. That little graveyard above, at that time it was filled full up of bodies; the [Poor Law] Union had no way to buy coffins for them. There would be a bag made, and the body put into it, that was all; and the people dying without priest, or bishop, or anything at all. But over in Connemara it was the dogs brought the bodies out of the houses, and asked no leave.[13]

The Gregory family was active in supporting the workhouse at Gort. Opened in 1841, it was the first institution of its kind in County Galway and was intended to be a last refuge for the poorest of the poor. People greatly feared ending up in a workhouse, and the establishments were unpopular. That at Gort was built to hold a maximum of 500 residents but, during the famine, came to house 3,643 in the main building and ancillary premises. Lady Gregory was a patron of the institution. One of the repercussions of the controversy surrounding the 1911 production of Synge's *Playboy of the Western World* by Gregory's Abbey Theatre in Dublin, this being the play that James O'Shaughnessy subsequently reviewed for the *Chicago Tribune,* was that some nationalists in County Galway (encouraged by a local priest) stopped children from Gort making customary visits to Gregory's Coole Park estate.[14]

Fiddler Raftery and Mary Hynes

The grandfather of James and Gus O'Shaughnessy and their siblings in Chicago may once have danced to the fiddle of the famous Raftery (Antaine Raiftearaí, 1799–1835). At the close of the nineteenth century, Lady Gregory wrote,

Yeats' tower at Kiltartan, looking across a partly flooded Newhall townland, sketched
by Lady Gregory's son Robert before 1918. Photograph courtesy Colin Smythe.

Raftery died over sixty years ago; but there are many old people still living
. . . who have seen him, and who keep his songs in their memory. What
they tell of him shows how closely he was in the old tradition of the bards,
the wandering poets of two thousand years or more. . . . Raftery's little
fiddle helped to make him welcome in the Ireland which was, in spite
of many sorrows, as merry and light-hearted up to the time of the great
famine as England had been up to the time of the Puritans. "He had no
place of his own," I am told, "but to be walking the country. He did well
to die before the bad years came. He used to play at Kiltartan cross for
the dancing of a Sunday evening. And when he'd come to any place, the
people would gather and he'd give them a dance; for there was three times
as many people in the world then as what there is now."[15]

One of Raftery's best known poems celebrates a young woman called
Mary Hynes (Máire Ní Eidhin), "the shining flower of Ballylee" ("an pó-
sae gléigeal 'tá i mBaile Uí Laí"), who died young. When Lady Gregory

established a branch of the Gaelic League at Gort in 1899, the president of the league and a future president of independent Ireland, Douglas Hyde (1860–1949), attended the event. Hyde wrote down a Gaelic version of the poem from Tommy Hynes of Kiltartan whom he met and who was related to the girl.[16] It is not known if Mary Hynes, whose father came from County Galway and who married James O'Shaughnessy in Chicago in 1907, was also related to "the shining flower of Ballylee" celebrated by Raftery. Mary Hynes of Ballylee interested W. B. Yeats, who refers to her directly or indirectly in a number of his own poems and whose revised edition of *The Celtic Twilight* published in 1902 contains a lengthy discussion of both her and Raftery, including passages about Kiltartan and the death of Hynes there. An old man brought Yeats a little way from the mill and the castle at Ballylee and showed him the old foundation of the Hynes house, "but the most of it is taken for building walls."[17]

In an incidental reference to local superstitious beliefs, Yeats adds that an old weaver, whose son was "supposed to go away among the Sidhe (the faeries [spirits]) at night" said that "Mary Hynes was the most beautiful thing ever made" and was much sought-after to be a bride: "My mother used to tell me about her, for she'd be at every hurling [a sport played by men], and wherever she was she was dressed in white." People thought her too beautiful for her own good, as Yeats explained in that same account:

> Those who are much admired are, it is held, taken by the Sidhe, who can use ungoverned feeling for their own ends, so that a father, as an old herb doctor told me once, may give his child into their hands, or a husband his wife. The admired and desired are only safe if one says "God bless them" when one's eyes are upon them. The old woman that sang the song thinks, too, that Mary Hynes was "taken," as the phrase is, "for they have taken many that are not handsome, and why would they not take her?"

Folklore in County Galway

The countryside from which members of the Shaughnessys departed for America was, like much of rural Ireland, steeped in such ancient folklore. This was one of the springs of inspiration for the great national intellectual movement of which the Celtic Revival and the Anglo-Irish Literary Revival were aspects. Lady Wilde, Lady Gregory, W. B. Yeats, and Douglas Hyde were foremost among those who were interested in Irish folklore. The latter three not only knew the Kiltartan area but also engaged with its inhabitants in discussions about traditions and beliefs. Yeats later recalled spending time at Coole Park about 1897, being brought by Lady Gregory from cottage to cottage. Every night she wrote out what she had heard, in the process "discovering that vivid English she was the first to use upon the stage." Yeats said that "when we passed the door of some peasant's cottage, we passed out of Europe as that word is understood."[18] Had James O'Shaughnessy's father stayed at home in County Galway and not himself passed out of Europe then it is quite possible that, had he survived the Great Famine, he would have been one of those local peasants who shared their folklore with Yeats and Lady Gregory. For her *Kiltartan Poetry Book*, Gregory translated Raftery's praise of Mary Hynes, and some of those verses might have come from the mouth of a Shaughnessy before the famine when gazing across Newhall to its neighboring townland where she lived: "There is sweet air on the side of the hill, when you are looking down upon Ballylee; when you are walking in the valley picking nuts and blackberries, there is music of the birds in it and music of the Sidhe."

Yeats regarded folklore variously as a source of artistic inspiration, an aspect of the broader world of the occult in which he was interested, and a therapeutic refuge from the misery of life for peasants. He was a student of "fairy" lore, "preferring to spell it 'faery,' which suggested occultism rather than archness" says a biographer.[19] "Fairy" is a somewhat misleading word into which to translate the old Gaelic term "Sidhe." The English word may connote charming Victorian tales for children, whereas the spirits to which Irish folktales refer had a strong psychological reality and a cultural complexity that made them part of the daily life of many people in the era before electric light. Yeats knew of a number of people around Gort and Kiltartan who believed in such spirits, although he admits that a local doctor thought that a man who was said to "go out riding among them at night" was simply "mad."[20]

Yeats was conscious of the sensitivities of those to whom folklore seemed sacred, and he observed that such people did not readily share stories. "You must go adroitly to work," he advised anyone who wished to hear them relate their tales. He adopted a Socratic attitude of intellectual curiosity in respect to the "truth" of folklore and scoffed at skeptics who dismissed it all as simple nonsense: "even a newspaper man, if you entice him into a cemetery at midnight, will believe in phantoms, for everyone is a visionary, if you scratch him deep enough. But the Celt is a visionary without scratching." In 1888 he distanced himself from those whom he thought had misused ordinary people for literary purposes, including in this category Samuel Lover and Thomas Crofton Croker:

> Croker and Lover, full of the ideas of harum-scarum Irish gentility, saw everything humorised. The impulse of the Irish literature of their time came from a class that did not — mainly for political reasons — take the populace seriously, and imagined the country as a humorist's Arcadia; its passion, its gloom, its tragedy, they knew nothing of. What they did was wholly false; they merely magnified an irresponsible type, found oftenest among boatmen, carmen, and gentlemen's servants, into the type of a whole nation, and created the stage Irishman. The writers of Forty-eight [1848], and the famine combined, burst their bubble.[21]

The Haunting in Missouri

When James Shaughnessy and other immigrant members of his family fled harsh famine in Ireland and bought land in northern Missouri, they became part of a small and broadly dispersed Catholic community there. Many such immigrants brought with them from rural Ireland a perspective rooted in an ancient world of spirits and magical powers predating the arrival of Christianity in Ireland. Finding themselves living in America, especially in isolated homesteads scattered among hills or across prairies, they were unlikely to abandon immediately their folklore, or the idea that ghosts and other supernatural forces might haunt them. When civil war erupted in the United States, its physical disturbances created conditions in which any fears and uncertainties multiplied. In 1864 John Shaughnessy, an uncle of the future adman, and his wife, Hannah, who was also an Irish emigrant, had a particularly severe upset in Missouri. The story of that upset is a remarkable one and is worth telling, not least because it was recorded with such conviction by John Hogan. As bishop of St. Joseph, Missouri, Hogan attended the first Vatican Council in Rome and was not inclined to be fanciful. His account of the haunting of the O'Shaughnessys is reproduced in full in appendix 2. It records how, in temporary accommodations during the Civil War, the family was "subjected to terrors of an extraordinary kind." These included loud knocking noises that were so strange and unusual that they caused dogs to howl and fowls to fly off their roost. The house itself seemed to sway at night. Sometimes a man, "strange and unknown to them," would appear and disappear.

With tales such as this in his own family it is not surprising that at least one of the younger generation of the O'Shaughnessys was to be drawn into journalism. Hogan wrote,

> The strange visitor that was so often seen around the premises, was noticed by persons outside the house, to pass directly from the door; and yet, upon inquiry, the inmates had no knowledge of the presence of such a person amongst them. These facts were testified to before me, by persons living in the house, and by outsiders — Catholic and non-Catholics — who had gone to the house through curiosity, or to find out the imposition, if such had been practised there. Several testified, these were chiefly men, that when they heard the noises, and the hammering on the floor under their feet, where there was neither space nor cellar that they hastened out of the house, and could not be induced to return there. Those that I examined were persons above suspicion of collusion or deceit; and I found that were I were to continue the examination, as many as forty could be produced, witnesses of these facts, and present when they had occurred.

Hogan was subsequently summoned to attend an old man who was dying and who lived in a little house adjoining the haunted premises occupied by John Shaughnessy and his family, and who had been resident there when Shaughnessy took possession of the place. When the old man died, wrote Hogan, "It was whispered among the mourners that he who was that day laid to rest had been once a noted magician in Chariton County; and that the extraordinary occurrences . . . of late, must have resulted from his presence as a dweller there." Hogan was so astonished by the whole affair that when he wrote about it in 1892 he sent his account before publication to John Shaughnessy's brother James for formal verification. The latter, whom

Hogan describes as "a surviving witness, most intimately connected with these events" confirmed the account and added that, "The old man who used to set charms was named David Condon. . . . The ghost story is true as you related it."[22]

What is not clear from Hogan's account but is evident from the census is that the family name of John Shaughnessy's wife, Johannah, was also Condon. The likelihood that she was related to this "old man" David seems high.[23]

One wonders if this "old man who used to set charms" was the same "old man" whom the Mulhollands were tempted to summon when their daughter Catherine was very ill, but whom Fr. Hogan then vigorously resisted. A reader may have surmised, until this reference to Condon occurs, that "the old man" mentioned in the context of Catherine's illness was perhaps a Native American. However, the name "David Condon" suggests that "the old man" was in fact Irish and perhaps some kind of "faith-healer," of whom there are still quite a few in Ireland even today. W. B. Yeats referred to such a person in County Clare in Ireland at the end of the nineteenth century as "an old witch-doctor."[24] While some people attribute the ostensible powers of faith-healers to natural gifts, persistent respect for them may also be regarded as a superstitious remnant of ancient Irish beliefs. Hogan's disapproval echoed that of St. Patrick and early Christian missionaries in Ireland when they contended with pagan practices and views of the world.

The Book of Kells

As their fortunes in America improved, not least due to the educational efforts of religious orders on the prairies, Irish families did not abandon quickly the culture of their homeland. Both James the journalist and Thomas Gus O'Shaughnessy the artist, in particular, became interested in the Celtic Revival, that movement on both sides of the Atlantic that took various forms but that generally encouraged artistic initiatives and the study of old manuscripts. The movement underpinned political demands by the Irish for independence from Britain.

American interest in old Irish arts and crafts was stimulated by the erection of not one but two "Irish villages" on the mile-long midway at the great world exposition in Chicago in 1893. As mentioned earlier, members of the

O'Shaughnessy family were among the many millions who visited that vast fair. Thomas was especially inspired by Irish motifs and later came to be regarded as the foremost exponent of the Celtic or Gaelic Revival style of design in the United States. Sometime around the turn of the century he traveled to Ireland and studied art in the old country. He spent hours at Trinity College Dublin sketching pages of the most renowned Irish illuminated manuscript, the Book of Kells.[25] The development of arts and crafts was at the time gathering pace in Ireland, not least as a result of efforts to persuade the Catholic Church to employ Irish artists. The stained glass creations of Harry Clarke, as well as the cooperative glass and mosaic works of An Túr Gloine (The Glass Tower) came to be highly regarded.[26] Harris notes, "The linkage of craft revival with national or ethnic identity was not unique to Ireland at the turn of the century. In Finland, in Hungary, in Bohemia, Palestine, Catalonia and elsewhere, hand production of jewelry, ceramins, furniture, rugs and textiles, was linked both to economic self-sufficiency and collective self-consciousness."[27]

Eugene O'Growney and Maynooth

James O'Shaughnessy also visited Ireland, and more than once. During his visit to Europe in 1894 he "came to Ireland to see one of the greatest men of his time, and that was the late Fr. Eugene O'Growney," — as he would proudly tell us and Irish advertising agents thirty years later in Dublin.[28] O'Growney (known in Irish as Eoghan Ó Gramhnaigh) was professor of Irish language, literature, and antiquities at the Catholic college of Maynooth, County Kildare, not far from Dublin and the principal place where Irish priests were trained. He was also one of the founding members of the Gaelic League, editor of the *Gaelic Journal* and a prolific correspondent and writer until his untimely death in California, to which he had traveled for medical treatment.[29]

Irish-Americans, including representatives of the Gaelic Societies, warmly welcomed O'Growney when he landed at New York in November 1894. Although ill in the United States, he offered Chicago's *New World* (which, "having an immense circulation, is about to start a Gaelic column"), his services to conduct for some months its planned Gaelic column which would be based on a revision of his best-selling book of instruction in the Irish language,

Fr. Eugene O'Growney, before 1894. From O'Farrelly (ed.), *Leabhar an Athar Eoghan*, p. 7.

Simple Lessons.[30] After he died in Los Angeles in 1899, Irish-Americans in Chicago received his remains with great ceremony as they were being returned to Ireland for burial. The Irish-born priest Andrew Morrissey, president of the University of Notre Dame and an acquaintance of the O'Shaughnessys, celebrated a special mass in Chicago in O'Growney's honor.[31]

Stones of Gort

It is not known if James O'Shaughnessy traveled to Gort when he visited Ireland between 1894 and 1901, although it seems likely that he would have done so. He wrote in 1912 that he had earlier "foot toured" Ireland. Gus almost certainly went there. A sketch by him at that time appears to feature the medieval St. Flannan's Oratory in Killaloe, County Clare, which is twenty-four miles from Gort.[32]

Early in 1912, when she was in the United States with her Abbey Theatre players, Lady Gregory told a story that raises the intriguing possibility that the "well-to-do man" from America who is mentioned in it was in fact one of the O'Shaughnessys:

I was passing not long ago by a roofless, long-deserted cottage near Kiltartan and a neighbouring woman told me that a few years ago a well-to-do man had come from America, son or grandson of the last who lived there and had taken two stones from the wall, taken them back to America. It has always been so. That little Ireland has held the hearts of men through the ages.[33]

Shortly after telling this story, Lady Gregory attended the same Chicago performance of *The Playboy of the Western World* for which James O'Shaughnessy was in the audience, as noted earlier when considering his unenthusiastic review of it for the *Chicago Tribune*. There is no reason to believe that they met and discussed Newhall or his family's origins in County Galway. However, O'Shaughnessy's disdain for her company's play may have had some very personal roots in the relationship between supplanting Anglo-Irish landlords and their dispossessed old Gaelic tenants.

To some of those who lived beyond the gates of big houses such as Lady Gregory's Coole Park, and to the descendants of others who had fled Kiltartan during famine, it may have seemed that Gregory and Yeats, despite their good intentions, toyed with traditions for their own occult, romantic, or political purposes. As Ireland modernized and as the Catholic Church made a determined effort to have its members shrug off ancient superstitions that had long heavily influenced many of them, emergent Irish and Irish-American Catholic middle classes that had been educated in new schools were eager to put folktales and a rough, rural way of life behind them. When writers displayed peasant life on the stage and not mere folklore in books they touched a raw nerve, and reactions could be heated. Many Irish who had risen from poverty preferred to celebrate Ireland's more distant medieval past, recalling it as "the land of saints and scholars."

Illinois Foundation for Gaelic Studies

We have seen that the O'Shaughnessy brothers were closely involved in both setting up and helping to run the Irish Fellowship Club in Chicago. In addition to occasionally transporting soil and shamrock from Ireland, the club supported a more serious cultural initiative. During the fateful year of 1916, as war took its toll across Europe and as rebellion erupted in

Ireland, American newspapers reported the establishment at the University of Illinois of an Irish Fellowship Foundation for the promotion of Gaelic studies: "This foundation is the immediate result of a presentation of the cause of Irish history and literature by President E. J. James and Dr Gertrude Schoepperle at a recent meeting of the Irish Fellowship Club in Chicago." James O'Shaughnessy was then the club's corresponding secretary. It was expected that Joseph Lloyd, the former co-treasurer of the Gaelic League in Dublin who in 1915 had lost his job as editor when the league decided to discontinue publishing books, would be appointed for the first year of the foundation. However, the job actually went to the Rev. Andrew O'Kelleher of the University of Liverpool. Lloyd never recovered from the decline in his fortunes.[34]

Terence MacSwiney, Hunger Striker

Members of the O'Shaughnessy family were politically active on behalf of the Democratic Party, as noted earlier, but Thomas also made a statement about Irish politics. He did so in a striking way, through his art, by dedicating a window at Old St. Pat's Church in Chicago to Terence MacSwiney (1879–1920). MacSwiney had been elected lord mayor of Cork City in Ireland but was arrested by British forces for participating in the struggle for Irish independence and died while on a protesting hunger strike in an English jail on October 25, 1920. Less than one month later it was reported from Chicago that the "'spontaneous memorial' to Lord Mayor MacSwiney of Cork, who died after a long hunger strike, from the Irish people of Chicago is in place. It is almost ready for solemn dedication next Wednesday at high noon. It is a massive window in St. Patrick's Roman Catholic church, Adams and Desplaines streets."[35] Containing fifty panels and reportedly weighing almost two tons, it was said to embody the only examples in the United States of certain fine ceramic and mosaic arts. Maume writes that MacSwiney "thought religious and political idealism inseparable."[36] So a church window was an apt tribute to him. Noting that Thomas Gus O'Shaughnessy was the artist, the *Chicago Tribune* disclosed that he had met MacSwiney, perhaps during the former's visit to Ireland at the turn of the century when MacSwiney cofounded the Celtic Literary Society. In any event, it was said of Gus, "He knew the late lord mayor of Cork when a young man." O'Shaughnessy donated three and a half months of his labor to making the window. The *Tribune* reported, "The window is unique in that it is a memorial begun before the death of the man it honors. The commission was given Mr. O'Shaughnessy by the Rev. William J. McNamee, pastor of the church [and his late wife's uncle], three days after the lord mayor was imprisoned and began his hunger strike."[37] A guide, apparently written by O'Shaughnessy himself, states, "The story built into the window is a brief synopsis of the story of Ireland, from the glorious, happy past to the tragic, glorious present. . . . To represent the holiness of Liberty, this panel is rendered in the colors of the Irish Republic. The green, white and orange of the Republic are complemented by the deep blue, crimson and purple of ancient Ireland." Because of events in Ireland, where a war of independence was in progress, political sentiments were running high among Irish Americans at the time. While most of the window is taken up with Irish religious figures and imagery,

> [i]n the center panel at the base of [the] window is shown the soul of Terence MacSwiney being borne to Heaven. Beneath him the palms of martyrdom; on either side the fires of trials and persecution. Above him the Cross of St. Bride [Brigid], which typifies the ideal of the Irish people, in their devotion to law, order and chivalry.
>
> To the extreme right and left at base of window are shown the chaos brought upon the world by England's wars of conquest.
>
> The cause which Ireland has served, for which Terence MacSwiney has died, is embodied in the window in the inscription, "For the Glory of God, for the Love of Mankind."[38]

Irish-American Admen in Ireland

In July 1924, James O'Shaughnessy went to London for the major international advertising convention then scheduled. He also took the opportunity to visit again both his father's homeland and Antwerp in Belgium, where he had spent time as a young man. In a special press release that recognized his importance to their sector of the economy, the Associated Advertising Clubs of the World announced his visit to England and spoke in glowing terms of his contribution to US advertising. It remarked, incidentally, "Mr

Thomas O'Shaughnessy's window at Old St. Pat's
Church, Chicago, depicting Irish patriot Terence
MacSwiney being borne to heaven by angels, 1920.

O'Shaughnessy is bringing quite a party with him to London, which in-cludes the charming Mrs. O'Shaughnessy, formerly Miss Mary Hynes of Missouri, Miss Mary, his daughter, a high school miss, and Miss Aimee Hynes, a niece, also from Missouri."[39]

The international advertising convention was held in conjunction with the British Empire Exhibition at Wembley, London, and ran July 13–17, 1924. Various trips were organized for the week following the convention, mostly within Britain but also one each to Northern Ireland, the Irish Free State, and the French battlefields of World War I. The leaders of the visit to the Irish Free State were Homer J. Buckley, Bernard J. Mullaney, and James O'Shaughnessy. Each of these was associated with the Irish Fellowship Club in Chicago.

In 1909, when he was employed as secretary to Mayor Fred Busse of the Republican Party, Mullaney had shared a platform with Francis O'Shaugh-nessy as one of the club's St. Patrick's Day speakers. Mullaney, formerly a political reporter on various Chicago newspapers, spoke then on "The Irishmen's mission in America." That same year he declined, for family reasons, the mayor's offer to appoint him chief of police, but he did become the city's commissioner for public works. In April 1915 both Mullaney and James O'Shaughnessy, along with John Hopkins and 37 other residents of the state of Illinois, were constituted as the Illinois Chapter of the American Irish Historical Society.[40] During World War I, Mullaney was "borrowed" by Samuel Insull, energy entrepreneur and chairman of the State Council of Defense of Illinois, to establish a news and editorial service through which, "by mixing patriotic appeals with political and economic pressure, he [Mullaney] enlisted Illinois editors as active propagandists, dissemina-tors of information of Illinois' part in the war, and publicists for the State Council of Defense." Insull had responded enthusiastically to the initia-tives of George Creel's Committee on Public Information.[41] Mullaney, a brilliant publicist and former newspaperman, became after 1919 the vice president for public and industrial relations at the Peoples Gas Light and Coke Company of Chicago.[42] Bradley adds, "Mullaney was at the center of a 25-million-piece literature blitz by the gas and electric utility industries in the 1920s to gain public goodwill and achieve favorable state regula-tion instead of municipalization." He describes him as a "public-relations ace."[43]

For his part, Homer J. Buckley had been secretary of the Irish Fellowship Club in 1907, when O'Shaughnessy was its president. By 1911 he and O'Shaughnessy were directors of the Chicago Association of Advertisers, and the work of both men is honored today by their inclusion in the Advertising Hall of Fame of the American Advertising Federation. Buckley was often introduced in the United States as "the Father of Direct Mail" and was even said to have coined the term *direct mail. His Science of Marketing by Mail* was published during the year in which he visited Ireland.[44] One wit observed that the energetic Buckley "belongs to and organised more advertising clubs than Heinz has pickles." It was not long before members of the public noticed that direct selling was a mixed blessing and some humorous verses in 1923 referred to Buckley in this context:

> Oh, here is the man who invented
> The one-cented drive and two-cented,
> And clutters the mails
> With bushels and bales,
> Till the mailmen are Buckley-demented.[45]

Meeting President Cosgrave

A delegate in London later wrote warmly about the pleasures of a trip that he made to Scotland after the conference, adding, "The other excursions were on a similar scale of unstinted hospitality, and those who went to Ireland were the most exposed of all to the dangers of too-generous hosts." He claimed that a London paper had reported that an American delegate of well-known "prohibition" or anti-alcohol views had accepted an invitation to the Belfast tour, but canceled it when he found that one of the features was a visit to a famous distillery: "He then booked for the Dublin trip, and when he got to Dublin he was straightaway escorted through the largest brewery in the world [Guinness]. He acquiesced, saying that his principles wouldn't hold out any longer."[46] While this makes a good story, it may not be true. For, far from being whisked straight to a brewery, 150 delegates who journeyed on from the London convention to the newly independent Irish state were met at Dun Laoghaire port, near Dublin, by members of the Publicity Club of Ireland. These had secured for their visitors exemption from a search of their luggage by customs officials, and they used their own cars to ferry their guests to various hotels.

That evening the guests enjoyed musical entertainment at a banquet in the Metropole Hotel on Dublin's main thoroughfare, O'Connell Street. They were officially received there by William T. Cosgrave, the prime minister (known then as "president") of the Irish Free State, who also presided at the banquet. This level of official repect for the visitors, mainly Americans, was on a par with that afforded them in England where the UK prime minister and the Prince of Wales had addressed delegates.

Ireland was recovering from a war of independence, and from a bitter civil war in 1922 and 1923 that followed the division of the island into two political units, one becoming the Irish Free State and the other remaining part of the United Kingdom. With reports of recent atrocities in the papers, Cosgrave was eager to reassure foreigners that Ireland was stable, observing that "many descendants of exiles who left this country in sad and troublous times had come back to see what was happening here, to refute the slanders and allegations made against Ireland. . . . He hoped that the visitors would bring back with them a message that this country is a safe country for tourists, and that it is a safe country for business."[47]

Homer J. Buckley was the first to respond to Cosgrave. He was soon followed by James O'Shaughnessy, who recalled that "his father left this country in dark days." Purporting to be impressed by what he had already seen in Ireland, on this his second visit, he praised local advertising agents and promised them, "All the secrets they had in New York were at their disposal. No man could fix confines to advertising or its expression and there was a great future before them." He was later to arrange to make himself available not just to Irish advertising agents but to Cosgrave himself.

On the following morning the delegates traveled by train to the scenic tourist destination of Killarney in County Kerry, where "a good deal of the afternoon was spent in boating on the lakes."[48] Thus, it was only on their third day in Ireland that they visited a brewery, and that was just one of a number of stops on a tour of Dublin that also included Jacob's, a biscuit (cookie) factory, and the offices of a leading daily newspaper, the *Irish Independent*. Guinness hosted a lunch for them. Afterward, they visited the police headquarters, where they were greeted by the minister for justice, Kevin O'Higgins. Three years later, O'Higgins would be assassinated by civil war enemies who had never forgiven him for his role in that conflict.

In the afternoon, Governor-General Tim Healy received the delegates in "unpropitious" weather at a garden party at his official residence in the Phoenix Park. The "Lady Correspondent" of the *Irish Independent* expressed her disappointment that "none of the women who have made good in the great world of advertising, several of them Irish-American, had come to Ireland" from London. There were said to have been more than two hundred such women at the convention. James O'Shaughnessy spoke to her about the AAAA and told her that "the manager of his big advertising establishment is a woman, who has power at engaging and dismissing the men on the staff." The unnamed "Lady Correspondent" reported in turn that O'Shaughnessy was accompanied to the garden party by his wife, "smartly dressed in blue and grey, and his daughter and [also his] niece Ms Hynes."[49]

Among those who had met the delegation at Dun Laoghaire and who also attended the garden party was Kevin J. Kenny, my grandfather and the founder of what came to be regarded as Ireland's first full-service advertising agency. Also a founder of the Publicity Club of Ireland, he would soon go on with others to establish an Irish equivalent of the AAAA. Among others who attended Tim Healy's garden party was W. B. Yeats, the poet and now senator in the new state. It is tempting to imagine Yeats and O'Shaughnessy in conversation about Kiltartan, where the adman's father had lived as a child and where the poet and his family had acquired the medieval Ballylee tower. "My country is Kiltartan Cross, my countrymen Kiltartan's poor," Yeats wrote in a poem to commemorate the death of Lady Augusta Gregory's son Robert in World War I, this Robert being a son and grandson of the very Gregorys who had been landlords of James O'Shaughnessy's father and grandfather. Where Lady Gregory and Yeats had turned the Hiberno-English dialect or language of Kiltartan into poetry, James turned that same linguistic inheritance into journalism and advertising copy. Theirs was a romantic if benign vision of Ireland viewed from the big houses of the Anglo-Irish ascendancy. His was a more practical and bourgeois view of the world as seen from the perspective of an Irish-American family that had struggled to survive its history and to rise in society. If Yeats regarded advertising as part of a "filthy modern tide," that in his poem "The Statues" he depicted as threatening to wreck the ship of ancient Irish values,

O'Shaughnessy regarded it generally as a useful force for economic growth and development.

That evening most of the US visitors left for Britain, but James O'Shaughnessy was not among them.[50] He traveled to County Galway to visit his ancestral home. Tom Grehan later said that O'Shaughnessy "gave two whole days to Gort."[51] Grehan, himself also from County Galway, was the most progressive advertising manager of any Irish newspaper in the early twentieth century and had attended the London convention.[52]

Rotary Club, Dublin

O'Shaughnessy addressed the Dublin Rotary Club on July 28. This had been the first Rotary Club chapter ever to meet outside the United States. Three days later the Publicity Club met to hear him:

> Mr. "Jim" O'Shaughnessy of New York, one of the leaders of the recent delegation to Dublin of American Advertising Men, and regarded in the States as "The prince of advertising men" gives a talk today to the Publicity Club of Ireland, at Clery's Restaurant. . . . And a very large attendance is expected. Mr. O'Shaughnessy is an interesting and witty speaker, and his address is being looked forward to.[53]

O'Shaughnessy told the Publicity Club that he would like to see advertising grow in Ireland. He declared that advertising in America had come to be a national service, not simply because of the skill of the advertising agency, nor due to the vastness of their markets, nor to the media, but to "a happy fusion of the interests of all." He thought that Ireland had a circulation for her markets proportionately equal to America's and that there was no city of its size that had come under his notice that was better equipped for productive circulation than Dublin: "The circulation of the daily newspapers and periodicals was a big factor in the promotion of advertising, and in a national advertising service that helped to create new wants and so to advance civilisation." He said that the advertiser knew that in buying space he was investing in something that would generously repay his outlay.[54]

To any of his Dublin listeners who had read reports of his speech in Boston in 1919, his optimism about the potential of a local market may have sounded somewhat familiar. In Dublin he also reverted to that rhapsodic or almost mystical tone that he had struck when speaking to the American farming press:

> It was not fully or generally understood that the advertiser wanted to serve his fellows in a wider and fuller degree. He was the kindliest man they knew. He wanted to be of still greater service to his fellow-workers, and to get a big reward out of the better opinion of the larger number of his fellow-men. It was not for cash alone that the big advertiser worked.
>
> Civilisation was based upon the number of people's wants. Advertising created more wants in the minds of the people, and the more they wanted the higher they were climbing. Thus, the growth of advertising meant the happy development of civilisation.

While we might now be tempted to regard the 1920s as a more innocent era than that in which we live today, undoubtedly even then some of his Dublin listeners thought James O'Shaughnessy was overstating both the philanthropic nature of his business and its benign effects on culture. It is not known if he kissed the Blarney Stone on one of his visits to Ireland.

James Wept

At the end of O'Shaughnessy's speech, Tom Grehan on behalf of the Publicity Club presented him with a Claddagh gold ring. Claddagh, then still a small fishing village in Galway, has given its name to a form of ring that is regarded as a token of affection. It consists of two hands clutching a single heart under a crown. Grehan later recalled, "The effect of this was remarkable. He simply broke down and wept. When he pulled himself together he just said one thing which I shall never forget. 'Gentlemen,' said he, 'I want to tell you that not all of the money I have ever possessed could buy me anything I would value as highly as that ring.'"[55]

From Ireland the O'Shaughnessys traveled on to mainland Europe and later sailed home from Cherbourg on board the *George Washington*. Before leaving Ireland, O'Shaughnessy, Buckley, and Mullaney, as the committee heading the visiting delegation in Dublin, signed a letter to the Publicity Club of Ireland expressing their gratitude and pointing out that most of the delegates had been in the country for the first time and that "the impressions that they have received of Ireland cannot be measured in a cash value of dollars and cents, but will come back to the Publicity Club and all Ireland in hundreds of ways that comprise prestige, good-will and mutual understanding."[56]

Three years later, Buckley and O'Shaughnessy were prevailed upon to send congratulations to Galway on the reestablishment of its port and the commencement of a steamship service there. O'Shaughnessy considered "Galway . . . the front door of Europe."[57] Two months later he showed great foresight when he wrote to Tom Grehan, the Galwayman and advertising manager of the *Irish Independent,*

> The next big job for Galway is to make an air port. Galway could be the popular eastern terminus of transatlantic air travel. All they would need to do would be to make a landing field, with the usual equipment to take care of 'planes when they land. Galway could make a tremendous hit if they would advertise quickly in this country that they had or were immediately building an air port for receiving and caring for aeroplanes arriving there from the U.S.A., and also facilities for the next flight on their way.[58]

Galway did not act quickly enough on O'Shaughnessy's advice. When an international airport was later opened west of the River Shannon it was in the neighboring county of Clare, and for decades this was at least as successful as he had foreseen such an airport might be.

First Patron of the Irish Association of Advertising Agencies

In August 1929, within months of his becoming business manager of *Liberty,* O'Shaughnessy found himself again in Europe, this time among about 2,000 US delegates at the International Advertising Convention (Welt-Reklame Kongress) in Berlin. He was the general chairman of the transportation committee for the event.[59] When the Berlin convention ended, he and his wife, two daughters, and some of the other delegates traveled to Dublin.

The *Irish Independent* reported that twenty members of a famous advertising organization in Philadelphia known as the "Poor Richard Club"

O'Connell Street, Dublin, May 1928. Courtesy National Library of Ireland.

were also in town as was a party of twelve "Publicity Women," mostly from Providence, Rhode Island, and nearly all of Irish descent. The paper noted that the latter were to be guests at a lunch organized by the Publicity Club of Ireland that was expected to include among its other guests "Mr. James O'Shaughnessy, one of the foremost advertising experts in America."[60]

O'Shaughnessy was also guest of honor at a special luncheon organized for him by the new Irish Association of Advertising Agencies, on Thursday September 5, 1929. The association's chairman W. E. O'Keeffe explained that they greatly appreciated O'Shaughnessy's visit, "which proved beyond doubt his continued interest in the welfare of Ireland in connection with advertising." O'Shaughnessy, "in the course of a highly interesting address," foresaw a great future for Ireland under self-government: "He stressed, however, the necessity for hard work in order to achieve success." Did he mean to suggest by this that Irish people then were too inclined to take it easy? He said that five years after his last visit, he was more convinced than ever that "every Irishman had a wonderful chance to make good in his own country — if he could only work hard enough." He also traced the history of American advertising and expressed his opinion that "Co-operation is absolutely essential in all business today, and I hope Irish advertising men will stick together and do their utmost to uplift their profession to its proper place in the world of industry and commerce."[61]

The meeting ended with the Irish Association of Advertising Agencies electing O'Shaughnessy as its first patron. It was a signal honor for the son of an impoverished emigrant.[62]

On the day after this luncheon in his honor, James O'Shaughnessy sailed from Cobh for New York, once more on board "the famous United States floating palace, the *George Washington*."[63]

TEN An Irish Leader in America

Having met the Irish prime minister in Dublin in 1924, James O'Shaughnessy hoped to be of some service to W. T. Cosgrave when he visited the US in 1928. No doubt it pleased O'Shaughnessy that the Chicago club of which he had been a prime mover was instrumental in securing the first visit to America by a leader of the Irish Free State. Yet Cosgrave was to find himself perhaps too closely associated with some of Chicago's controversial citizens.

Cosgrave, whose title "president of the executive council" was then the Irish equivalent of "prime minister of the cabinet," received a remarkably enthusiastic welcome from Irish-Americans. Very large crowds turned out to greet him in New York and Chicago. For many Irish emigrants and their descendants the creation of an independent state in Ireland, even if it did not include the territory of the entire island, represented at least the partial fulfilment of long-cherished aspirations for their country of origin. Cosgrave's visit provided an opportunity to celebrate that achievement.

The civil war that followed the partitioning of Ireland and the birth of the Irish Free State in 1921 had been brief but bitter. Éamon de Valera and others rejected the treaty with London, but most nationalists supported it as a practical measure of progress toward better political arrangements. Once the civil war ended in defeat for de Valera, Cosgrave's government had its hands full repairing infrastructure, building up new institutions of state, and avoiding further violence. Until the general election of June 1927 de Valera and his allies boycotted the Oireachtas (parliament) in Dublin. On July 10, 1927, Minister for Justice Kevin O'Higgins, a member of Cosgrave's cabinet, was assassinated by some of his old civil war enemies. In August 1927 Cosgrave's government barely survived a vote of confidence.

While Cosgrave was busy in Ireland coping with political and paramilitary challenges, Ireland's envoy in Washington was aware that the new state needed to cultivate good relationships with Irish-Americans for both economic and political reasons. Timothy Smiddy (1875–1962) now urged Dublin to consider sending a senior minister to Chicago for the next St. Pat-

Timothy A. Smiddy, Ireland's envoy extraordinary and minister plenipotentiary to the USA, with Mrs. A. L. MacFlat, secretary, Irish Legation, Washington, DC, 1 Dec. 1925. Courtesy Library of Congress.

rick's Day festivities. For some time Smiddy had wanted Cosgrave himself to visit the United States, expressing concern in 1925 about harmful publicity relating to Ireland that he felt was deterring tourists. Minister for Posts and Telegraphs J. J. Walsh also told Cosgrave, "This country is being maligned shamefully throughout the length and breadth of America."[1]

Michael Faherty and "Big Bill" Thompson

On August 30, 1927, Smiddy wrote, "I have given Mr Michael J. Faherty, President of the Board of Local Improvements of the City of Chicago, and Mr Rodger Faherty (his son), President of the Irish Fellowship Club, Chicago, a letter of introduction to the President [Cosgrave]." In this letter, headed "*un*official [italics added] and confidential," he told Dublin that Michael Faherty "is a staunch friend of the Irish Free State and especially admires the constructive work of the Cosgrave government." Faherty Senior himself had been the third next president of the Irish Fellowship Club after James O'Shaughnessy. Smiddy noted, "His son Roger is most anxious to get one of the Ministers to be the guest of the Irish Fellowship Club and principal speaker on next St Patrick's night. The Club will liberally defray all his expenses to and from Chicago to Dublin." The envoy added, "My object in writing to you on the subject is to tell you confidentially it might be worth while to bestow a little extra courtesy on Mr Faherty. He is very wealthy and is apt to be generous in any cause worthy of support."[2]

Smiddy did not mention the fact that, three years earlier, Michael J. Faherty had been charged with paying substantial bribes to a paving company during construction of the Michigan Boulevard Bridge in Chicago. Admittedly, Faherty had been found not guilty. Clarence Darrow and Patrick H. O'Donnell had successfully defended him, the former arguing ingeniously if not disingenuously that the payments were made to save the city money by getting the bridge completed on time. Faherty was also embroiled with Chicago's extrovert mayor, "Big Bill" Thompson, in long-running legal battles with the *Chicago Tribune.* Irked by the *Tribune's* continuing criticism of him, including assertions that he had failed to support the war effort and that his political machine was looting the city treasury, Thompson had in 1918 personally sued the paper for defamation. Then in 1920 he had instituted, ostensibly and unusually on behalf of the city of Chicago, another libel suit against the newspaper, this time claiming $10 million in damages. It is believed to have been at the time the biggest demand for libel damages in the history of the United States, and the *Tribune* fought it as an attack on the freedom of the press. The newspaper also, in 1921, instituted in turn its own lawsuit against Thompson as mayor and Michael J. Faherty as president of the Board of Local Improvements, and others. It sought an order that certain monies paid by the city be returned to the city. An officially authorized Irish record of the tour later described Michael J. Faherty, who was instrumental in getting Cosgrave to visit America, as "Mayor Thompson's chief lieutenant (and the biggest Irish leader in Chicago)." He has been depicted elsewhere as Thompson's "demon of energy" and accused of "wild prodigality," his motto ostensibly being, "Go ahead on the jump and straighten out the legal end later."[3] Wendt subsequently wrote, "If the *Tribune* could require Thompson and his friends to be personally responsible for misused city funds, millions more could be recovered from 'expert fees' alone, since scores of Thompson ward leaders and cronies had been paid from hundreds to thousands of dollars each during the mayor's six years in office. The bill for the return of such sums could ruin Big Bill Thompson, though he was a wealthy man."[4]

By April 1923 Thompson as plaintiff had lost his and the city's libel actions. The Illinois Supreme Court declared, "Prosecution for libel on government is unknown to American courts." Journalists welcomed the decision, although Hearst's papers did not join publicly in the media celebrations. Although the libel proceedings by Thompson had ended, the *Tribune*'s "expert fees" action against him, Faherty, and others was to rumble on until 1929. If Smiddy knew of these cases, and it is difficult to see how he could not, he deemed them unworthy of reference in his "unofficial and confidential" letter to Dublin in August 1927.[5]

All Sane Irishmen

Cosgrave decided to call another general election, hoping to strengthen his government's position. In September 1927 he again won, although not as convincingly as he had hoped. The Irish Fellowship Club's secretary, Kevin Kelly, then followed up Smiddy's letter of August by writing in late September to Cosgrave to say that "all sane Irish Americans are happy at your election," and to point out that he and Michael Faherty, whom he described as "the city builder," would soon be in Dublin. His endorsement of one party in an Irish general election seems at variance with the heading on the notepaper of the Irish Fellowship Club that he used. This proclaimed that his club was "non-political, non-sectarian." In October Kelly sent Cosgrave an American press report of a luncheon in Paris that had been hosted by the Chicago municipal commission for those French who had just then facilitated a Chicago delegation's inspection of the Paris underground railway system. In a speech at that luncheon Irene Montonya, head of the Chicago Board of Local Improvements, described Faherty as "one of the greatest American builders." Faherty subsequently traveled from France to Ireland, where Cosgrave met him. Kelly later wrote to thank Cosgrave for the meeting and added, "Mr Faherty reiterates what he said in Dublin that a visit from you and Mrs Cosgrave would be to the benefit of the Irish Free State, because it would show to the people of Ireland that the people of America are perfectly satisfied with your government and have no sympathy with de Valera and his opposition forces."[6]

Vatican Competition for American Funds

As envoy in Washington, Smiddy felt strongly that the opportunity should not be missed to fly Ireland's flag in America, even if Cosgrave himself could not go. He first won over Patrick McGilligan, the minister for external affairs in Dublin. Smiddy himself had given a lecture a few years ealier at the Irish Fellowship Club and told McGilligan that the club "is one of the most respected clubs in Chicago. It is non-political but a strong supporter of the Irish Free State." He recalled that presidents Taft and Roosevelt had spoken at it, and that its banquet for Cardinal Patrick O'Donnell, Catholic Primate of Ireland, had been one of the biggest of its kind given in Chicago on the occasion of the Eucharistic Congress in June 1926: "I am convinced that such a visit would be productive of excellent results, and the magnitude and publicity of the reception would help to weaken the influence of de Valera." He predicted accurately that Chicago would give a "most spectacular" reception to Cosgrave if he went, and assured Dublin confidently, "There need be no fear of any manifestation of hostility from anyone in Chicago that would in any way mar the dignity of the event."[7]

McGilligan was persuaded by the argument. A memorandum that the secretary of his department sent to the "executive council" (cabinet) in December 1927 referred bluntly to the material benefits of such a visit. The secretary was happy to play up the hyphenated loyalties of emigrants and to explain that the Catholic Church was already raising money from Irish-Americans:

> It has been frequently said by friendly and influential Irish-Americans in the course of the past few years that we cannot expect Irish-Americans to take an interest in the Saorstát [Free State] if we persist in ignoring their existence. There is no doubt whatever that the great body of Irish-American opinion worth having is passively on our side and it only requires a little nursing to become active. The Vatican is at present drawing huge revenues from Irish-American millionaires simply because it never loses a chance of flattering their vanity. The Pope recently sent a special envoy to New York to marry the daughter of an illiterate Tipperary man who had amassed five millions in a little over twenty years. It is well known that this individual and a considerable number of similar types are ready to invest their money in Ireland if given the proper encouragement and publicity. It is time to begin a definite campaign which should include a complete change of attitude in our press towards the United States of America.

McGilligan urged the government to agree to at least a short visit to America by Cosgrave or his vice president, Ernest Blythe, "with no other public object than to make a few speeches" with the intention of "getting in touch with most of the influential Irish-Americans." His department pointed out, "The opportunity is now put into our hands by the Irish Fellowship Club."[8]

Radio and Other Media Hookups

Concrete plans for a visit to Chicago were soon made. Smiddy told Dublin that Faherty was working closely in Chicago with Edward Hurley, former chairman of the US Shipping Board, and D. F. Kelly, a prominent business-man: "Mr Faherty is getting a Mayor's Committee of a hundred business leaders for the welcome and arrival of the President. They have arranged for the finest suites at the Drake Hotel." Patrick Crowley, president of the New York Central Railroad, put his private railway carriage at the disposal of Cosgrave for the journey from New York to Chicago and thence to Washington. Positive media coverage was also desirable, and Smiddy noted that arrangements were being made for broadcasting speeches in Chicago and elsewhere, "and hooking up from these centers with all the various radio centers in the United States." Robert R. McCormick had invited Cosgrave to visit the *Chicago Tribune*.

James O'Donnell Bennett, "a notable journalist of Chicago and who wrote a very noteworthy article in the *Chicago Tribune* on the Eucharistic Congress" was expected to deliver a special article for the *Chicago Tribune* on the occasion of Cosgrave's visit. O'Donnell Bennett, "the dean of journalists" as he was then known, was soon to write for the *Chicago Tribune* a syndicated series of sensational stories under the title "Gangland" that in 1929 told "the true yet incredible tale of what has happened in the under-world of Chicago during the last five years. The story of a war."[9] It was a "war" that did not deter W. T. Cosgrave from coming to Chicago.

To enable a special radio hookup to happen coast to coast, so that Cosgrave might reach an audience of "about thirty millions of people from the Irish Fellowship Club," Edward Hurley contacted the chairman and managing director of the Radio Corporation of America and stated that he and "some Chicago friends" would pay for the broadcast. Hurley also got in touch with Will Hays, the first president of the Motion Picture Producers and Distributors Association of America, and "asked him to give instructions that special care be given to the pictures taken of President Cosgrave and his party and that these pictures with suitable captions be exhibited in the various cinema theatres in America." Smiddy wrote that Hays had promised to comply with the request.[10] Hays, a former postmaster general, held a key position in the film industry and became one of the best known Americans of his day. But he could scarcely have "instructed" local movie theaters to screen pictures of a foreign politician visiting America. In any event some newspapers gave the visit considerable attention. Hearst's *New York American,* for example, reported that Cosgrave "will be visiting the largest Irish city in the world" en route to Chicago. It noted that the "300,000 population of his capital city, Dublin, would have a tough time in a tug-of-war or hurling match with the New York Irish. We have here more than 200,000 who were born on the Emerald Isle and three times that number born of Irish parents."[11]

Tough Travel

Cosgrave's American trip was challenging both physically and politically. It was also a public relations success. Fears that demonstrations by Irish immigrants or Irish-Americans who had opposed the government of the Irish Free State in the recent civil war might somehow mar Cosgrave's visit proved unfounded, as Smiddy had foreseen. Éamon de Valera happened to be in New York at that time, but Cosgrave "disclaimed any intention of seeking out the Republican chief" when asked if he might do so.[12]

On the morning of January 21, 1928, the Irish prime minister arrived from New York at La Salle Street Station, Chicago, on board an overnight train laced with ice and snow. Among those who had arranged to travel with him by rail was James O'Shaughnessy, willing to take time off from the 4A's in Manhattan to make the journey.[13] Waiting on the platform for Cosgrave in Chicago was a remarkable party of about two hundred city aldermen and others in top hats and morning suits, stamping their icy feet on the cement platform in an effort to keep warm. Their formal dress was a sign that the Irish had arrived socially and were no long poverty-stricken. Also present was Police Captain Patrick J. Collins, "a brother of the famous Michael Collins, who was killed in the recent civil war in Ireland."[14]

Anomalous among so many men in tails and top hats was the city's mayor,

Ireland's President W. T. Cosgrave (left) and Chicago's Mayor Bill Thompson
on a cold Chicago day, January 1928. Courtesy Chicago History Museum,
Chicago Daily News collection DN-0084734

William Thompson, wearing his distinctive soft gray fedora and a coat of
raccoon in which he "fairly enveloped" Cosgrave. The latter, who had had
a rough crossing to America, now found himself contending directly with
a Chicago winter. Thompson, wrapped in thick fur, told him, "I've brought
my open car, so the people could see you. I don't know but what [*sic*] it's
too cold for you. What do you think?" O'Donnell Bennett reported, "The
president evidently thought well of the mayor's red open car and into it
the pair stepped. A squadron of mounted police road in front of them,
the American flag and the flag of Chicago in their first rank. Judge Marcus
Kavanagh, Edward Hurley, and some two score other Chicago notables of
Irish ancestry followed in closed cars."[15] The fact that they followed mounted
police necessarily slowed their pace in the icy air. At least one photograph of
Cosgrave and Thompson in the open red vehicle suggests by the look on the
Irish leader's face that he was not entirely comfortable with the arrangement.

Shortly before Cosgrave arrived in Chicago, Smiddy noted that "Mr.

Michael J. Faherty and his Committee have had large posters printed of President Cosgrave and are displaying them in the most advantageous parts of downtown Chicago." One of these, draped in the Irish national colors of green and white and orange, was hung on the city's main train station. James O'Donnell Bennett wrote that Chicago welcomed Cosgrave and his party "not as fawners for funds," but as men "doing their work in the building of a state newly come into the comity of nations." Headlines proclaimed his "Huge Chicago Welcome," and photographs of his American visit show people lining the sidewalks of Chicago and New York at least six deep in places. Chicago's *Herald-Examiner* shouted, "Throngs Hail Cosgrave."[16]

Big Banquet

As many as five thousand guests attended a banquet in Cosgrave's honor that the Irish Fellowship Club organized at the Stevens Hotel. Desmond FitzGerald, a senior government minister who accompanied Cosgrave and who was the father of a future highly regarded Irish prime minister (Taoiseach Garret FitzGerald), wrote, "It was a night of unqualified joy to the Irishmen of Chicago. Living thousands of miles from Ireland they heard the story of work done there and not the story of internecine strife."[17]

As planned, Cosgrave's address to the Irish Fellowship Club's Chicago banquet was broadcast live to millions of radio listeners across the US. Back in Galway the *Connacht Sentinel* reported that thousands of Irish radio listeners had been able to pick it up. W. S. Bateman of Dublin, for example, did so on his three-valve radio set. Next morning, Cosgrave attended Sunday mass at Old St. Patrick's Church in Chicago, greeted by its pastor Fr. William McNamee, the uncle of Thomas O'Shaughnessy's late wife. O'Shaughnessy's work was visible on the walls and in the windows for Cosgrave to see. As the Irish leader left Old St. Pat's that morning "the organ pealed forth the strains of the Saorstat National Anthem."[18]

Al Capone's Shadow

Mayor William Thompson of Chicago, who was known as "Big Bill" Thompson, also hosted a function for Cosgrave. He was a most controversial mayor and a popular demagogue who is said to have accepted campaign funds from Al Capone. Contemporary authors wrote vividly of Thompson's rise, his successful courting of the black vote, and his "hollow appeals to free Ireland."[19] Another controversial figure present was the notorious "Bathhouse" John Coughlin, regarded as "spectacular dean of Chicago's board of aldermen." Back in 1911, during a rally chaired by Thomas O'Shaughnessy, Charles Merriam and others had strongly condemned Coughlin's "partnerships with vice and crime." But Coughlin survived the political challenge and now made a speech in which he told Cosgrave, "As the son of a Connaught man and a Limerick lass, who were forced to leave Ireland in the old, bad days of tyranny, it is the proudest honor of my life to present you resolutions of welcome adopted unanimously by our board of aldermen."[20]

Faherty or others appear to have convinced Cosgrave that various unsavory rumors about Chicago's mayor were unfounded, or else Cosgrave simply decided for political reasons to ignore them. Almost gratuitously it seems, before he left the city, he endorsed Thompson: "I want to say a good word about that great and grossly libeled man, Mayor William Hale Thompson. If I were not experienced in politics I would have expected to meet a roughneck. I found him to be a big, kindly, genial American, so bubbling over with plans for the betterment of his city that he talked about hardly anything except the plan to connect Chicago with the sea and make her America's greatest city." He would again put in a good word for Thompson when he got to Washington, claiming there once more that the mayor of Chicago had been libeled.[21] Cosgrave was in America partly to boost investment in Ireland, and diplomatic niceties require visiting dignitaries to be pleasant. The prime minister of the new state, desperate for economic stimulus, had learned of Faherty and Thompson's plan for new waterways around Chicago. These might mean jobs for Irish emigrants and new trade links between Ireland and America. Thompson promised, "We are going to treat with Ireland at the rate of $7 a ton by water one way or another. By means of new waterways which — economically speaking — will move our western farmers and manufacturers nearer to your Ireland, and which will do the same for Irish producers in their dealings with us."[22]

However, given Thompson's controversial reputation, did Cosgrave have to go quite so far in seeming to endorse him? If one account of Cosgrave's visit is correct then the explanation for this endorsement may be that he felt indebted to Thompson for leaning on Irish-Americans and Irish emigrants who otherwise might have disrupted his tour because they opposed his policies in Ireland. The *Irish Independent* reported, "It is freely stated that Mayor Thompson passed the word to the local Irish stalwarts to keep quiet or some of them would soon be out of a job."[23] Smiddy had earlier given Dublin an assurance that there would be no hostility in Chicago, and Thompson made it clear from the outset that he was taking care of his Irish visitor. The *Chicago News* described the scene as the mayor escorted Cosgrave from the station: "If one can picture two of the three bears in the old nursery tale, the papa bear and the little bear, they might form a picture of that walk down the platform."[24] When the little bear's train later crashed on its way to Ottawa, Canada, claims that the incident was an attempt on Cosgrave's life caused Secret Service officers to rush mounted police to the scene under orders to make a complete investigation. Cosgrave had been in no hurry to come to America, and these rumors point up the importance of Thompson's persuasive influence in deterring possible Irish Republican troublemakers. For who but his civil war enemies whould have wished to harm Cosgrave in America? In fact, the crash was discovered to have been an accident.[25]

Many who attended the Irish Fellowship Club's banquet in Chicago were reportedly "diehards" who came to the event thinking de Valera's "no compromise" platform on the partitioning of Ireland a better one than Cosgrave's. However, speaking at the banquet, Faherty warned Irish-Americans against interfering in Irish politics: "Let the Irish people take care of themselves. They are well able; any encouragement given to the disturbers of our race is a crime against the Irish people in America and Ireland." Cosgrave was no doubt grateful for this and relieved that, when he spoke, "nearly every one in the room was on his feet cheering."[26]

Favorable Media Coverage

Cosgrave appreciated the favorable media coverage that he received on his tour, particularly it seems from the Hearst group. As his train pulled out of Chicago for Washington he told John T. Burke, "Universal Correspondent" of the *Herald and Examiner,* "I cannot forbear recalling my welcome by the staffs of the *Herald and Examiner* and the *American.* May I add, and I think the occasion appropriate, that Ireland will never forget William Randolph Hearst, who has always been one of her best and truest friends."[27] Publicity surrounding Cosgrave's visit had some of the hallmarks of informed "media management" and it may be noted that the wily adman and journalist James O'Shaughnessy had made arrangements to accompany Cosgrave not only from New York to Chicago but also when the latter went on to Washington to meet President Coolidge, who had formally invited Cosgrave to visit the United States. However, it has not been possible to confirm what, if any, particular advice this founding member of the Irish Fellowship Club gave the traveling party.[28]

One year after Cosgrave met Coolidge, the latter was succeeded as president by another Republican, Herbert Hoover. To face Hoover in the election, the Democrats had chosen Al Smith as their candidate. Smith, the first Catholic nominated by a major political party for that high office, identified himself with Irish-America even though only one of his grandparents was an Irish Catholic. Three decades would pass before a candidate from an Irish-American Catholic background became president.

Dry Wit

Cosgrave visited the US during the era of Prohibition (1920–1933), when alcohol was illegal there and could only be bought under the counter. He generally avoided commenting on the ban, but while in Chicago he was asked what he thought of Prohibition, and he replied, in a flash of dry humor, "That is not one of Ireland's many problems."[29]

The Irish leader's return to Ireland was an occasion of celebration, with an immense crowd turning out to see him.[30] His visit had been for Irish citizens a moment of national pride after the disastrous civil war, not least because so many Irish emigrants and descendants of Irish emigrants lived in North America. Reading contemporary reports of popular excitement surrounding Cosgrave's trip, one is reminded of the scenes of jubilation that marked the visit to Ireland of a much more charismatic politician, President John F. Kennedy, in 1963.

ELEVEN

The Best in the Business

In 1928 James O'Shaughnessy decided to quit his job as chief executive of the American Association of Advertising Agencies and to become a consultant. He was then aged sixty-three and had been eleven years at the helm of the AAAA. The reputation that he enjoyed was reflected in the fact that by 1928 he was also lecturing to postgraduate business students at Columbia University in New York City. He had been invited to share with them his extensive knowledge of advertising agency procedures and practice.[1]

Sack of Gold

Even while still at the AAAA, James apparently had taken on some private and lucrative counseling work. His clients included "for many years" the Hotel Belmont in New York, and also *Liberty* magazine, which the *Chicago Tribune* group launched in New York in 1924.[2]

When he was leaving, his colleagues arranged for him a farewell lunch at which William H. Johns, on behalf of the 4A's, presented him with a cloth sack, "which he said, contained 125 double eagles (about £500) showered upon him from his friends in the Association from coast to coast."[3]

O'Shaughnessy wrote to Tom Grehan, advertising manager of the *Irish Independent* newspaper, and told him that he was stepping down as executive secretary in order to concentrate on his consulting work. He explained that one reason for making the change was to get rid of a great many routine tasks and said that he supposed that he was the only person anywhere in his new line of activity: "What I am doing is giving counsel or advice or managerial direction to whoever thinks he needs it. I am engaged by way of retainer and with various fees as the work indicates." He added that his clients, "so far," were publishers of newspapers and magazines, advertising agencies, advertisers, and bankers, also associations: "I have been almost overwhelmed with offers and I feel very happy with the business aspect of the change."[4]

One of his new clients as a counselor was the agency association that he had just quit. His new business address was 420 Lexington Avenue. This towering block by Grand Central Station in Manhattan was known as the Graybar Building and also housed the J. Walter Thompson Company.

He was in demand as a speaker, too. In November 1928, for example, he went straight from addressing the convention of the American Newspaper Publishers Association at Virginia Beach to the District of Columbia, where he delivered a talk to the Washington Advertising Club in the ballroom of the National Press Club.[5]

Liberty's Business Manager

When the owners of the *Chicago Tribune* launched *Liberty* magazine in 1924, they promised themselves the largest magazine circulation in the world.[6] This locked them into a struggle with the *Saturday Evening Post*, the leading publication in their particular market. So they put responsibility for *Liberty* into the hands of the legendary Max Annenberg, that "life-long friend of Mr. O'Shaughnessy." Both men had once worked at the *Chicago Tribune* and at Hearst's *Chicago American*.[7] Annenberg had remained in Chicago as circulation manager of the *Tribune* until 1919, "mightily helping it to prosper." Then his chiefs transferred him to New York to work on their *Daily News*, in which he was reputed to have become a heavy stockholder.[8]

Max later claimed that he was the one to induce O'Shaughnessy to resign his position with the 4A's and to go into business for himself: "*Liberty*, he said, had been Mr. O'Shaughnessy's first client, at the highest fee ever paid for advertising counsel, namely, 100 dols. a word."[9]

Liberty was said to have "more of the far-reaching whole family appeal than any other magazine printed," with articles for both men and women in areas that included sports, business, cooking, fashion, and beauty — and a special feature for children.[10] But by 1929 it needed a boost in its advertising revenue, for Annenberg was not having the same success with admen in respect to advertising as he had long had with newsdealers in respect to circulation. *Time* magazine was critical of his performance at *Liberty*, observing that "advertising men are different from newsdealers. They must be coaxed, cannot be driven." The writer noted that *Liberty*'s advertising did not keep pace with its readership: "'Trick' layouts, a special testimonial

issue, salesman's 'thermometers' in the office and other features of the
hard-driving Annenberg technique, did not bring in the business as fast
as required." The owners of *Liberty* looked to a seasoned professional who
had a knowledge of both editorial and advertising to solve their problems:

> Rather than demote General Manager Annenberg, a new title of Business
> Manager was created for the man now called in to build up *Liberty's*
> advertising. And the man is an old time *Liberty* counsellor, the best in the
> business, grey-haired James O'Shaughnessy, longtime Executive Secretary
> of the American Association of Advertising Agencies (Four A's), famed
> as a goodwill-maker as well as for his knowledge of advertising, one of
> the most universally popular practitioners in a highly temperamental
> profession.[11]

It was praise indeed to be dubbed "the best in the business" by *Time*
magazine. *Liberty's* owners on Park Avenue had been very eager to have
him. They announced his retention as the magazine's advertising counselor
in the spring of 1929 and had already for the period March 15 to December
31, 1928, paid him a "salary" of $12,039.80 in total.[12] *Time* later remarked on
the fact that *Liberty* had been a very particular project for the owners of
Chicago's leading newspaper, publisher Joseph Medill Patterson's "especial
pride." In 1924 he set himself to challenge the *Saturday Evening Post*: "He
aimed at a slightly more jazz-loving level of the public than *Satevepost's*
audience is supposed to be. Spending some $14,000,000 he got as high as
2,470,882 readers. (*Satevepost* has been more than 3,000,000.) In 1929 he
prophesied: 'We estimate that in 1935 *Liberty* will have the largest magazine
circulation in the world.' He even showed a graph of the future, in which
Liberty topped *Satevepost* jauntily (*Time*, July 1, 1929)."[13]

The weekly *Liberty* boasted of a "circulation" of more than 2.25 million, a
term that *Time* here equated with readers rather than sales. While still just
a consultant to *Liberty*, O'Shaughnessy had told its readers that two methods for getting more contacts for advertisers were open to it. One was to
keep its present size and to increase circulation, but that would necessitate
an increase in rates. The other was to change its format, reduce the cost
of production, and turn the savings into additional circulation. This way,
"The manufacturer would receive more for his advertising dollar. A distinct
economy in selling would be accomplished." The company chose the latter

Liberty magazine,
28 June 1930.

route beginning in January 1929, and O'Shaughnessy forecast that it would increase its circulation by half a million within six months. Rates remained unchanged. Five months later, he wrote, "*Liberty* has asked me to become its business manager and I have accepted. In identifying myself completely with *Liberty* I feel that I am joining another great national undertaking in advertising — an undertaking of proportions so large as to satisfy any man's highest ambitions." He added, "I have previously been associated with the company which owns *Liberty*. The growth of the *Chicago Tribune* under the present management has been a superb, outstanding event in the history of publishing." Boasting of the *Tribune*'s diversification into timberlands, shipping, paper mills, and radio, James O'Shaughnessy tempted faith as the great Wall Street crash approached by predicting "a great future" for *Liberty*.[14]

The magazine's successful profile at this time saw it being mentioned comically by Groucho Marx, in a movie released in August 1929 in which

Groucho played a hotel manager addressing employees: "Well, what makes wage slaves? Wages! I want you to be free. Remember, there's nothing like Liberty — except Collier's and the Saturday Evening Post." *Collier's* had been founded in 1888 by an Irish immigrant, Peter F. Collier, and by 1929 it reportedly had a circulation of "well over 2,000,000." The *Saturday Evening Post* claimed one of nearly 3,000,000. Colonel Robert R. McCormick, editor and publisher of the *Chicago Tribune* and godfather of *Liberty* magazine, reportedly let O'Shaughnessy known that he wanted their magazine "to have the biggest circulation on this or any other planet."[15]

An Old Acquaintance

During 1929 the new business manager of *Liberty* met Albert Johnson, an old friend from his days in Missouri. Johnson was by then a prominent member of Congress "but otherwise the same as when he disdained the prunes at the Ogden house with such high gesture that you will recall somewhat impaired their standing as a delicacy for dessert. Of course, that was a critical crowd and not so easy to please." So O'Shaughnessy told May Montgomery, another acquaintance from their time in St. Joseph. The comment was in his reply to a letter from her in November 1929. He described the changes to his own life as well: "I am still working hard, as you can imagine, and I have children strung out all the way from grammar school to college." He added that he had never "got out of the atmosphere of publishing" but that he believed that he was now "looked upon as an advertising man more than anything else, and have been for years." Remarking that he had only been back to St. Joseph once since leaving it nearly four decades earlier, he mused, "I think I would be willing to make a trip back to St. Joe if all four of us could sit down together at the same table again in the Ogden house, but I would insist upon giving the prunes their old place of honor on the table. This is a far away wish, but it is pleasing to think about it."[16]

Wall Street Crash

While the circulation of *Liberty* rose, the US economy collapsed. The Wall Street crash of late 1929 signaled the beginning of a long economic depression. James O'Shaughnessy and Max Annenberg struggled on, the former writing to the latter during 1930 with a suggestion for a feature that he thought might attract some of those advertising revenues that were becoming more elusive. He was just back from lunch with Stewart Mims and Bill Day of J. Walter Thompson who had eagerly suggested to him "that a series of stories be run in *Liberty* that would show women's achievements or progress, using famous women characters of history and great events in which women cut the big figure." They had even proposed "the man [!] to write the stories," one "Perequine [*sic*] Acland of The Lodge, Greenwich, Connecticut."[17]

Acland, whose first name was actually Peregrine, was a Canadian war hero whose hard-hitting novel about a soldier, *All Else Is Folly*, had been published in New York, Toronto, and London in 1929 to some critical acclaim. Ford Madox Ford wrote its preface, and Bertrand Russell read and endorsed the book. The son of a journalist and civil servant, Acland himself dabbled in journalism but was employed from 1925 to 1929 by J. Walter Thompson. There he worked closely with Stanley Resor. For his part, Sims is said to have "sacrificed" his position as a professor of history at Yale for a job in advertising and to have decried "the effeminizing presence of women in business." Yet, here he was, eager for *Liberty* to advance the image of women in history as "the big figure" by having another adman write about them. Perhaps Resor's wife, the renowned copywriter and executive Helen Lansdowne, was behind the idea.[18]

By April 1931, reported *Time*, "*Liberty's* circulation, always 99% newsstand, was claimed to have reached over 2,400,000." Yet the anticipated increase in advertising continued to elude its executives, and its owners suddenly cut their losses:

> The publishing world long had known that *Liberty's* advertising was being ridden to death by hard-boiled General Manager Max Annenberg, concerning whose acquaintance with Chicago's famed Scarface Al Capone an interesting testimonial was published last week in Big Bill Thompson's [pamphlet] "The Tribune Shadow." Annenberg once promised a 250,000 circulation growth at no increased page-rate and got thereby many an advertiser. Forthwith he cut *Liberty's* page-size, lost in goodwill what he had made in profit. James O'Shaughnessy, expert on advertising, was called in (*Time*, July 29, 1929), but could not revive the invalid. Advertising

makes a magazine pay; *Liberty* did not pay. It ailed, grew thinner, was printed on cheaper paper. Still it remained Capt. Patterson's pride. He was satisfying his readers. Some people thought he might run *Liberty* a while longer and then close it up. Few people suspected he would ever let it go into other hands.[19]

But he did, selling it to Macfadden publications, home of *True Story* and a dozen other popular magazines: "In the city-rooms of the *Chicago Tribune* and the *New York Daily News,* editors gasped and whistled to themselves as they took in the story. Their employers, Col. Robert Rutherford McCormick and Capt. Joseph Medill Patterson, suddenly, unexpectedly, had sold their nickel-weekly *Liberty* to Bernarr Macfadden!" *Time* noted the fact that "ruddy-complexioned and hazel-eyed" James O'Shaughnessy, who "thrived on hard work," was out of a job.[20]

After *Liberty*

After *Liberty* was sold, James O'Shaughnessy faced a period of uncertainty at a time of economic depression. He had in 1929 told May Montgomery that "I have children strung out all the way from grammar school to college." Now in his late sixties, O'Shaughnessy was relieved to find a new job as vice president and sales manager of the Outdoor Advertising Association, which represented a medium that he had so eloquently defended against its detractors seven years earlier. It was to employ him from 1931 to 1935. On January 11, 1932, he wrote to his old acquaintance Max Annenberg. The *Tribune* owners had reassigned Annenberg to the tabloid *Detroit Mirror,* founded by Bernarr Macfadden in 1929 as the *Detroit Daily* and subsequently transferred to the *Tribune* group as part of its deal with that publisher for the acquisition by Macfadden of *Liberty.* O'Shaughnessy confessed to Annenberg, "It was a long haul getting reset — much longer that I thought it would be — much longer than I wanted it to be. Conditions, however, were as bad as you said they were going to be." He claimed to have had many propositions, but "Things could not be rushed." He told Anneberg that it was due to the latter's "foresight and thoughtfulness and fine consideration" that he had been able to "get over the dead spot in the road." He still spoke highly of *Liberty,* which was "the work of two master minds — Joe Patterson's and yours" and suggested that "time will show that it was a success in everything but the fending off of a world calamity, and no magazine or any other sort of a publication was able to do that." He wished Annenberg success with the *Detroit Mirror*.[21]

Unsurprisingly for someone who was now promoting outdoor advertising, he was not especially enthusiastic about the current value of radio to advertisers. Yet, given the evident public interest in radio, including as a medium for political communication during the visit of W. T. Cosgrave, he would not underestimate its potential. In November 1931, he told the Inland Press Association, "The radio is not a big factor today . . . though it is a major medium. It is here to stay. . . . It will soon find its technique. It is very clumsily handled today, and advertisers are not satisfied with it."[22]

Art and Outdoor Advertising

Later in 1932 he returned to the theme of art and advertising, one he had employed during 1929 in an address to the Guild of Freelance Artists of The Authors' League of America.[23] This theme now served the interests of his new employer, the Outdoor Advertising Association. In February 1932 he submitted to *Printers' Ink* a discourse entitled "What is 'Art for Art's Sake?'" It appears to have been too abstract or too extravagant a piece for that practical journal, because a note scribbled on the copy that is among his papers at Duke University tells us that it was "not used." When rejecting a second article by him that same year, on the more concrete topic of "Distress Copy," the editor of *Printers' Ink* explained that he faced "very stringent space limitations."

Yet the content of O'Shaughnessy's 1932 unpublished essay on art is both amusing and informative, linking as it does some of the greatest artists in the history of Western civilization to later advertising techniques and giving us another insight into the author's tendency to exaggerate the benefits of advertising even by the standards of his own industry. Having told his intended readers that "Art is the spritely hand-maid of advertising" as well as "the good step-mother of advertising," he reminded them that, for its part, advertising had given art "a better allowance." He thought, "The engaging beauty of a modern page advertisement in a newspaper, the alluring charm of a magazine page glorifying a commercial offer, the serene majesty of a great outdoor advertisement — are all contributions to aesthetics, man-ifolded into the high virtue of material service. Advertising intrudes the fragrance of its beauty into every mind. Its 'art for art's sake' does exactly that social service."

Where his contemporary Bruce Barton pictured Jesus as a successful adman, O'Shaughnessy just knew that the great masters of painting would have been at home in a modern agency:

> If Rubens or Velasquez or Rembrandt were here today, can you imagine them as failing to appreciate the opportunity of the poster panel with its heroic proportions, its epic themes, its inspiration in service and the joy it gives in knowing it will be seen, even by those who are too materialistic to go to museums?
>
> Would Jordaens or Hals have grabbed the opportunity of illustrating a page advertisement in the newspaper? I think they would, and that Raphael and de Vinci would be reaching for a chance to do a page advertisement for the magazines.

He also referred to someone who had greatly impressed and influenced his own brother Thomas. This was a European who had visited Chicago: "Some quarter of a century ago Alphonse Mucha shocked the world by mak-ing a series of poster advertisements. He was accused of commercializing his divine art. Later on copies of Mucha posters were sought by ponderous museums. That differentiates between art for indolence and art for service." He thought that "modern minded artists" were courageously breaking the old shackles and that "In this very year of 1932 some of the master work of the great artists has enriched the outdoors across the country. It is being said that indications of a new school of American art have within this very year appeared on the panels of poster advertising and in magazines and in newspapers."[24]

In 1935 James resumed his freelance counseling for both national and international corporations and kept working until his death. Changing with the times, he became associated for a while with Independent Broadcasters and delivered at colleges and elswhere various guest lectures in marketing.[25]

Notre Dame and Knute Rockne

There were certain constants in James O'Shaughnessy's adult life. One was his interest in Ireland. Another was his involvement with the media. The third was his loyalty to the Catholic Church, within which one of his sisters and two of his daughters became nuns.[26] His siblings, too, were important to him, as was the O'Shaughnessys' continuing relationship with Notre Dame. James now hoped that his own son Colman would become a student there, and in 1926 he paid a deposit for him to do so. However, in September of that year Notre Dame President Matthew Walsh told James that he was "badly disappointed" to learn that Colman had not in fact registered. If Arch Ward's description of that university at the time is accurate then it may not have been the most attractive destination for a sensitive or troubled person. In giving an account of Frank Leahy's football exploits there, Ward wrote: "The University of Notre Dame, a man's school whose purpose is to train American boys for men's work, wastes little time in orienting its charges."[27]

James kept in touch with Walsh, once sending him a copy of the *New York Journal* and suggesting "Tunney" as a guest lecturer at Notre Dame. He appears to have been referring to the Irish-American boxer Gene Tunney who defeated Jack Dempsey in 1926, and again in 1927, to become world heavyweight champion. Tunney's relative intellectualism and general public reticence and abstemiousness marked him out from more popular pugilists, according to McCarthy.[28]

By 1931, Colman had gone to study at South Bend, where he became the honorary secretary of Notre Dame's Metropolitan Club. His father feared that he was neglecting his work and wrote apologetically to Charles O'Donnell, who in 1928 had succeeded Walsh as president of Notre Dame, and asked him to call in Colman and to have a word with the young man. O'Donnell did so. He found Colman "wholesome" and frank, but exceedingly regretful that "a certain journal of his fell under eyes for which it was never intended and that an entirely false understanding of the record resulted." He reassured James, "Lots of good men, as we all know, have been unsatisfactory beginners," and added, "The boy is doing well, is interested in his work, and receiving Holy Communion, he tells me, nearly every day."[29]

During 1931, the famous Notre Dame football player and coach Knute Rockne died in a plane crash on his way to take part in the production of a film entitled *The Spirit of Notre Dame*. His sudden passing shocked Americans. At his funeral in Notre Dame, in the same church in which Rockne had been welcomed as a convert to Roman Catholicism, college president Charles O'Donnell delivered his eulogy. James O'Shaughnessy seems to have written an editorial salute entitled "The Power That Was Rockne" that appeared in *Advertising Age* on April 4, 1931. James also visited Notre Dame that year to give a talk on advertising to students in the new Commerce Building of the College of Commerce there. His address was reported to be "full of the philosophy of selling and contained many observations on human nature."[30]

Irish Fellowship Club Celebrations

James O'Shaughnessy did not attend a special Past Presidents' Day organized by the Irish Fellowship Club at the La Salle Hotel in Chicago on December 15, 1934.[31] He sent his regrets to the club's president, former Congressman George E. Gorman, writing that the club had by now become "an overtowering realization of my glamorous dream more than thirty years ago. Its influence for good has grown to be more than nationwide." Two years later he was also unable to travel to a special celebration in honor of the club's first president, Edward Dunne. He wrote to Michael Faherty, "It is a fine tribute to our racial stock that the Club has been able to present year after year in its presidency, a man who has been an honor to his race and a credit to its citizenship." Not everyone might agree that each past president of the club was as worthy of such praise as was Edward Dunne.

In 1953 the Irish Fellowship Club published a short pamphlet to celebrate the fact that it had been more than half a century in existence. Although subtitled "Its History and Objectives" this contained little or no historical detail about the club except a list of past presidents and a few sweeping generalizations. One of these was that its founders, whom the author does not name, were "young men who were steeped in the story of Ireland's long struggle for freedom." The pamphlet's flowery language celebrates Ireland and Irish culture, declares its support for a united Ireland under one republic, and highlights the good work of the club in promoting Ireland and in assisting Chicago charities. The anonymous author is keen to point out that "The cast of mind of the Irish has been important in the Empire

[*sic*] building work of America." Perhaps the most interesting aspect of the pamphlet is that, at a time when the House Committee on Un-American Activities was drumming up the anti-Communist "Red Scare" and the Korean War had continued to involve US forces, club members yet again felt it necessary to confront that hyphen in their immigrant status:

> The freedom loving Irishman quickly is transformed into a freedom loving American. If he likes to be called an Irish-American there is no allegiance to a foreign power implied. The phrase merely particularizes his Americanism, as Charles Carroll of Carrollton particularized his Americanism. [Carrollton was the only Catholic to sign the American Declaration of Independence.]
>
> The Irish-American glories in his Irish parentage. He is a natural patriot. Wolfe Tone, Robert Emmet, and de Valera are types of the Irish patriot. When he becomes an American, he transfers his innate love of home and country to the home he has made far from the green hills of Ireland. He is loyal to the land of Washington and Lincoln as ever he was to the land of Brian Boru [an Irish king whose forces defeated the Vikings] and Saint Patrick and tho' evil days may befall him, never will he sink so low or become so blind as to traduce the country of his adoption by flying the flag of the Communistic party line.[32]

It is not surprising to discover that the club's guest for the St. Patrick's Day banquet in 1954, just one year later, was Joe McCarthy. This Republican senator for Wisconsin led political and personal attacks on individuals who were actual or alleged Communists or who were suspected of being "soft" on Communism.[33]

When the Irish Fellowship Club published a centenary history in 2001, it contained much information that the 1953 pamphlet had not. Its author, Thomas O'Gorman, paid James O'Shaughnessy the compliment of referring to him not only as "the Club's fifth president" but also as "its most dynamic catalyst at its founding."[34]

TWELVE

Missouri to Manhattan

Immigrants deal with their emotions in a variety of ways when they live far from their home country. For James Shaughnessy, like so many others, migration had been a matter of sheer necessity. He fled a terrible famine in Ireland during the 1840s rather than end his days starving by the side of the road or terminally ill in a workhouse infirmary. He had little reason to reflect calmly on his cultural identity or to fret about his feelings as he landed in the new world and sought employment that would pay for the necessities of life.

But things were different for his children. His decision to go west to Missouri proved to be a happy one, as he met Catherine, his future wife there, and as her family helped both him and his brothers to acquire land so that they could become farmers. Notwithstanding the fact that Missouri suffered greatly during the Civil War, and that his wife had almost died at the age of nineteen, James and Catherine went on provide for their children in ways that James could not have done in Ireland as a person of his social class there. His children grew up benefiting from the opportunities that America offered them, while learning also to appreciate the culture of the old country in which their family had its roots. The children of immigrant families make many journeys. Those who were Irish-American at that time found their experiences reflected in the works of writers such as Finley Peter Dunne and James T. Farrell.

Young Lonigan

In 1932 James T. Farrell's first novel was published. *Young Lonigan: A Boyhood in Chicago Streets* tells the story of a fictional Irish-American who had been born thirty years earlier, just two years before the birth of Farrell himself in that same city. Farrell (1904–1979), the grandson of Irish immigrants, would continue to write novels about the fate of members of Chicago's immigrant Irish community, some of whom remained poor while families such as the O'Shaughnessys prospered and rose in society. Reinforced by the closed structure of ethnic neighborhoods in Chicago, the pervasive influence of an Irish Catholic background on the consciousness of some immigrants was such that Farrell could tell Ezra Pound in 1932, "As to the Irishness of it [*Young Lonigan*], I generally feel that I'm an Irishman rather than an American."[1]

Woodrow Wilson, dead eight years at the time, would most probably have disapproved of Farrell's formulation. Albeit hyperbolic, it dispensed entirely with both the hyphen and the hyphenated identity of an Irish-American in a way that left the author proudly proclaiming himself not an American but a foreigner. It is doubtful if any of the O'Shaughnessys felt that way, notwithstanding their links with the old country. For they became solidly established in the Midwest as citizens of the United States, and their desire to learn more about Ireland and their Irish heritage did not displace or diminish that allegiance.

Material Prosperity

Moving to live in New York from 1917, James O'Shaughnessy appears to have coped better with his material prosperity than did Finley Peter Dunne, another Chicago resident who made the move to Manhattan. James advanced from the financial uncertainties of journalism to advertising, and to a secure niche as chief executive of the American Association of Advertising Agencies. He eventually became a comfortable suburban consultant. He was a Catholic whose sister was a nun and two of whose daughters also entered the convent. And any "Irish disrespect for the pursuit of tidy bank balances and business careers," such as Ibson perceives among Irish-Americans, was not obvious in his case. If Ibson is right that "the Irish have had a singular relationship with American culture's worship of success" and that "[t]hat relationship is grounded in Catholic otherworldliness camouflaged as a seeming Irish similarity to Anglo-Saxon Protestants," any such otherworldliness was no bar to business in the case of James O'Shaughnessy. It may, however, explain his tendency to rhapsodize the benefits of advertising as a creative and social and even moral force. Finley Peter Dunne, on the other hand, found it very difficult to cope with his material success when he moved from Chicago to New York. He no longer penned Dooley pieces and appears generally to have neglected his writing talents in favor of other pursuits.[2]

Deaths

James O'Shaughnessy died aged eighty-five on November 27, 1950. Thomas reprised his own design of the Irish Fellowship Club's banquet program of 1910 for its half-centenary banquet in 1951, but he did not take part in those festivities "due to the recent death of my brother James."[3] Thomas himself died on February 11, 1956, "in relative obscurity" according to Barton, although the *Chicago Tribune* did report briefly the passing of this "stained glass [and] mural artist, noted for his work [and] credited with initiating Columbus Day."[4] While Thomas may be regarded as being at least as important in the world of Irish-American visual art as was his brother James in the business of advertising, his passing was not marked as much as that of James.

It was a sign of the respect in which the advertising industry held James O'Shaughnessy that, when he died, the busy weekly trade publication *Printers' Ink* devoted both an editorial and a full-page obituary to him. The author of this obituary noted that O'Shaughnessy "is credited with doing more than any other person to set up standards of agency operation and to establish standarised advertising rates," and added that getting the 4A's established "called for a lot of leg work, more than the average diplomacy and, as one of the pioneers in advertising put it, 'a heap of personality, of which Jim had plenty.'" In an editorial in that same issue of *Printers' Ink* in which the obituary appeared, it was said that

> A modern generation that accepts the agency system today as a natural evolution of advertising's growth in this country may overlook the patient and delicate task that had to be performed to get individual agencies to meet with one another, to join together as a group and to agree on practices satisfactory to all.
>
> Jim O'Shaughnessy had the engaging Irish personality ideally suited to the job of making the important advertising agents of the early part of the century sit down and talk things over.[5]

Hall of Fame

In December 1950, the editor of *Printers' Ink* concluded his observations on the life of the late James O'Shaughnessy by recalling the fact that the latter had made an "important" contribution to the idea of an advertising Hall of Fame and remarked that "the best tribute we can pay to Jim here is to suggest that his name be considered for the Hall of Fame of the Advertising Club of New York as soon as the rules allow."[6] This recommendation was accepted. In 1953 James O'Shaughnessy was inducted posthumously into the Advertising Hall of Fame of the American Advertising Federation, not simply as the former chief executive but also as one of the cofounders of the AAAA. The tribute to him that the Hall of Fame today posts on its website recalls his work in helping to organize the modern agency system and further credits him with being "instrumental" in forming the Advertising Agencies Corporation after World War I. It concludes by noting that "O'Shaughnessy was always interested in engaging youth in advertising and served as marketing lecturer at several universities." He was also the first president of the New York chapter of the American Marketing Association. The Hall of Fame's footnote to his lifetime of achievement was a fitting memorial of an Irish-American who rose from humble immigrant origins in the Missouri countryside to become a respected Chicago journalist and one of the most widely known admen in the United States.

Advertising came to play a central role in popular culture during the twentieth century, and by writing an account of the foundation and development of the American Association of Advertising Agencies under the executive guidance of James O'Shaughnessy this author has demonstrated that sector's rising power and influence. Indeed, as was seen earlier, George Creel and others who were involved in planning the late entry of the United States into World War I appear to have recognized at least as soon as the agencies themselves did so that advantages would flow from the creation of an effective national association of agencies in 1917.

Supporting one another, James and the other O'Shaughnessy boys from Missouri rose through the social strata of American society beyond their father's modest status as boot-maker, small farmer, shoe-seller, insurance salesman, and realtor. By identifying that dynamic, it is easier to see what motivated them. James was the son of a poor Irish Catholic and never forgot his origins. If he was conservative, the moral values of his upbringing informed his journalism and inspired his benign view of advertising and of those who worked in it. "Famed as a goodwill-maker," he tried to be consistently constructive and positive.

The story of James O'Shaughnessy's career also reflects and illuminates the rapid development of us media between 1890 and 1935. Having worked as a journalist, he successfully made the transition to advertising and became in that field "one of the most universally popular practitioners in a highly temperamental profession," as *Time* put it. By contextualizing his and his brothers' achievements within his family's circumstances and within the framework of Irish-American concerns the overall contribution that immigrants can make to the United States in general and to American culture in particular are better understood.

Rags to Riches

As a chief executive in brand new offices overlooking Madison Square in Manhattan, James had "made it." His brother Thomas found his life harder, torn as he was between art and the need to earn a living by producing prosaic forms of illustration. John and Francis worked steadily as attorneys, with Francis enjoying a day in the sun as the first alumnus of Notre Dame to deliver a commencement address at that university, admittedly as a late substitute for another invited speaker. If theirs were not exactly "rags to riches" stories, with that of James coming closest to one, the collective fate of the O'Shaughnessy boys was one that many children of immigrants might envy.

Emigration from Ireland did not end in the nineteenth century and has resumed in recent years. It has continued or commenced from other countries too. The sons and daughters of immigrants today are still driven to seek a level of financial security that many of their parents do not enjoy.

A number of contemporary factors favored the O'Shaughnessy children as they grew up in Missouri. Once civil war across the country had ended, the United States began a period of continuing — if sometimes interrupted — expansion and economic growth. There were new opportunities to go to school and college. Settled immigrants created networks of personal and professional support for those of their own ethnic or national backgrounds. The us population overall continued to increase as more immigrants arrived and as new settlements were created and expanded in the West. Chicago in particular was a boomtown and a magnet for young people from places like Missouri to which it was connected by good rail and river transport. Going up to that windy city, people benefited from its need for energetic workers in law and in newspapers among other employment sectors. Newspaper sales soared in the early twentieth century, and an increasingly literate and more prosperous citizenry found time to appreciate art. There was time, too, for organized sport, which Martin O'Shaughnessy surely appreciated as the first captain of the official Notre Dame basketball team. If he shone somewhat less brightly than his brothers after he left university, this simply illustrates the fact that there is never a guarantee of prosperity and success. Most people manage at best to fare modestly well financially.

The O'Shaughnessy sisters appear not to have shared the professional aspirations of their brothers or, if they did, had no opportunity to realize such ambitions. Reared in an orthodox Catholic family, two married and the other became a nun. One of the former died in childbirth, leaving her parents to raise her son. They did so willingly, and her father was also no doubt happy to be helping her sister to build a house in Missouri at the time of his own death.

Creative and Public Life

The contributions that the O'Shaughnessy brothers made to American society were both consistent and remarkable. Their two outstanding legacies are in the fields of advertising and art, but their efforts also oiled the wheels that kept Chicago running. They were involved in its cultural, social, political, and legal institutions.

Advertising played a pivotal role in the creation of a consumer society in the United States and elsewhere during the twentieth century. Its signal importance was recognized by James Joyce, who made a study of it and whose groundbreaking novel *Ulysses* is not only regarded as a literary masterpiece but is also a hymn to the role of advertisements in our imaginative life. Its hero, Bloom, is an adman of the old school, while its language is imbued with the concepts and copy of contemporary advertising in the early twentieth century. The content of advertisements is often subjected to critical analysis today, but the practice of the trade or profession itself has received too little notice given its cultural and economic importance. Suspicions about its moral and aesthetic values may prejudice our judgment of its significance, not least because as consumers we are guiltily implicated in its ideology and pleasures.

James O'Shaughnessy never apologized for being an adman, or for advertising. Indeed, he was seldom slow to sing its praises. During his years as chief executive of the American Association of Advertising Agencies the reputation of advertising rose to a point at which current and future presidents of the United States publicly enthused about it. Franklin D. Roosevelt was even moved to declare in 1931 that if he were starting life over again, he might well go into the advertising business in preference to almost any other. While James certainly cannot be given all of the credit for a change in public opinion about advertising, his skills and achievements were widely recognized in his day on both sides of the Atlantic and ought not to be forgotten now. In highlighting them in this volume, it has been both necessary and desirable to devote time to the emergence of the association that he steered from 1917 to 1928, especially because that particular story had not to date received the attention that it deserves. The role of George Creel and the catalyst that was World War I are shown to have been particularly relevant to the association's development.

The other principal area in which the O'Shaughnessys of Missouri left their mark nationally was in art, with Thomas winning recognition for his innovations in respect to the creation of glass and in its use for decorative purposes in churches and elsewhere. His work on Old St. Pat's Church in Chicago is generally recognized as his greatest achievement and is part of the cultural heritage of the United States. While some people regard artifacts of the Gaelic or Celtic Revival as simply handicrafts or decorative embellishments rather than high art, such a categorization is unduly crude, for the Gaelic Revival was an important part of the process of redefining national identities in an era overshadowed by imperialism, and the process of creation that was involved helped people to realign their perspectives and open their minds to new ways of thinking. While such work may be unfashionable today, Thomas O'Shaughnessy's vision continues to inspire some artists.

The family's contributions to journalism and public life are, in at least one respect, no less notable. By their prominent roles in founding and sustaining as presidents or otherwise the Irish Fellowship Club in Chicago they were party to an institution that helped to propel the Irish into power for many decades in that city and that provided a platform from which visiting Irish leaders might be heard in America stating their case for political and economic support at home. The club also helped to counter representations of Irish-Americans as badly behaved or buffoonish immigrants. It played a central role in facilitating the remarkable first visit of any leader of an independent Irish government to the United States.

The O'Shaughnessy boys were active in many ways, supporting the University of Notre Dame long after some of them graduated from it, and joining the Knights of Columbus as a manifestation of Catholic activism. Thomas the artist was not obliged to press for Columbus Day to become a public holiday, but he did so willingly and successfully and has been remembered gratefully for that achievement as well as for his stained glass.

In law and politics, too, they played a part, with James at one stage an enthusiastic "boomer" for the newspaper owner William Randolph Hearst when the latter aspired to become president. James and Francis were also closely associated with Edward Dunne, the humane and liberal mayor of Chicago and later governor of Illinois. Thomas devoted himself at one point to trying to effect change and reform by supporting the campaign of a reforming Republican for mayor, the respected academic Charles E. Merriam.

Both Thomas and James also worked for newspapers, the former as an illustrator on a number of Chicago titles and the latter as a reporter or manager on a range of publications from St. Joseph through Chicago to Manhattan. While the comic strips that Thomas drew for some years no doubt amused readers of the *Daily News,* he may have found them a galling if financially essential distraction from his vocation as an artist. He grew bitter about the failure of Catholic authorities to give him more work, and even aspects of what he was asked to do for his best-known project at Old St. Pat's in Chicago appear to have disappointed him. James found journalism more satisfying.

It cannot be said that James made the same sort of nationally significant contribution to American journalism that he made to the practice and profession of advertising. But it was a distinct honor for him to be described later by the *Chicago Tribune*'s famous Washington correspondent Arthur Sears Henning as having been a "star reporter" at that newspaper in 1899. The sparing use of by lines until more recent times means that it is difficult to know exactly what O'Shaughnessy wrote for the papers, but three examples in the first appendix give one a taste of his style. Bright and affable, his work as an aspiring "muckraker" was appreciated by the distinguished publisher of Hearst's *Chicago American* when James moved to it. James had started out as a journalist in Missouri, and much later in life he took on the challenge of making a success of *Liberty* magazine in Manhattan. But along the line in Illinois he grew tired of journalism and diverted most of his energies into the more lucrative field of advertising.

A different kind of service to society was represented in the choice made by one of the sisters of James and Thomas to become a nun. Their father had set an example for such service when he sat on at least one school board as well as supporting other charitable or benevolent organizations after he settled in Missouri. As an immigrant who fared well in a new land, he had the pleasure of seeing his children contribute to American society in a number of remarkable ways that demonstrated just how much they had benefited from being citizens of the United States.

Not all immigrants or their children get the breaks that James Shaughnessy and later his family came to enjoy after he fled famine in Ireland during the nineteenth century. Those wishing to enter the United States today, for example, may encounter many legal barriers that simply did not exist in earlier days. Environmental and other global factors limit the possibilities of economic growth everywhere. If there is a moral in the story of the O'Shaughnessys of Missouri it is not that one can get rich quickly by emulating them but that even back then, in relatively auspicious circumstances, any success that they achieved was in large part attained through personal commitment, mutual support, and sustained effort.

APPENDIX ONE Journalism of James O'Shaughnessy

The Missouri Waif

(St. Joseph, 1889)[1]

The little body of THE HERALD waif was laid to rest yesterday afternoon in Calvary cemetery. The remains were conveyed from the Home of the Friendless and escorted only by those who had taken upon themselves its care — Miss May Montmorency [*sic*] and the three young men of THE HERALD's local staff. It was borne silently to its last resting place . . . that city of white shafts and marble crosses, and high up on the quiet hillside where the long soft grasses grow in summer time, the little grave was dug.

'Twas a strange funeral, and when the little white casket was lowered into the grave, to the group of strollers in the cemetery who gathered there in idle curiosity, it may, indeed, have seemed so. No priest, no prayer, no tear, or sound except the falling clods. There was no need of priest or prayer. The holy minister of God had cleansed its soul with the sacred water of baptism, and long before it knew the sin of this world, its soul was taken to a better land, where pain, privation and neglect are never known. No prayers were needed by that sinless soul. No tears were shed, as those who knew the little waif in life, knew that it was with the infant souls in Heaven and dared not wish it back where sin prevails.

The sexton slowly shoveled in the crumbling clods, and when the grave was filled he shaped a small mound of clay and planted at the head a wooden cross, on whose white arms was written the name, MADONNA-RODY O'SHAUGHNESSY-JOHNSON.[2] The silent mourners turned away and the curious crowd gathered nearer then to read the simple epitaph and wonder on the strangely curious name.

THE CHICAGO TRIBUNE: SATURDAY, JULY 1, 1899.

The Spanish-American War

(Cuba, 1898)[3]

The trenches and blockhouses at Daiquiri and Siboney had been charged and taken without the sight of a Spaniard or the firing of a shot by the land forces. The fight of the Rough Riders and black troopers at Guasimas five days before had taken place before all of the troops were debarked. It was by easy stages of reckoning, therefore, that so many of the soldiers and camp followers had formed and were holding a vague sort of opinion . . . that the campaign meant hunger and discomfort and nothing more. . . . It was then the firm opinion of every one whom I heard express himself that the Spaniards would not fight.

At sundown the transports moved out to the horizon line and to the west from Siboney one could see dimly in the distance the blue smoke from the funnels of the warships on the blockading station before Morro Castle . . . .

Columns of mounted Mambises of Cuban soldiers were moving back and forth in restless, nomadic fashion. It was being discussed by the soldiers whether they would fight. Those who were in the fight at Guasimas were saying they would not. The remainder of the army seemed loath to relinquish the opinion it had formed in the United States of the bravery of the Mambises.

Many officers and camp followers were complaining because [General] Garcia had signalized his arrival at Siboney by issuing an order that no Cubans should act as servants to Americans. The enervating climate was causing men to wish for servants who never had thought of a such a thing before in their lives.

Horses were in such demand that almost fabulous sums were offered for them and no questions asked. Many of Garcia's men had two and three pack horses besides their mounts, but none was for sale. Money was not of much value. A can of meat or a sack of tobacco was of more value in a trade than a handful of coin.

Foreign attachés who went out to the front this day were compelled to return to the beach at evening for food and shelter. The distance was variously estimated at from six to eleven miles. I always accepted the latter estimate of the distance as nearer correct. Hospitality in the army camps at the front was unknown. Regimental commanders in many instances issued orders that no guests should be received at meal times. These orders more often were intended for correspondents than any one else, for they were at liberty to walk over the mountains to the beach whenever they were hungry . . . .

A single trail extended from Guasimas out beyond the Aguadores River. There it divided: to the north Caney, to the west San Juan. It was so narrow that only in places was it wide enough for a man on horseback to pass a wagon. Into this trail the cavalry moved to advance towards San Juan to be ready to take up the fight when Lawton came swinging down on the Holguin road from Caney, and not till then. Although the firing became heavy far off on the left, its sound came no nearer.

Cavalry, infantry, and artillery were moving, halting, tangling, and glutting the trail. The sun was blazing fiercely, and the distant rattle and roar of battle was as far away on the left as when it began. Way was made for artillery to pass. The cavalry was to be in advance. The infantry of [General Jacob] Kent's command was pressing on, pausing, halting, and advancing again, and sharing the narrow road with the troopers.

The second ford of the Aguadores was crossed. The red tiles could be seen on the old building on a hill to the left that was afterwards to become the objective point of Kent's division. Here was a small, sandy flat, and here a jam of men and guns was formed. It was here the men of the Seventy-first New York set up a cheer, and it was here, and behind and in front of the ford that most of those fell who died to make San Juan a name to live in American history. The Spaniards in the red roofed house and in the trenches in front of it found the range of that mass of men jammed in the trail about the ford, and that is why it is called the "bloody angle." The sending up of the observation balloon served to bring the fire of the enemy on those who were resting in comparative safety farther back waiting to advance.

It was 12:20 o'clock when the head of Wikoff's brigade crossed the ford, and the men were deployed quickly to the left and exposed to the fire from the trenches. It was here Wikoff fell. He was a hero of the civil war, and one who had done more than his share of Indian fighting, and had lost an eye in battle. It is believed he was killed by a Spanish sharpshooter in a tree behind the American lines. Lieutenant Colonel Worth of the Thirteenth Infantry succeeded to the command of the brigade, and he almost immediately was wounded. Lieutenant Colonel Liscum of the Twenty-fourth [African-American infantry regiment, nicknamed "Buffalo Soldiers"] succeeded Worth, and he dropped with a Spanish bullet in his shoulder. Lieutenant Colonel Ewers of the Ninth Infantry then took command of the brigade, which had lost three commanders in thirty minutes.

The brigade under Pearson came up and crossed the knoll a little farther to the right and came down into the flat. Hawkins' brigade on the right of the division was crossing the flat in skirmish order to the sunken road under the lee of the strongly intrenched and vigorously defended blockhouse hill. Best's light battery was firing at intervals, and Parker's Gatling guns were sweeping the line of white straw hats and blue jackets that surmounted the yellow clay strips on the brow of the hill. The cavalry division was moving up to the slope of the next two hills on the right, which also were intrenched and being manfully held by straw-hatted Castilians.

A charge was made across the flat and straight for the blockhouse. The men came up out of the sunken road, scaling the steeper side of the steep hill. The Gatling guns were raking the trenches. A white flag was waved on the hillside. It was a signal for the machine guns to stop their hail to let the infantry charge. The Spaniards were leaping from the trenches. A cheer came down the hillside.

The retreat from the blockhouse was followed by the desertion of the five hills of the San Juan chain, and the outer defenses of the city were taken.

Lawton was still fighting at Caney. San Juan Hills had been taken contrary to orders. But then the fight of the Rough Riders at Guasimas was made and won contrary to orders. After the hills were taken there was no feeling of security. The cavalrymen sent to Kent for reinforcements. Bates was hurried back from Caney when that village finally was taken, and his brigade was intrenched that night on the left of the blockhouse hill.

The arrival of three regiments of volunteers that afternoon at Siboney was welcomed as a providential coming. The Ninth Massachusetts Volunteers were debarked in haste, dumped in the surf, hurried out over the hills to the front without stopping for supper or blanket rolls, and put in Bates' brigade to help hold the San Juan Hills.

Playboy of the Western World

(*Chicago, 1912*)[4]

Why Irishmen should feel themselves incited to interference on seeing these Irish actors in "The Playboy of the Western World" goes over my head as fairly as Kathleen-ni-Houlihan went over the heads of those who made up the audience at the Grand last night.

I saw no one making his way yawningly out during the show. Therefore I take it, if there were any in the audience of Irish heritage he was like myself, not there to be merely entertained. And not there to be thrilled. And not there to experience the downpull of his moral standards. Like me, he must have been there to observe for some critical purpose.

I remained until the play was finished. I did it so that I might be able to write this after honestly saying I had sat it through. I suppose the others who remained to the close were impelled by some sense of duty.

The play is not salacious at all, comparatively speaking. I have seen many plays that were filthier in any one of various scenes than this play is in its whole length. In that respect it will prove perhaps a serious disappointment.

It is not an attack on any particular church. But considered in the light of a layman's knowledge of Christian doctrine it negotiates a somewhat slimy contact with the average American view of Christianity. I gathered my notions on this subject in Missouri, where I was born and where I passed my early years. But I know something of the Irish notion too. I am heir to it. And I have foot toured Ireland. The Irish are an intensely Christian people — Catholics and Protestant, both here and in Ireland. Their Christianity may be latent, but it never dies. So it is not any surprise to me that any sort of Irishman would feel unpleased while listening to this play. I do not mean that he would be impulsive in displeasure, but rather accusingly wondering why he was there.

It is just Irish enough to be extremely remote from truth. It is Irish in some of its habiliments. Some other of its wrappings were brought from cities larger than any in Ireland. Still there is enough of the Irish in its aspect on which to base an argument.

As a piece of handicraft I regard it as Irish in its execution, but not in its construction.

As a piece of literature, "The Playboy of the Western World" is a vapid hoax.

Its cleverness is not sufficiently in evidence to justify it on that score. It is unpretty, but not enough so to excite anybody mentally. Even its squalor is labored and uninteresting.

The only thing about this whole "Playboy" affair that really interests me is the press agenting it has. This is good work. As an advertising expert I consider it the finest thing of its kind. Even the declining Manchu dynasty of Ireland has seemingly been ransacked in the interest of press agent efficiency.

The Irish-American of any generation who would throw an egg or a dead cat over the footlights at the "Playboy" is certainly not of any class of my acquaintances.

No Irish-American, I am sure, would interfere with the performance of his own volition. They are too tender-hearted.

The "Playboy," however, may do a great deal of good by calling attention to the rising school of clever young writers in Ireland, of whom Synge, who confected the "Playboy," could hardly be called one in spirit.

A Missouri-
Irish Haunting

Bishop John Joseph Hogan Recalls[1]

It was now the autumn of 1864, the fourth year of the [civil] war. The wildest terror overspread North Missouri. Bushwhackers and guerillas were everywhere. Murders, robberies, and burnings were of daily occurrence. And above all places, Chariton County was the theatre of dark and atrocious crimes. The Mulhollands and Shaughnessys abandoned their homes, and fled for greater safety; some to Brookfield, some to St. Catherine's, and some to Center Point. I noticed that these terror-stricken refugees were regular attendants at Mass at Brookfield, on days appointed for Mass there — the fourth Sunday of each month. One of the Shaughnessys, with his family, occupied temporarily the vacant residence of a Squire Sportsman, close by the railroad, on the east bank of East Yellow Creek, near Center Point; the Squire having fled from the place and gone to California at the beginning of the war. The Squire's log mansion, the first built and longest inhabited house in that part of the country, did not, as the event proved, entirely suit the tastes of the newcomers. No doubt it was so, because they were the first to make the sign of the cross within its walls, and to shake the holy water over its foundations. We have heard of a strong city long ago, the walls of which fell down, when assaulted by the prayers of the servants of the Lord, and if the Missouri Squire's log castle did not come down so readily in a tumble, it was, as we shall see, because there was in it unbeknown, "a strong armed man determined to keep his court." (St. Luke 11:21.)

On a Sunday after Mass at Brookfield, the Center Point Shaughnessys, attended by many of their neighbors, called on me for consultations and advice. They said that since they had occupied the Sportsman residence, they were subjected to terrors of an extraordinary kind. That, commencing with sunset, and between that time and nightfall, loud knocking noises were frequently heard, within, outside, and under the floor of the house; and that these noises were so strange and unusual as to cause the dogs to howl, and the fowls to fly off their roost. They said also, that at these times, a man, strange and unknown to them, was usually seen walking outside, around the house, and from the house to an outside kitchen, close by the end of the house, and that upon search being made for him, he was nowhere to be found. Furthermore, they averred, that during the hours of the night, the beds, doors, windows, and furniture of the house rattled and shook, and that the house itself seemed to move and sway on its side. Yet, when they arose and lighted the lights, the commotion usually had ceased, and nothing seemed disturbed, or out of order. The strange visitor that was so often seen around the premises, was noticed by persons outside the house, to pass directly from the door; and yet, upon inquiry, the inmates had no knowledge of the presence of such a person amongst them. These facts were testified to before me, by persons living in the house, and by outsiders — catholic and non-catholic — who had gone to the house through curiosity, or in order to find out the imposition, if such had been practiced there. Several testified, these were chiefly men, that when they heard the noises, and the hammering on the floor under their feet, where there was neither space nor cellar that they hastened out of the house, and could not be induced to return there. Those that I examined were persons above suspicion of collusion or deceit; and I found that were I to continue the examination, as many as forty could be produced, witnesses of these facts, and present when they had occurred. There was nothing left for me to conclude, that these terrified people were convinced, as I was by their testimony, that the case was one of supernatural agency.

BEELZEBUB CAST OUT

Mr. Shaughnessy and his wife besought me to go with them to their house, to stay with them there that night, and to say Mass for them there the next morning. For this I did not feel prepared, especially as I was convinced that I would have to meet there a vexing evil spirit. I replied that I was not ready just then, but that I would soon appoint a time to be with them, of which I would give them due previous notice, so all could assist at Mass and receive the sacraments. Mindful of the rebuke of Our Lord to his Apostles, who, although having received power from Him to cast out devils in His name (St. Luke 10:17), were nevertheless unable to do so, for want of certain necessary virtues in themselves (St. Mark 9:28); I thought it to be my duty, and in a measure necessary for my safety, to make a spiritual retreat of some days in prayer and fasting. Accordingly I entered into retreat. But scarcely had I begun, when I was obliged to go on a sick call, east of Center Point, in the direction of Macon City. Having attended the sick call, it was in order for me to insist with myself on keeping a good rule I had made with myself for my better guidance; never to delay unnecessarily at a place from home, after my duty there had been complied with. So, taking the first train that came along, which happened to be a freight train, I was soon on my way westward, towards Brookfield and Chillicothe. Naturally my mind reverted to the Sportsman Log House, now a place of grave concern to me, towards which the train was hurrying, and close by which the train was to stop, at a water tank at East Yellow Creek. I remembered, from my many former journeys on freight trains over the same place, that with the engine at a stop, taking water at the tank, the caboose, always the hindmost car of the train, rested so near the Sportsman house, as to be within a few feet of it, across the fence, by the side of the track. Accordingly, as the train approached the place, I prepared myself for the opportunity by holding the ritual open in my hand, with the words of Exorcism on the page before me. Going out on the rear platform of the car, as it came to a stop at the spot, I read from the ritual, the command to the evil spirit in possession of that place, in the name and by the power of Jesus, to depart therefrom, and never again to return thereto. Soon again the train was on its way. I was convinced that the work I had to do was done. In about a week I made inquiries whether my presence would be needed at Mr. Shaughnessy's, at East Yellow Creek. The word came back that the causes for my going there no longer existed.

"FROM AN ILL END DELIVER HIM, O LORD."
Litany for a soul departing.

Some time afterwards, I was again called to Mr. Shaughnessy's, of East Yellow Creek, but upon another business — to attend a sick man, who lived in a little house adjoining, and who was resident there when Mr. Shaughnessy took possession of the place. Arrived at East Yellow Creek, I entered the dark but not otherwise altogether uninviting little abode. I found the patient, an old, decrepit little man, very sick, and almost in immediate danger of death. I explained to him the mercies of our Heavenly Redeemer, the Son of God, who died on the cross to save sinners, and who was ever willing to pardon sinners if they would but repent of their sins, and return to Him with sorrow for what they had done, and with love for Him in their hearts. For hours I stayed by the side of this poor sick man, leaving him betimes to himself to think of himself and his God; then again returning to encourage him with suggestions and promises by renewed hopes and consolations. Through God's all-powerful and merciful grace, my prayers and exhortations were not in vain. The poor dying man put his hope and trust in God, and continually prayed to God for mercy and pardon. Seeing his good dispositions I administered the last Sacraments to him, according to his great needs. Then, helping him to make his thanksgiving, and to renew his acts of Faith, Hope and Love for God; also recommending to him to invoke the patronage and intercession of the Blessed Mother of God, and that of St. Joseph, I imparted to him the Last Blessing and Plenary Indulgence for the dying. Reluctant to leave the dark little cabin that was now a sacred place, I fondly cast a last look on the paling features of the poor man that was so dear to me. Then with a fast throbbing heart, and with eyes suffused with tears, I left that ever memorable humble scene, on which God had so mercifully cast the light of His Heavenly Countenance. Shortly afterwards, the soul of the dying Christian departed. His mortal remains were borne by loving hands, and laid side by side with the saintly dead, in the secluded little cemetery, set apart in that neighborhood for Catholic burial, in a grove on the hillside, on the verge of the prairie. It was whispered among the mourners, as they departed from the sacred place, that he who was that day laid to rest had been once a noted magician in Chariton County; and that the extraordinary occurrences at Squire Sportsman's of late, must have resulted from his presence as a dweller there.

The foregoing narrative, prepared by me in manuscript, word for word as it appears in print, was sent by me to Mr. James Shaughnessy, a surviving witness, most intimately connected with these events; my purpose for writing to him having been, to test the reliability of my memory of the facts I have recited. His answer to me is as follows: "Padgett, Chariton County,

Missouri, April 12, 1892. Right Reverend John J. Hogan; Bishop of Kansas City; Administrator of St. Joseph. Right Reverend and Dear Bishop: I received the manuscript you kindly sent me. I find it correct as I remember it. The old man who used to set charms was named David Condon. It was my brother John who lived at Sportman's. The ghost story is true as you related it. We thank you for your kind remembrance of my wife's parents — Mr. and Mrs. Mulholland; and we are greatly pleased that you have not forgotten any of us. My wife and daughter, the subjects of your narrative, send you their most respectful filial obedience and regards. Kneeling, we ask your blessing, and will ever pray for your welfare. Your humble servant, Jas. Shaughnessy."

Notes

ONE Missouri Settlers

1. Schrier, *Ireland and the American Emigration,* 5.

2. McCaffrey, *Irish Diaspora in America,* 62–69.

3. US Census 1860, at Milford, MASS, *sub* Thomas Shaughnessy (aged 35); US Census 1900, at Chariton County, MO, *sub* Thomas Shaughnessy (aged 76); Massachusetts Historical Commissions, *Milford,* 8–9. This Thomas was born in 1823, and so was older than James, but did not enter the United States until 1856.

4. Hogan, *Missouri and Memoir,* 181. Not until 1860 was a railway bridge built across the Mississippi, from Chicago to Davenport, Iowa, about 140 miles north of Hannibal, Missouri.

5. *Ballou's Pictorial Drawing-Room Companion,* Mar. 14, 1857, 168; O'Laughlin, *Irish Settlers,* 60; Towey, "Irish Americans in St. Louis," 139–59; McCandless, *History of Missouri,* 2, and Parrish, *History of Missouri,* 3, *passim.*

6. US Census 1870, Chariton County, MO, *sub* "Shaunessy" (James, Thomas and John); Anon., *Howard and Chariton Counties,* 506; Anon., "Obituary" [1]. Also in 1861 his brother John became father to a boy born in Boston, Massachusetts, whom he named James.

7. Edwards, *Illustrated Atlas of Chariton,* 46; *Plat Book of Chariton County,* 28.

8. Miller, *Emigrants and Exiles,* 315; Miller, *Ireland and Irish America,* 348, who notes that 27 percent of German, 25 percent of British and 46 percent of Scandinavian immigrants then worked in US farming.

9. Miller, *Ireland and Irish America,* 253.

10. O'Shaughnessy, "250th anniversary," 210; O'Gorman, *Irish Fellowship Club,* p.161, under James O'Shaughnessy in the biographies of its presidents.

11. Anon., *History of Linn County,* 121–22, 642–43; Anon., "Obituary" [1]; *Chicago Daily News,* Apr. 22, 1948; Hogan, *Missouri 1857–1868,* 3–5, 9–11, 73; Miller, *Ireland and Irish America,* 259. Hannibal was home to Samuel Clemens ("Mark Twain") who left it in 1853 aged eighteen. It appears under fictional guises in Twain's *Tom Sawyer* and other works (Rasmussen, *Twain,* ii, 712–14).

12. Chariton County, MO, Keytesville Courthouse, Deeds, Book Q, 170–71 (Mar. 31, 1857); Anon., *Howard and Chariton Counties,* 505–6 for Demsey, described in 1883 as having been "a man of considerable note" in the county. There is today a Demsey Road at Salt Creek.

13. Hogan, *Missouri 1857–1868*, 6–8, 37–41, including a striking description of the circumstances in which some slaves were transported.

14. Chapman, *Buchanan and Clinton Counties*, 550–52.

15. Hogan, *On the Mission in Missouri*; Payton, *Irish Wilderness*; Brown, *Irish-American Nationalism*, 353–54.

16. Hogan, *Missouri 1857–1868*, 156–60.

17. Ibid., 160.

18. 1860 US Census gives Catherine's birthplace as Pennsylvania; Chariton County, MO, Keytesville Courthouse, Register Book AB, 40 (filed Apr. 22, 1864) records Hogan's name on the register of marriages where he is identified as "Catholic Priest"; Hogan, *Missouri 1857 1868*, 118; O'Shaughnessy, "General James Shields," 115.

19. Chariton County, MO, Keytesville Courthouse, Deeds, Book W, 233–34 (Feb. 5, 1864). There is no prefix "O" on the surname on this deed.

20. Hogan, *Missouri 1857–1868*, 161–62.

21. James, b. July 1865, John P., b. Aug. 1868, Thomas Augustin, b. Apr. 1870, Francis, b. Feb. 1872, Anna/Annie, b. Mar. 1873, Martin, b. Jan. 1876 and Mary, b. Oct. 1882 (birth years except Lizzie from 1900 Federal Census). Lizzie married Thomas Berney but died aged thirty in childbirth at Long Beach, California, in 1894. Annie married one William Cullen (US Censuses 1900 and 1910; http://www .findagrave.com/cgi-bin/fg.cgi?page=gr&GRid=59436262 and =58744744). Lizzie's child would be born safely even as she expired and be named James and reared by his grandparents Catherine and James.

22. Anon., *History of Howard and Chariton Counties*, 382.

23. Ibid., 405.

24. Hogan, *Missouri 1857–1868*, 162–69. See appendix 2.

25. 1870 US Census at Chariton County, MO, sub O'Shaughnessy; Passport application of James O'Shaughnessy Junior, 1924 (via ancestry.com); *Printers' Ink Monthly*, Aug. 1929, 16.

26. Chariton County, MO, Keytesville Courthouse, Deeds, Book 3, 263 (Indenture, Sept. 25, 1869).

27. North Missouri Railroad Co., *Facts for Emigrants*, 24.

28. Anon., *History of Howard and Chariton Counties*, 374.

29. Hogan, *Missouri 1857–1868*, 7; Obama at the White House, St. Patrick's Day 2011 and Dublin, May 23, 2011.

30. Hogan, *Missouri 1857–1868*, 23, 123–24; Baskin, *Clinton County*, 368; *New York Times*, Oct. 16, 1866.

31. Chapman, *Buchanan and Clinton Counties*, 550; Anon., *History of Linn County, Missouri*, 65; Conard, *Encyclopedia of the History of Missouri*, v, 441.

32. Anon., *Howard and Chariton Counties*, 714; Hogan, *Missouri 1857–1868*, 1–3, 15,

25, 34–5.

33. AIHS, "Biographies"; Anon., "Obituary" [1].

34. *Columbia Statesman,* Mar. 3, 1876.

35. Miller, *Ireland and Irish America,* 348.

36. *Columbia Missouri Statesman,* Mar. 3, 1876; US Census 1880 *sub* James Shaughnessy; *Moberly Daily Monitor,* Aug. 25, 1883; *Printers' Ink Monthly,* Aug. 1929, 16; Enclosure with letter from James O'Shaughnessy to George O'Gillingham, Feb. 13, 1931 (Duke MSS, O'Shaughnessy Papers, Box 1, File 7); Anon. "People Talked About," 8; Katzenberger, *Phi Delta Phi,* 337; Minogue, *Loretto Annals,* 177, 236; Waller, *Randolph County,* 184–85; *Chicago Daily News,* June 5, 1931; *Moberly Monitor Index,* Nov. 17, 1972; Saloga, "Stained Glass."

37. AIHS, "Biographies"; O'Shaughnessy, "General James Shields," 121; Anon., "Obituary" [1].

38. O'Shaughnessy, "General James Shields" (Nov. 12, 1914), 113, 121–22.

39. Anon., "Obituary" [1].

40. *Catholic Tribune,* Mar. 9 and 16, 1889.

41. Hoye, *St. Joseph,* 455. Information in the 1890 directory appears somewhat out of date as it gives the family's home address on Faraon and not North, to which the records of the local De La Salle Brothers college indicate that they had moved about 1887.

42. For St. Joseph in 1882, including fine earlier sketches, see Anon., *Linn County,* 103–28.

43. Quotation cited but undated on the City of St. Joseph's home webpage (http://www.ci.st-joseph.mo.us/history/history.cfm); O'Laughlin, *Irish Settlers,* 59, 152–63; Burnett and Luebbering, *German Settlement in Missouri, passim.*

44. [Rutt], *Buchanan County and St. Joseph, Mo,* 550–51 (introduction states these chapters were first published in the *Daily News*); De La Salle Brothers, *Mississippi Vista,* 167–78. The De La Salle religious order, founded by Jean-Baptiste de la Salle, came to be known as the "Christian Brothers," and its members are to be distinguished from the Irish "Christian Brothers" whose order was founded by Edmund Ignatius Rice.

45. I am grateful to Brother Robert Werle FSC, archivist, for searching the De La Salle Christian Brothers Archives — Midwest District, at Christian Brothers University, Memphis, TN. The family was at 1120 Faraon St. in 1886–1887, but at 917 North St. the following year. In the class list for 1887–1888 there appears only Augustin Shaughnessey. No other Shaughness[e]y (nor O'Shaughness[e]y) is found in the record book, and none appears to have graduated there.

46. Bonner, "History of Illustration": *Music Trade Review,* Nov. 1, 1919; McNamara, *Heavenly City,* 13; Barton, "Celtic Revived," 85. On 23 November 1892 Thomas wrote a homesick letter to his brother Frank on paper headed "City Editor's Desk" of the office of the daily *Pueblo Chieftain* (U. Notre Dame, CTAO 1/07).

47. Enclosure with letter from James O'Shaughnessy to George O'Gillingham, Feb. 13, 1931 (Duke MSS, O'Shaughnessy Papers, Box 1, File 7); Anon. "People Talked About," 8; *Printers' Ink*, Dec. 8, 1950.

48. ibid., AIHS, "Biographies," 546.

49. Davitt, *Fall of Feudalism in Ireland*, 204–5; O'Day, "Media and Power: Charles Stewart Parnell's 1880 Mission to North America," 202–19.

50. *Catholic Tribune*, Mar. 2 and 23, and June 22, 1889.

51. Ibid., Mar. 2 and 9, 1889.

52. Johnson, "Reminiscences" (Jan. 28, 1934).

53. If "Montmorency" was indeed Montgomery then Johnson may also have erred about her spouse being a Kentuckian, or perhaps that relationship soon ended, for Montgomery married Preston R. King from Atchison, Kansas, in 1894.

54. Olson, *Owen*, ch. 3.

55. May Montgomery King to James O'Shaughnessy, undated but 1929; James O'Shaughnessy to May Montgomery King, Kansas City, Nov. 8, 1929 (Duke MSS, O'Shaughnessy Box 1, File 3); *Nevada* [Missouri] *Daily Mail*, Oct. 19, 1886; *New York Herald*, Jan. 13 and 21, 1867; Organ, *County Press of Missouri*, 275, 286, 296; Dudley Clarke, *Lineage Book*, 289; Conard, *Encyclopedia of the History of Missouri*, vol. 3, 42.

56. Johnson, "Reminiscences" (Jan 28, Feb. 4 and 18, Mar. 11, 1934).

57. Hillier, "Albert Johnson," 193–94, 208.

58. Rutt, *Buchanan County and St. Joseph, Mo.*, 309–10.

59. Letter from James O'Shaughnessy to May Montgomery King, Nov. 8, 1929 (Duke MSS, O'Shaughnessy Papers, Box 1, File 3).

60. Chicago Historical Society, *Encyclopedia*, at "Illinois and Michigan Canal."

61. Johnson, "Reminiscences" (Jan. 28, 1934).

TWO   James O'Shaughnessy, Star Reporter

1. Organ, "County Press of Missouri," 111, 116; O'Laughlin, *Irish Settlers*, 36–42.

2. Walsh, *World's Debt to the Irish*, 328–29; Glazier, ed., *Encyclopedia*, 484–87 (by Terry Galway).

3. *Catholic Tribune*, June 29, and July 6, 1889; *American Newspaper Directory*, 1886, 341; Ayers, *Annual 1890*, 1,890; [Rutt], *Buchanan County and St. Joseph*, 185, 316, 358; O'Laughlin, *Irish Settlers*, 36–42. Born in Dublin in 1837, Francis Graham was the son of a Protestant builder who converted to Catholicism when he married.

4. Ayers, *Annual 1888*, 285; Chapman, *Buchanan and Clinton Counties*, 447–8; AIHS. "Biographies," 456. The Ayer's annual catalog does not in every case give consistently similar information for each year, and details of the editor of the *Catholic Tribune* are omitted for other years during the 1880s.

5. Anon, *Linn County*, 61; Conard, *Encyclopedia of Missouri*, v, 440–41; Organ,

"County Press of Missouri."

6. Anon., *History of Linn County, Missouri*, 128.

7. *Catholic Tribune,* June 29, and July 6, 1889, for the policy of its new owners, Michael Lawlor and Peter Nugent,

8. Johnson, "Reminiscences" (Jan. 28, 1934).

9. Ibid. See appendix 1 for the report by O'Shaughnessy.

10. His grandniece Brigid O'Shaughnessy kindly furnished the author with a copy of this photograph.

11. *New York Herald,* June 11, 1894; US Department of State, Passport Application, 1924. Accessible online (e.g., via ancestry.com); AIHS, "Biographies," 546; *Printers' Ink,* Dec. 8, 1950, 72.

12. Press release (Duke MSS, AAAA Records, AF2); *Printers' Ink Monthly,* Aug. 1929, 16; Farnum, *Pawnee Bill,* 11.

13. Associated Advertising Clubs of the World press release, 1924 (Duke MSS, AAAA Records, AF2).

14. Rhodes, *Ethnic Press,* 141–42.

15. Bonner, "Illustration."

16. Mott, *American Journalism,* 561.

17. *New York Times,* June 1, 1907; *Daily Globe,* Apr. 27, 1944; Finnegan, "Social Responsibilities of the Newspaper," 168; O'Gorman, *Irish Fellowship Club,* 169; *This Is Your Life,* May 9, 1956 (posted by his great-grandson Thomas J. Loarie on YouTube http://www.youtube.com/watch?v=TlhtyvxJqIc).

18. James O'Shaughnessy to Morrissey, Aug. 21, 1897 (University of Notre Dame MS UPEL 55/28).

19. Brown, *Correspondents' War:* Dunne, *Peace and War;* Fanning, *Finley Peter Dunne and Mr. Dooley: The Chicago Years,* 185–200; Fanning, *Mr. Dooley and the Chicago Irish, passim;* Fanning, "Dooley Reconsidered," 72–83.

20. Hearst, *Hearst,* 60; Mott, *American Journalism,* 533–35.

21. Hearst, *Hearst,* 54–57.

22. Ibid.; Emery and Emery, *The Press and America,* 249–56; Campbell, *Yellow Journalism,* 71–150; Campbell, *The Year That Defined American Journalism: 1897,* 137.

23. Gleijeses, "1898," 685 note 12, 692–95; Nofi, *Spanish-American War,* 46–47.

24. Gleijeses, "1898," 710–11.

25. *Chicago Daily Tribune,* June 29, 1899.

26. Ibid., June 29, and July 1, 1899 ("In Front of Santiago a Year Ago Today").

27. Ibid., June 29, 1899.

28. Ibid., July 1, 1899.

29. Parker, *Rear-Admirals Schley, Sampson and Cervera,* 283.

30. Brown, *Correspondents' War,* 435.

31. James O'Shaughnessy to Andrew Morrissey, Oct. 5, 1898 (U. Notre Dame MS

UPEL 66/16).

32. Email to author, Feb. 27, 2012. I am grateful to Ms Kindig for sending me photographs of the flags.

33. O'Gorman, *Irish Fellowship Club,* 161.

34. Simpson; *Harper's Pictorial History of the War with Spain,* ii. 342–44; Nofi, *Spanish-American War,* 150–51; McCaffrey, *Inside the Spanish-American War,* 91–108.

35. AIHS, "Biographies," 546–47 (says he was there for the *Chronicle*); Conner to Editor, *Grays Harbor Washingtonian,* Feb. 4, 1934 (says he was there for *the Inter-Ocean*); *Printers' Ink,* Dec. 8, 1950, 72; Anon. "People Talked About," 8; Matsen, "The Battle of Sugar Point."

36. O'Brien, "The Chicago Press and Irish Journalists," 125; Funchion, "Irish Chicago," 86.

37. James O'Shaughnessy to Andrew Morrissey, Feb. 27, 1899 (U. Notre Dame MS UPEL 74/05).

38. Stone, *Fifty Years a Journalist,* 229–30.

39. Brown, *Correspondents' War,* 433.

40. Underwood, *Chronicling Trauma,* 114–16.

41. Francis O'Shaughnessy to Andrew Morrissey, Aug. 21, 1900 (U. Notre Dame MS UPEL 111/27).

42. Henning, "Colorful Reporters of 1900."

43. Henning, "New Reporter Is Last Hired, So First Fired."

44. Henning, "Colorful Reporters"; Henning, "New Reporter"; *Los Angeles Times,* Dec. 27, 1900.

45. James O'Shaughnessy to Andrew Morrissey, July 3, 1899 (U. Notre Dame MS UPEL 74/11).

46. *Dublin Daily Express,* July 22, 1898; *San Francisco Call,* Oct. 4, 1899; Stone, *Fifty Years a Journalist,* 239; Arceneaux, "News on the Air," 168.

47. Enclosure with letter from James O'Shaughnessy to George O'Gillingham, Feb. 13, 1931 (Duke MSS, O'Shaughnessy Papers, Box 1, File 7).

48. Charles Edward Russell, *Bare Hands and Stone Walls,* 137.

49. Ibid., 131–47 with cartoon; Mott, *American Journalism,* 573–75; Vaughn, *Encyclopedia of American Journalism,* 309–10.

50. Emery, Emery and Roberts. *The Press and America,* 217.

51. Koenigsberg, *King News,* 270–72.

52. Lundberg, *Imperial Hearst,* 67.

53. AIHS, "Biographies," 546–47.

54. Enclosure with letter from James O'Shaughnessy to George O'Gillingham, Feb. 13, 1931 (Duke MSS, O'Shaughnessy Papers, Box 1, File 7); Associated Advertising Clubs of the World press release, 1924 (Duke MSS, AAAA Records, AF2).

55. *Chicago Daily Tribune*, Sept. 20, 1906; *Chicago Blue Book 1908*, 111; AIHS, "Biographies," 546–47.

56. Digby-Junger, "'The Main Rendezvous for Men of the Press,'" 85.

57. Davis, "The Journalism of New York," 217.

58. *Time*, Aug. 28, 1933.

59. Norton Smith, *The Colonel*, 136–37.

60. Ibid., 137–38.

61. *Time*, July 29, 1929 ("Specialist Called").

62. *The Day Book* ("An Adless Daily Newspaper"), July 14, and Aug. 7, 1913; Lundberg, *Imperial Hearst*, 152–63.

63. Kilroy, *The Playboy Riots, passim*.

64. Richards, "Brogue Irish," 47; Kibler, "Pigs, Green Whiskers, and Drunken Widows," 489–94.

65. *New York World*, Nov. 26, 1911; O'Donovan, "Aim of Irish Players," 101. Leading roles in the touring *Playboy* were performed by O'Donovan as Christy Mahon, Eithne McGee as Pegeen Mike, and Sara (Sally) Allgood as the Widow Quinn. Allgood would later be nominated for an Academy Award for her part in the film *How Green Was My Valley* (1941).

66. Watt, "Irish American Drama," 99.

67. Gregory, *Our Irish Theatre*, 241–45.

68. Hammond, "Playboy."

69. Gregory, *Our Irish Theatre*, 203–06.

70. *Boston Sunday Globe*, July 8, 1923; Estrin, *Conversations with Eugene O'Neill*, 39–40; Shaughnessy, *Down the Nights and Down the Days*, 23–24.

71. Hammond, "Playboy," in *Chicago Tribune*, Feb. 7, 1912.

72. Gregory, *Our Irish Theatre*, 239–40.

73. *Chicago Tribune*, Feb. 7, 1912.

74. Ibid.

75. Lockwood Williams, *School of Journalism*, 3. The École Supérieure de Journalisme in Paris taught journalism earlier but did not offer a distinct journalism degree until later.

76. *Advertising and Selling*, May 5, 1926, 92.

77. Williams, *School of Journalism*, 395.

THREE Rising Fortunes in Chicago

1. Meagher, *Columbia Guide to Irish American History*, 103.

2. Johnson, "Reminiscences" (Jan. 28, 1934); Shanabruch, *Chicago's Catholics*, 42, 114–15. See also Meager, *Inventing Irish America*, 240–44.

3. Nilsen, "Irish Language in New York," 253; Glazier, ed., *Encyclopedia*, 470–74;

Meagher, *Inventing Irish America*, 240–44; Meagher, *Columbia Guide to Irish American History*, 268–69.

4. O'Neill, *Catholic Directory of Illinois 1906–1907*, 180–81 (2220 Lincoln to 4705 North Winchester); Anon., "Obituary" [2].

5. Meagher, *Inventing Irish America*, 16, 240.

6. Miller, "Assimilation and Alienation," 89–90; Doyle, "Irish in Chicago," *passim.*

7. Skerrett, "Irish Americans in Chicago," 117–38.

8. Burns, *Notre Dame Story*, i, 18.

9. Ibid., i, 135.

10. *Chicago Law Directory 1913–1914*, 4, 80; *Ottawa* [Illinois] *Free Trader*, June 17, 1910; Hope, *Notre Dame*, ch. 19; Burns, *Being Catholic*, i, 33. University of Missouri archivist Gary Cox emails me that John "is listed as a junior in the Law Department in the 1894 Catalog."

11. AIHS, "Biographies," 546–47; *Scholastic* 53, 411 (Apr. 24, 1920).

12. Francis O'Shaughnessy to Andrew Morrissey, Aug. 21, 1900 (U. Notre Dame MS UPEL 111/27); Burns, *Being Catholic*, i, 33.

13. Correspondence between Gus and James O'Shaughnessy and Andrew Morrissey relating to outstanding bills (U. Notre Dame MSS UPEL 55/17, 55/26, 61/40, 74/05, 74/07, 74/18, 111/10). Angela Kindig, archivist at Notre Dame, emails Feb. 17, and June 11, 2012.

14. Hope, *Notre Dame*, 257; Moore, "Academic Development, University of Notre Dame," ch. 5.

15. Burns, *Notre Dame Story*, i, 79; Heisler, *Fighting Irish*, 14.

16. *Notre Dame vs. Kentucky, Jan. 26, 1946.* Sports program. University of Kentucky, KY Digital Library. http://eris.uky.edu/catalog/xt79gh9b637v_9/text?

17. Burns, *Notre Dame Story*, i, 136–37; Glazier, ed., *Encyclopedia*, 144; Sperber, *Notre Dame Football*, 79–81.

18. *Scholastic*, Dec. 9, 1932, p. 18; *Spokesman-Review*, Feb. 15, 1981 (Spokane, WA). Also *News and Courier*, Feb. 15, 1981 (Charleston, SC); Heisler, *Fighting Irish*, 14–15.

19. *Spokesman-Review*, Feb. 15, 1981 (Spokane, WA); also News and Courier, Feb. 15, 1981 (Charleston, SC); Burns, *Notre Dame Story*, i, 79.

20. Francis O'Shaughnessy to Morrissey, Aug. 21, 1900 (U. Notre Dame MS UPEL 111/27); Burns, *Notre Dame Story*, i, 31.

21. *Scholastic*, 46, no. 37 (Junes 1913, p. 603); *Scholastic*, 51, no. 12 (Jan. 12, 1918, p. 200). Martin O'Shaughnessy to Andrew Morrissey (U. Notre Dame MSS UPEL 102/01 and 05 and 12); US Census 1910.

22. Anon., "Obituary" [2]; Thompson, *Knights*, 117, 303, and 313 for photos of Francis and Thomas; Egan and Kennedy, *Knights of Columbus*, ii, 72, 93.

23. Skerrett, "Catholic Dimension," 47

24. Cronin and Adair, *Wearing of the Green*, passim.

25. Crimmins, *St. Patrick's Day*, 5.

26. O'Growney to MacNeill from Phoenix, AZ, Mar. 16, 1899 (NLI MS 10,875, file no. 12, with obituary clipping for Murphy).

27. Cited at Overland, *Immigrant Minds, American Identities*, 2–3.

28. Cited in Drury, *Chicago in Seven Days*, 83.

29. *Chicago Daily Tribune*, Sept. 23, 1904; McLaughlin, *Irish Chicago, passim*.

30. Shanabruch, *Chicago's Catholics*, 236–37. Between 1880 and 1910 the Irish-born population of Chicago rose from 44,411 to 65,963, but the German-born population increased from 75,205 to 182,281. Taking into account men and women with at least one foreign parent, the respective figures in 1910 were 138,858 Irish and 319,551. From 1880 to 1910 the total of those born in Bohemia and Moravia who settled in Chicago more than quadrupled to 50,063, and Poles flooded in so that by 1910 there were 126,059 compared to just 5,536 thirty years earlier.

31. Shanabruch, *Chicago's Catholics*, 105, 237 (table 9).

32. Michael O'Shaughnessy posted the photograph on the internet before he died.

33. *Scholastic* 51, 200 (Jan. 12, 1918).

34. *Chicago Daily Tribune*, Jan. 8 and 9, 1918.

35. Anon., "Obituary" [1]; Anon., "Obituary" [2].

FOUR Hyphenated Immigrant Loyalties

1. Chicago Daily News, *Notable Men*, 44, 121, 161, 164, 314, 356.

2. Quoted at Onahan. "Sixty Years in Chicago," 79–80.

3. Fleming, *America in World War I*, 62–6; Buckley, *New York Irish*, 10–11.

4. Hart, *Woodrow Wilson*, 28–32, 138.

5. Joyce, *Editors and Ethnicity*, p. 17 note 37.

6. When President Kennedy visited the Republic of Ireland in 1963 he presented to its parliament the second green color of the 69th New York and spoke of that particular flag's origins in 1862.

7. O'Gorman, *Irish Fellowship Club*, 25–31, 161.

8. Wilson to O'Donnell, Mar. 18, 1918 (Chicago History Museum MS).

9. Ward, "America and the Irish Problem," 76, 80–81.

10. Miller, "Assimilation and Alienation," 87–88; Carroll, *American Opinion and the Irish Question*, 155.

11. Kelly, *The Shamrock and the Lily*, 6.

12. Diocese of Springfield, IL. http://www.dio.org/dedication/ under "Nave." (June 9, 2013); O'Shaughnessy, "Window Story," 47.

13. Ibson, *Will the World Break Your Heart?*, 105, citing Amory, *The Proper Bostonians*, 346.

14. Lears, *Fables of Abundance*, 219.

FIVE The Irish Fellowship Club and Chicago Politics

1. O'Gorman, *Irish Fellowship Club*, 5, 94; record relating to Irish Fellowship Club (City Council, Chicago, MS "Journal," Oct. 3, 2001).

2. O'Gorman, *Irish Fellowship Club*, 3–6.

3. The twenty-first triennial conclave of the American Knights Templar had taken place in Chicago in 1880, and the thirty-first would be held there in 1910.

4. Chicago Daily News, *Notable Men*, 9; Glazier, ed., *Encyclopedia*, 148.

5. *Chicago Daily Tribune*, Mar. 16, 1903.

6. O'Gorman, *Irish Fellowship Club*, 3–6, 86 (Truman), 89 (de Valera), 107 (O'Kelly), 117 (Lynch), 145 (Robinson).

7. AIHS, "Biographies," 517, 546; Koenigsberg, *King News*, 273–74; *Chicago Daily Tribune*, Jan. 14, 1904.

8. O'Gorman, *Irish Fellowship Club*, 3–6.

9. Carroll, *American Commission*, 9; Finegold, *Experts and Politicians*, 138–44; Morton, *Justice and Humanity*, 17.

10. Sullivan, *Dunne: Judge, Mayor, Governor*, 13–15, 38–39.

11. *Los Angeles Times*, Dec. 18, 1905.

12. *Chicago Daily Tribune*, Mar. 3, 1906; Carroll, *American Commission*, 9; Morton, "Illinois' Most Progressive Governor," 218–34.

13. Tarbell, "How Chicago Is Finding Herself," 127.

14. McCaffrey, "Irish-American Politics," 175.

15. Francis O'Shaughnessy to Matthew Walsh, and Walsh's reply, Apr. 1924 (U. Notre Dame MS UPWL 16/51).

16. *Chicago Daily Tribune*, Apr. 2, 1911; Finegold, *Experts and Politicians*, 157.

17. Chicago Historical Society, *Encyclopedia*, at "Era of 'Hinky Dink' and 'Bathhouse John'"; Wendt, Kogan and Jore, *Lords of the Levee*.

18. *Chicago Daily Tribune*, Apr. 2, 1911.

19. Lombardo, *Organized Crime in Chicago, passim*.

20. Shanabruch, *Chicago's Catholics*, 42, 71, 115.

21. Redmond, *The Chicago Convention*; Finerty to Redmond, Mar. 3, 1903, May 10, and June 28, 1924 (NLI MS 15,236/7); Ward, "America and the Irish Problem," 65.

22. *Chicago Daily Tribune*, Sept. 23, 1904.

23. O'Gorman, *Irish Fellowship Club*, 11.

24. Watt, "Irish American Drama," 98–9.

25. *New-York Daily Tribune*, Mar. 19, 1907; *Marion [Ohio] Daily Mirror*, Mar. 19, 1907.

26. Howard, *St. Joseph County, Indiana*, i, 517. Other speakers included Peter J. Muldoon, the Roman Catholic auxiliary bishop of Chicago, whose career in the church hierarchy was not to rise as high as his supporters hoped (Shanabruch,

Chicago's Catholics, 41).

27. *Kentucky Irish American,* July 6, 1907.

28. *Chicago Daily Tribune,* Sept. 27 and 28, 1908; Wendt, *Chicago Tribune,* 360.

29. Patrick Egan to Redmond, Feb. 18, 1910 (NLI MS 15,236/5. 26 items); *Sacred Heart Review,* 43 no. 14 (Mar. 26, 1910), 1.

30. *New York Times,* Mar. 18, 1910; O'Gorman, *Irish Fellowship Club,* 94.

31. *Evening Independent* (St. Petersburg, Florida), Mar. 17, 1910.

32. *Chicago Tribune,* Mar. 12, 1910.

33. *Evening Independent* (St. Petersburg, Florida), Mar. 17, 1910.

34. *Waterville Times,* NY, Mar. 18, 1910.

35. *New York Times,* Mar. 17, 1910; *Sporting Life,* Mar. 19, 1910; O'Gorman, *Irish Fellowship Club,* 14; Matthews, *When the Cubs Won It All,* 31; Roberts and Cunningham, *Chicago Cubs,* 81–155.

36. O'Gorman, *Irish Fellowship Club,* 13–14.

37. Press Club of Chicago. *Official Reference Book,* 25 gives him as son of "Patrick Charles and Bridget (Fahey)" (*sic*).

38. O'Gorman, *Irish Fellowship Club,* 161; Baker, "Plan of Chicago," 768.

39. Draper, J. "Planning Wacker Drive," 272.

40. William Howard Taft III, son of Roger, would become US ambassador to Ireland from 1953 to 1957, during the administration of President Dwight Eisenhower and with the active support of Roger — "who seemed to have lots of influence," according to Taft III himself (Taft interviewed by Kennedy, Apr. 30, 1987 [Association for Diplomatic Studies and Training MS]); Schmidt, *Dever;* O'Gorman, *Irish Fellowship Club,* 99, 163, 166.

six Gus and the Gaelic Revival

1. Fanning, *Mr. Dooley and the Chicago Irish,* 166–68, 199–200.

2. Harris, "Selling National Culture," 88, 90, and plates 10, 16, 42–48 and color plates 1, 2; Bowe, "Celtic Revival," 106. Johnson's work was exhibited in both the official display of the United Kingdom (of which all of Ireland was then still a part) and in at least one of the unofficial Irish villages.

3. Harris, "Selling National Culture," 85.

4. Ibid., 88, 90, 100; Barton, "Celtic Revived," 85. In fact Hart was an English philanthropist.

5. White and Igleheart, *Columbian Exposition,* 567–69 and 593–95 (with images); Bowe, "Irish Arts and Crafts Movement," 173–75; Beattie, "Cottage Industries," 66; Harris, "Selling National Culture," 96.

6. Mackay, "How Irish Colleens Were Chosen," 31–45; Oldham Eagle, *Congress of Women,* 746.

7. Oldham Eagle, *Congress of Women,* 746.

8. Morris, "Alice Milligan," 140–41; McCaffrey, *Irish Nationalism,* 6.

9. Curtis-Wilson, McCain, and Ray, "Irish Linen Story," 73; Bowe, "Imagining an Irish past," 107.

10. Holtz, *American Newspaper Comics,* 14–15, 388, and http://strippersguide .blogspot.ie/2007_09_23_archive.html on Aug. 2, 2013. O'Shaughnessy's strips included *Aesop up to Date, Easy Eddy* and *Friendly Fido,* as well as *Stub and Twist And Professor Butts.* He also contributed early to *Why Popkins Is a Bachelor* and *Tiny Tinkles,* adding "swan song" after his signature on his final strip for the latter in Sept. 1905.

11. *Chicago Daily News,* Dec. 30, 1903; Skerrett and Lesch, *Chief O'Neill,* xxiv, 293.

12. Chicago Historical Society, *Annual Report 1904,* 191, 202–4.

13. White and Igleheart, *Columbian Exposition,* 593–95, 567–69, including pictures.

14. Hennessy, "William from Galway," 3; Miller, *Emigrants and Exiles,* 285; Fitzpatrick, *Irish Emigration 1801–1921,* 11; Quinn, *Ireland and America: Their Early Associations,* 3.

15. Thompson, *Knights,* 237, 303, 313.

16. *Chicago Daily Tribune,* Aug. 5, 1908.

17. Fanning, *The Irish Voice,* 243; Norris, *Advertising and the Transformation of American Society,* 37–38 notes that in 1893 Samuel S. McClure, who was born in Ireland but arrived in America at the age of nine, produced the first issue of *McClure's,* a highly successful publication that within two years of its launch had a circulation of over a quarter of a million copies. It is said to have transformed the business of magazine advertising internationally.

18. *Chicago Daily Tribune,* Oct. 9, 1955.

19. *Pittsburgh Gazette Times,* Oct. 13, 1912.

20. *Tacoma Times,* June 17, 1912; *Chicago Daily Tribune,* Oct. 9, 1955; Abel, "Movie-Mad" Audiences, *1910–1914,* 28, 268. Ostensibly produced over three years, the film's "record budget" is said to have been bolstered from the coffers of the Knights of Columbus, and it featured nearly four hundred people in an "extraordinary number of scenes."

21. *Pittsburgh Gazette Times,* Oct. 13, 1912.

22. *Chicago Daily Tribune,* Sept. 1, 3, 4, 16, and 22, 1913, and Oct. 9, 1955.

23. Order Sons of Italy MS; Adams, "Illinois in 1956," 74.

24. *Chicago Tribune,* Oct. 9, 1955, and Oct. 12, 1992. *Chicago Daily News* online photograph archive includes images of Gus.

25. White and Igleheart, *Columbian Exposition,* 567–69, 593–95 (with images).

26. Barton, "Celtic Revived," 86, 94; McNamara, *Heavenly City,* 12–13; Walsh, *World's Debt to the Irish,* 409–10.

27. Walsh, *World's Debt to the Irish,* 409–10; Drury, *Chicago in Seven Days,* 82–3.

28. Barton, "Celtic Revived, 89–101; Skerrett, "Irish"; Skerrett, *At the Crossroads,* 24.

29. *Irish Times,* Mar. 19, 2012.

30. T[aylor], "O'Shaughnessy," 154–55. The window is preserved today in the Smith Museum of Stained Glass at Chicago's Navy Pier.

31. *Music Trade Review,* Nov. 1, 1919; Daley, *Mucha,* 19, 41–44. Thomas signed a souvenir program of the Bohemian Night dinner organized for Mucha in 1906 by the Palette and Chisel Club of Chicago ("Mucha Night, Guest Book" –paletteandchisel website). His granddaughter Brigid retains a sketch sent by Mucha to Thomas and signed by the artist with a friendly note.

32. *Chicago Daily Tribune,* Dec. 13, 1916; Saloga, "Stained Glass"; Barton, "Celtic Revived," 96.

33. *Chicago Daily Tribune,* May 2, 1916.

34. Ibid., Dec. 13, 1916; Saloga, "Stained Glass."

35. *Chicago Tribune,* Dec. 13, 1916, and Apr. 21, 1991; Thomas O'Shaughnessy to Rev. James O. McLaughlin, Miami, FL, July 13, 1923, and to Fr. James Cavanaugh (x2), Feb. 1934 (U. Notre Dame, MS CJWC 8/03); Saloga, "Stained Glass."

36. *Benedictine Voices: The News from Benedictine University* 32, no. 2 (Winter 2004). When Benedictine Hall was closed in the early twenty-first century, the windows were removed, cleaned, restored, and rededicated on Oct. 9, 2003. Four were placed in the St. Benedict Chapel in the Krasna Center and the others distributed to different buildings on the Lisle campus.

37. See http://www.findagrave.com/cgi-bin/fg.cgi?page=pv&GRid=80712143 &PIpi=51999993 for her death certificate. Barton, "Celtic Revived," 91, and Old St. Pat's Church for reference to Rose. See also Skerrett, "Canvas of Light," 9-10.

38. *Music Trade Review,* Nov. 1, 1919, quoting Charles E. Byrne of Steger and Sons Piano Co.

39. Gay, *Pleasure Wars,* 40–41; Dunne, "Molly Donohue," 6; Joyce, *Dubliners, passim.*

40. *Music Trade Review,* Nov. 1, 1919.

41. *Illinois Catholic Historical Review* 7, no. 1 (July 1924), 73, 150, 194–96, 204, 210–12, 219–20; Danckers, *Compendium of Chicago,* at Marquette.

42. *Chicago Tribune,* Mar. 4, 1936.

43. *Santa Cruz Evening News,* June 16, 1926.

44. The windows are reproduced at http://www.dio.org/dedication/ under "Nave." (June 9, 2013).

45. O'Shaughnessy, "Window Story," 47, 54.

46. Catalog of treasures of poetry and art in St. Stephen's . . . (Episcopal Diocese of Chicago MS, undated but after 1935, 1, pp 8–9); Dorn, "Sacramental Socialism of Irwin St. John Tucker," *passim.* In 1915 Tucker published his *Poems of a Socialist Priest*

(1915) with sketches by his wife, Ellen Dorothy O'Reilly, whom he had married on July 4, 1914. She was an illustrator with the *Daily Socialist* and a sister of Mary O'Reilly, one of the founders of the Chicago Teachers' Federation (Irwin St. John Tucker Papers, University of Illinois at Chicago, introductory note). Irwin and Mary each had an article on the front page of the *American Socialist* on Sept. 18, 1915.

47. Catalog of treasures of poetry and art in St. Stephen's . . . (Episcopal Diocese of Chicago MS, pp 8–9); *Chicago Daily News*, June 5, 1931; *Chicago Daily Tribune*, July 6, 1931. O'Shaughnessy also gave this church a sketch of his George Washington window in the cathedral at Springfield, IL, and "a plan for a Newspaper window, similar to that of the Artists" (ibid., 35). The Engraving Room at the *Herald and Examiner* donated a panel of the Last Supper, after da Vinci (ibid., 12).

48. Thomas O'Shaughnessy to Fr, John Cavanaugh, Feb. 15, 1934 (U. Notre Dame MS CJWC 8/3); *Chicago Tribune*, Mar. 4, 1934, Mar. 4, 1936, and Feb. 13, 1956; Adams, "Illinois in 1956," 74; Saloga, "Stained Glass"; Barton, "Celtic Revived," 85, 100.

49. Correspondence of James O'Shaughnessy (U. Notre Dame MS UPCO UPWL 16/44 and 47).

50. *Time*, Dec. 13, 1926; guide cited at http://www.irishlegends.com/pages /postcard/postcard_novoo.htm.

51. Walsh to Francis O'Shaughnessy, Dec. 29, 1925 (U. Notre Dame MS UPWL 16/49); Anthony, *Cram*, 141, 186–88.

52. Thomas O'Shaughnessy to Fr. John Cavanaugh, Feb. 10 and 18, 1934, and Memorandum for Superiors from John Cavanaugh (U. Notre Dame MS CJWC 8/3).

53. *Chicago Tribune*, Mar. 4, 1936.

54. *Scholastic* 78 (Apr. 23, 1943), 59–60; Thomas O'Shaughnessy to Roger Faherty, 1951, cited at O'Gorman, *Irish Fellowship Club*, 94.

55. Barton, "Celtic Revived," 85, 100.

56. *Chicago Tribune*, Feb. 13, 1956.

57. Opal Glass Studio http://www.opalglassstudio.com/history.html (June 9, 2013) and emails to this author.

58. Gruenke to Maher (Old St. Pat's MS; Old St. Pat's *Bulletin*, Jan. 3, 1993).

59. Thomas A. O'Shaughnessy Papers, 1892–2009 (U. Notre Dame MSS CTAO, listed at http://archives.nd.edu/findaids/ead/xml/tao.xm), for a list of some of his papers and sketches recently donated by his grandchildren. See also Skerrett, "A Canvas of Light."

SEVEN James at the Helm of US Advertising

1. Anon. "People Talked About," 8.

2. Associated Advertising Clubs of the World press release, 1924 (Duke MSS, AAAA Records, AF2).

3. *Chicago Daily Tribune*, Sept. 27 and 28, 1908; Wendt, *Chicago Tribune*, 360.

4. Stoltzfus, *Freedom from Advertising, passim*.

5. Enclosure with letter from James O'Shaughnessy to George O'Gillingham, Feb. 13, 1931 (Duke MSS, O'Shaughnessy Papers, Box 1, File 7).

6. *Chicago Daily Tribune*, Sept. 20, 1906; *Chicago Blue Book 1908*, 111; AIHS, "Biographies," 546–47.

7. US Census 1910 and 1920; (*New York Times*, Nov. 30, 1950). Their first child, known also as Mary, appears to have been christened "Mairin," a Gaelic name. Their other children were Colman, Bride, and Jane. They lived in Chicago on West Giddings Street.

8. US Census 1910 and 1920; AIHS, "Biographies," 546; *Printers' Ink*, Dec. 8, 1950, 72.

9. Mott, *American Journalism*, 593–97.

10. Coolsen, "Pioneers in Advertising," 83–84.

11. Stoddart, "Chicago — Wonder City of Advertising," 15.

12. Norris, *Advertising and the Transformation of American Society, 1865–1920, passim*.

13. *Printers' Ink*, Dec. 8, 1950, 72.

14. *Printers' Ink*, Oct. 19, 1911, 52; *Cedar Rapids Evening Gazette*, Nov. 25, 1911.

15. *Advertising and Printing*, Nov. 1912; Advertising Samples: O'Shaughnessy Advertising Company (Duke MSS, O'Shaughnessy Papers, Box 2, File 7); *Music Trade Review*, Oct. 3, 1915, and Nov. 6, 1915; *Printers' Ink*, Dec. 8, 1950.

16. O'Shaughnessy, "Modern Advertising and Modern Printing." This periodical was edited by C. E. Kimball and published in the Ravenswood neighborhood of Chicago where James's parents and some of his siblings still lived.

17. *Chicago Daily Tribune*, June 15, 1913.

18. Kenner, *The Fight for Truth in Advertising*; Bird, *This Fascinating Advertising Business*, 65–68.

19. Laird, *Advertising Progress*, 242.

20. Turnbull, "Genesis of the AAAA" (AAAA MS), 13.

21. Stoddart, "Chicago — Wonder City of Advertising," 16; *Printers' Ink*, Feb. 11, 1915, 50.

22. *Chicago Daily Tribune*, Oct. 10, 1915.

23. *San Francisco Newsletter*, Apr. 29, 1916, and *The Fourth Estate*, May 6, 1916 (clippings at Turnbull, "Genesis of the AAAA" (AAAA MS), Ex. 26–27). O'Shaughnessy Advertising Company cancelled checks, 1916, and advertising samples — O'Shaughnessy Advertising Company (Duke MSS, O'Shaughnessy Papers, Box 2).

24. O'Shaughnessy, *Paving Knowledge*; Library of Congress, *Copyright Entries*, 388; Anon., "Paving Men Advertise," 37–38 including one of the advertisements.

25. *Printers' Ink,* May 2, 1912, 64–66, and Sept. 26, 1912, 80; Thompson, *Knights,* 452–53.

26. *Printers' Ink,* Sept. 27, 1917, 85; Kilner, *Battery E in France: 149th Field Artillery Rainbow (42nd) Division,* 20, 43, 52, 89. Another of the agency's Illinois employees, George E. Schumacher, served at the Great Lakes Naval Training Station.

27. *Chicago Daily Tribune,* Apr. 27, 1917.

28. Proofs of Proceedings of the Conference of the American Advertising Agents Association, Feb. 23, 1900, and Association of General Newspaper Advertising Agents, Constitution and By-Laws, Apr. 1888 (Duke MSS, O'Shaughnessy Papers, Box 3, Files 1, 2). The chairman of the 1890 association was George Batten of New York, and its secretary was John Mahin of Chicago.

29. *Printers' Ink,* July 7, 1938, and Dec. 8, 1950.

30. Cleveland, *Agency Association Progress,* 6–7; Turnbull, "Genesis of the AAAA" (AAAA MS), Introduction and pp. 1–15; *Time,* Aug. 13, 1934. O'Keefe's copy of Presbrey's 1929 book is among the media archives of Dublin City University.

31. Lee, *The Daily Newspaper,* 360.

32. Turnbull, "Genesis of the AAAA" (AAAA MS), Introduction.

33. Creel, *How We Advertised America,* 3.

34. Kennedy, *Over Here,* 91; Vaughn, *Holding Fast the Inner Lines,* 5–6.

35. George Creel, *How We Advertised America,* 156.

36. *Printers' Ink,* Apr. 26, 1917, 86–88.

37. Creel, *How We Advertised America,* 155–58.

38. Ibid. William H. Rankin had been a vice president of the Mahin Advertising Company in Chicago when that company's president, John Lee Mahin Senior, and James O'Shaughnessy were both elected as directors of the Chicago Advertising Association. He later became known for his innovations in radio advertising (*Printers' Ink,* Oct. 19, 1911, 52, and Nov. 9, 1911, 45; Jacobs, "Advertising Agencies and the Adoption of Radio," 87–88).

39. *Printers' Ink,* Aug. 16, 1917, 20.

40. Proofs of Proceedings of the Conference of the American Advertising Agents Association, Feb. 23, 1900 (Duke MSS, O'Shaughnessy Papers, Box 3, File 1); *Printers' Ink,* June 7, 1917, 6; Turnbull, "Genesis of the AAAA" (AAAA MS), 16.

41. Printers' Ink, June 14, 1917, 65.

42. "Minutes of the Second Annual Meeting of the American Association of Advertising Agencies, Oct. 9–10, 1918" (AAAA MS), 90; *Printers' Ink Monthly,* Aug. 1929, 16.

43. Brown, "Irish-American Nationalism," 349; *Dictionary of Irish Biography* (Maureen Murphy on Ford).

44. Meyer, "Urban America in the Newspaper Comic Strips."

45. Turnbull, "Marshalling the Forces of Advertising" (AAAA MS), 1, and its

appendix for a copy.

46. Committee on Public Information, *Government War Advertising;* Creel, *How We Advertised America,* 156–58.

47. Turnbull, "Marshalling the Forces of Advertising" (AAAA MS), 1.

48. Creel, *How We Advertised America,* 156–58.

49. Turnbull, "Marshalling the Forces of Advertising" (AAAA MS), 2.

50. Kennedy, *Over Here,* 106.

51. Ibid., appendix.

52. Turnbull, "Marshalling the Forces of Advertising" (AAAA MS), its appendix for a copy.

53. History Committee, *Four Minute Men,* 12–13, 40; Kennedy, *Over Here,* 60–62, 69, 167.

54. Minutes of the Executive Board of the AAAA, Oct. 8, 1918 (Duke MSS, AAAA Records, AF2).

55. Turnbull, "Marshalling the Forces of Advertising" (AAAA MS), 2–3, who describes the surviving records of the division as "scant" and "sparse."

56. Ibid., 3.

57. *New York American,* Jan. 21, 1919.

58. Coogan, *Michael Collins,* 111–12; Maxwell, "Irish-Americans and the Fight for Treaty Ratification," 629.

59. Carroll, *American Commission,* 5, 8–20; Doorley, *Irish-American Diaspora Nationalism,* 53–62, 94–96.

60. Creel, *Ireland's Fight for Freedom,* xiii.

61. *Printers' Ink,* July 7, 1938.

62. Ibid.

63. Ibid.

64. Ibid.

65. Fox, *Mirror Makers,* 69.

66. *Printers' Ink,* July 7, 1938.

67. Turnbull," Marshalling the Forces of Advertising" (AAAA MS), 4–6.

68. Fox, *Mirror Makers,* 89–90.

69. *Boston Traveler,* Oct. 15, 1919; *Boston American,* Oct. 15, 1919; *Printers' Ink,* Dec. 8, 1950.

70. Minutes of the Executive Board of the AAAA, Jan. 13–14, 1920. (Duke MSS, AAAA Records, AF2).

71. "U.S. Will Advertise to Sell Ships," in *Advertising and Selling,* June 26, 1920, 26.

72. *Atlanta Constitution,* Feb. 4, 1921. Also see "US Shipping Board Advertisement Survey" (O'Shaughnessy Papers, Duke MSS, Box 3).

73. Turnbull, "Marshalling the Forces of Advertising" (AAAA MS), 4–7, and its appendix for AAC flyer. From 1921 until its demise, the corporation's president was

Charles W. Hoyt.

74. Stoddart, "Chicago — Wonder City of Advertising," 15.

75. *Printers' Ink,* July 7, 1938.

76. Letter from Benson to 4A's members, July 21, 1928 (AAAA MS at 4-A's NYC).

77. *Los Angeles Times,* Oct. 26, 1925; *Christian Science Monitor,* Oct. 22, 1926.

78. *Printers' Ink,* May 24, 1923, 20.

79. "Minutes of the Fifth Quarterly Meeting of the Executive Board, AAAA, New York, Oct. 8, 1918" (AAAA MS).

80. *Advertising and Selling,* Oct. 16, 1920, 14.

81. *Printers' Ink,* Oct. 17, 1918, 44–48.

82. Fox, *Mirror Makers,* 67.

83. Levin, *Edward Hopper,* 87. In 1920 Hoffman's play was made into a film of the same name, directed by Lawrence C. Windom.

84. *Printers' Ink,* July 5, 1917, 49–56, and Mar. 14, 1918, 76.

85. *Boston Traveler,* Oct. 15, 1919.

86. "Decennial Anniversary of the New York Council" (AAAA MS).

87. *Christian Science Monitor,* Mar. 22, 1923.

88. Benson, "How AAAA Works," 17–20, 125–32. Benson was the 4A's fifth president. Its first, William H. Johns, served two years because the war was still on. Johns was followed, in turn, by Harry Dwight Smith, Jesse F. Matteson, and Alfred W. Erickson. Benson would be succeeded in 1924 by Stanley Resor (Minutes of the Executive Board, Jan. 13–14, 1920, Apr. 12–13, 1921, July 12–13, 1921, Apr. 10–11, 1923, Apr. 8–9, 1924 [Duke MSS, AAAA Records, Box AF2]); Report of Morning Session of Annual Convention of AAAA, Oct. 10, 1923 (Duke MSS, AAAA Records, Box AF3)).

89. O'Shaughnessy, "The Meal Ticket of American Art"; *Advertising and Selling,* May 7, 1924, 34.

90. Lee, *The Daily Newspaper,* 361–62.

91. US Censuses 1900, 1910, and 1920; O'Shaughnessy Passport Application (NARA MS); *Printers' Ink,* Dec. 8, 1950, 72.

92. Greer, *Across with the Ad-Men,* 42, 210, 214, 226.

93. Cleveland, *Agency Association Progress,* 7–8. Cleveland had just begun, personally and anonymously, to fund a $1,000 award given annually by the American Association for the Advancement of Science, an award that continues since his death to be given in his name but that is now $25,000 each year (*Toledo-Blade,* July 30, 1951).

94. Associated Advertising Clubs of the World press release, 1924 (Duke MSS, AAAA Records, AF2).

95. O'Shaughnessy, "Constructive Cooperation," 84.

96. Presbrey, *History and Development of Advertising,* 527–28; Federal Trade Commission, *Report 1925,* 247–48; and *Report 1930,* 175.

97. See for example, O'Shaughnessy, "A.A.A.A. Service to Advertising," 14.

98. Address by James O'Shaughnessy (University of Illinois MS).

99. Elzey, "Jesus the Salesman," 151. In 1928 Barton, Durstine & Osborn merged with the Batten company, which was still being managed by William H. Johns, to form BBDO. Barton later served New York's 17th District as a Republican congressman.

100. O'Shaughnessy, "Advertising for the Country Newspaper," 13–16; Lockwood Williams, *School of Journalism*, 270–71.

101. *Los Angeles Times*, Jan. 2, 1927.

102. *Atlanta Constitution*, Jan. 22, 1928.

103. Forbes, "Early Years," 32; Coolidge, "Address."

104. Weltreklame (World Advertising) Congress, Berlin, 1912 (2 folders including booklet), and "Correspondence, 1929" (Duke MSS, O'Shaughnessy Papers, Box 2).

105. *Printers' Ink*, June 18, 1931.

106. Messinger, *Battle for the Mind*, 53.

EIGHT Two Midwestern Attorneys

1. Fratcher, *The Law Barn*, 16–17, for pictures of John graduating in 1895; Katzenberger, *Phi Delta Phi*, 337; *Scholastic* 3, 935 (June 2, 1928).

2. *New York Times*, July 3, 1909.

3. Lytle and Dillon, *From Dance Hall to White Slavery*, part 2, 107, 119–21, 124–25, 182.

4. *New York Call*, July 8, 1909; *Waterloo Semi-Weekly Courier* (Iowa), July 20, 1909.

5. *Waterloo Semi-Weekly Courier* (Iowa), July 20, 1909.

6. *New York Times*, July 2 and 12, 1909.

7. Abbott, *Sin in the Second City*, 182–3; McNeil, "The 'White Slavery' Panic," 60–61.

8. *Chicago Law Directory* 1913–1914, 4, 80; *Ottawa* [Illinois] *Free Trader*, June 17, 1910; Hope, *Notre Dame*, ch. 19; Burns, *Being Catholic*, i, 33. By August 1900 the brothers had taken offices in the Ashland Block; they later moved to the Otis Building on La Salle Street.

9. Lincoln Park, *Report*, 28–39, 46; *John Williams et al. v. City of Chicago et al.*, decided Jan. 8, 1917 (37S.Ct.142). O'Shaughnessy was one of six lawyers against Williams in the Supreme Court.

10. Matthew Walsh to Francis O'Shaughnessy, Jan. 6, 1928 (U. Notre Dame MS UPWL 10/61); O'Shaughnessy to Walsh, Mar. 5 and 27, 1923 (U. Notre Dame MS UPEL 16/58).

11. For Shields see p. 13, p. 15.

12. Chicago *Evening Post*, June 2, 1894; Fanning, "Dooley Reconsidered," 76.

13. Smiddy to McGillian, Jan. 9, 1928 (National Archives MS S4529); *Chicago Sun-Times,* Mar. 28, 1997; *Notre Dame Alumnus,* 6, no. 10 (June 28, 1928), 364; *Scholastic* 3, 935 (June 2, 1928).

14. Francis O'Shaughnessy to Matthew Walsh, May 16, 1928, and Walsh to O'Shaughnessy, May 21, 1928 (U. Notre Dame MS 16/43).

15. *Notre Dame Alumnus,* 6, no. 10 (June 28, 1928), 364.

16. *South Bend News Times,* June 4, 1928; *Notre Dame Alumnus,* 6, no. 10 (June 28, 1928), 364; *Scholastic* 3, 935 (June 2, 1928).

17. Walsh to O'Shaughnessy, June 9, 1928 (U. Notre Dame MS UPWL 5/24).

18. Glazier, ed., *Encyclopedia,* 775–76, for I. A. O'Shaughnessy. Marianne, the widow of Eileen and John J's son (John) Michael (1940–2009), has been helpful to the present author.

19. O'Donnell, *Dawn on Eternal Hills,* 33–5; James O'Shaughnessy to/from O'Donnell (U. Notre Dame MSS UPCO 6/124–6).

NINE Irish Roots

1. Death certificate and headstone of James O'Shaughnessy (Senior) give Aug. 18, 1842. US Census 1900 gives Aug. 1839. Anon., "Obituary" [1] gives his birthday as Aug. 15, 1838. It is quite possible that he himself did not know the exact date. Official registration of births in Ireland began later.

2. His entry in the US Census of 1910 gives the date of his departure from Ireland as having been 1848, although in 1924 one of his sons thought that it was "in or about 1852" (O'Shaughnessy Passport Application (NARA MS)).

3. Anon., "Obituary" [1].

4. Fahy, *Kiltartan,* 59. It is also found as "New Hall" in Galway.

5. This Colman, of Rinrush townland, states that some decades ago he removed the last stones of James Shaughnessy's old house in Newhall to use elsewhere. His own uncle Martin or "Matty" Shaughnessy immigrated to New York in the 1920s and has been identified as the man on the extreme left in a very well known photograph of eleven workers sitting on a girder having "lunch atop a skyscraper" high above Manhattan in 1932 (*New York Times,* Nov. 8, 2012)

6. Fahey, *Kilmacduagh, passim;* Blake, "O'Shaughnessy of Gort (1543–1783)," *passim;* Moran, *Galway,* 109–10, 176, 213, 220; Fahy, *Kiltartan,* 22.

7. Fahy, *Kiltartan,* 34–5. Coole Park house had become derelict by the 1940s and was demolished.

8. Fahy, *Kiltartan,* 78–91. Pigot's *Directory of Ireland 1824* and Slater's *Directory of Ireland 1856* give some Shaughnessys as traders in Gort, with one John Shaughnessy a bootmaker in 1856. The most substantial dwelling in the townland of Newhall in the 1830s was New Hall House, formerly the home of one Colonel Blaquiere and "in

a dilapidated state."

9. Thackeray, *Works,* v, 401–2.

10. *Galway Mercury,* Jan. 27, 1849, cited at Shovlin, *Journey Westward,* 105–6; Donnelly, *Great Irish Potato Famine,* 102, 110–12.

11. Gregory, *Sir William Gregory,* 139–41.

12. Moore Institute, at "Estate: O'Shaughnessy (Gort)"; Galway Public Library Database, at "New Hall" and "New Hall House"; Hunt, *The Abbey,* 23–24, 86; lines from "The Tower." The particular "foundations" to which Yeats refers were probably those of the Hynes family (below and Yeats, *Celtic Twlight,* 36); Smythe, *Robert Gregory 1881–1918: A Centenary Tribute,* 29. Neither the Yeats Estate not the National Library was able to say where the original sketch now is.

13. Gregory, *Kiltartan History Book,* 34–35; Fahy, *Kiltartan,* 84, 181; Census of Ireland, 1911, at Newhall for Ann Healy (aged 87).

14. Fahy, *Kiltartan,* 78; Hill, *Lady Gregory,* 310.

15. Gregory, *Poets and Dreamers,* 3, 34.

16. Hyde, *Raftery,* 11, 329–35; Fahy, *Kiltartan,* 188, 191–93.

17. Yeats, *Celtic Twilight,* 34–47; Hassett, "What Raftery Built," 97–98.

18. Yeats, *Autobiographies,* 399–400.

19. Foster, *Yeats,* i, 77–78.

20. Yeats, *Poetry,* 263–64.

21. Yeats, *Fairy and Folk Tales,* x-xviii.

22. Hogan, *Missouri 1857–1868,* 119–22.

23. Hannah Condon had been born in Co. Cork in 1832. She died in 1897. Her husband, John, uncle of James O'Shaughnessy Junior, died at Newhall, MO, on Sept. 16, 1905.

24. Yeats, *Autobiographies,* 401.

25. Bowe, "Celtic Revival," 107.

26. Sheehy, *Rediscovery of Ireland's Past,* 131–34, 156–57.

27. Harris, "Selling National Culture," 93.

28. *Irish Independent,* July 22, 1924.

29. Hickey, "Father O'Growney," 426–43; *Dictionary of Irish Biography.*

30. O'Growney to MacNeill, from Prescott, Arizona, 1895 (NLI MS 10,875, file no. 8).

31. *Freeman's Journal,* Nov. 30, 1894; O'Farrelly, *Leabhar an Athar Eoghan,* 28–34.

32. DN-0003078, *Chicago Daily News* negatives collection, Chicago History Museum. Although archived as "Painting of a cottage and trees," the word "Kil[l] aloe" is scrawled under O'Shaughnessy's signature and the "cottage" clearly resembles St. Flannan's. A related sketch of "houses at the base of a hill facing a river" (DN-0003080) also seems to be of Killaloe. Forty miles away, at Loughrea, Co. Galway, work began on the decoration of St. Brendan's Cathedral in 1897 as a

jewel of the Gaelic Revival. It is not known if Gus O'Shaughnessy ever visited it.

33. Gregory, "Why the Irish Love Ireland."

34. *Kentucky Irish American,* June 24, 1916, 1, col. 6; O'Kelleher and Schoepperle, *Life of Columcille,* ix; *Dictionary of Irish Biography,* at Lloyd for his subsequent breakdown. O'Kelleher devoted himself to editing and translating a manuscript life of St. Columcille that was in the Bodleian Library, Oxford.

35. *Chicago Daily Tribune,* Nov. 22, 1920.

36. *Dictionary of Irish Biography.*

37. *Chicago Daily Tribune,* Nov. 22, 1920.

38. Description kindly provided by Old St. Pat's Church, Chicago.

39. AAAA Records 1918–1998 (Duke MS AF2). His application to the Department of State for a passport for his trip to Europe listed his countries of destination as England, Holland, Scotland, Belgium, Ireland, Germany and France (O'Shaughnessy Passport Application [NARA MS]).

40. *Chicago City Manual 1909,* 25, for photo; *Kentucky Irish American,* Mar. 20, 1909; *New York Times,* Aug. 6, 1909; *Journal of the American Irish Historical Society,* 14 (1915), 111.

41. Illinois War Council. *Final Report,* 32, 158–61 (appendix viii); McDonald, *Insull,* 170.

42. Mullaney, *"Public relations";* Bishop and Gilbert, *Chicago's Accomplishments and Leaders,* 351; McDonald, *Insull,* 170, 184, 209; M. Goldstein, "From Service to Sales," 139.

43. Bradley, *Edison to Enron,* 156, 184. Less than two months before he departed for Europe, Mullaney gave an address to students of the College of Commerce at the University of Illinois in which he explained how he had helped to turn around the fortunes of the gas company, which had been in very bad shape, and defined the broad scope of what he meant by "public relations" (Mullaney, *"Public Relations,"* passim).

44. *Printers' Ink,* Oct. 19, 1911, 52; Buckley, *Marketing by Mail,* xiii; Bishop and Gilbert, *Chicago's Accomplishments and Leaders,* 77; Cox, *Sold on Radio,* 14; O'Gorman, *Irish Fellowship Club,* 168.

45. Print headed, "Homer J. Buckley Secretary-Treasurer Buckley, Dement and Co., Direct Mail Advertising Specialists" (Chicago, 1923).

46. Greer, *Across with the Ad-Men,* 121–22.

47. *Irish Independent,* July 22, 1924; *Irish Times,* July 26, 1924; *Weekly Irish Times,* July 26, 1924.

48. *Irish Times,* July 23, 2012.

49. *Irish Independent,* July 24, 1924. *Irish Times,* June 5, and July 24, 1924.

50. *Irish Independent,* July 24, 1924.

51. *Connacht Tribune,* Feb. 6, 1926.

52. Kenny, "Tom Grehan."

53. *Irish Independent,* July 29 and 31, 1924.

54. *Irish Times,* Aug. 1, 1924.

55. *Connacht Tribune,* Feb. 6, 1926.

56. *Irish Times,* July 30, 1924.

57. *Irish Independent,* May 21, 1927.

58. Ibid., July 5, 1927.

59. Weltreklame (World Advertising) Congress, Berlin, 1912 (2 folders including booklet), and "Correspondence, 1929" (Duke MSS, O'Shaughnessy Papers, Box 2); Mrs. O'Shaughnessy's Berlin Pin (Duke MSS, AAAA Records, AF7).

60. Grehan to O'Shaughnessy, Aug. 12 and 17 (Duke MSS, O'Shaughnessy Papers, Box 2, Files 2 and 9); *Irish Independent,* Sept. 2, 1929. For more on the publicity women see *Irish Times,* Sept. 3 and 4, 1929.

61. *Irish Independent,* Sept. 7, 1929, including photograph; *Ulster Herald,* Sept. 14, 1929. Among those present were Irish advertising pioneers Kevin J. Kenny, Brian O'Kennedy, and Charlie McConnell.

62. *Irish Times,* Sept. 6, 1929.

63. *Irish Independent,* Sept. 2, 1929.

TEN An Irish Leader in America

1. USA: Visit by Ministers 1928. Cabinet File (National Archives of Ireland S. 4529).

2. Ibid., for Smiddy to O'Hegarty, Aug. 30, 1927.

3. *Chicago Tribune,* Jan. 22, 1928; O'Kennedy-Brindley, *With the President in America,* 23; O'Gorman, *Irish Fellowship Club,* 48–51; Lewis and Smith, *Chicago,* 392–93, 402.

4. Wendt, *Chicago Tribune,* 475–76.

5. Three months after Cosgrave's visit, the *Tribune* would win its action and the defendants be ordered to pay $2.3 million. However, in 1930 this decision was overturned on appeal.

6. Kelly to Cosgrave, Sept. 20, Oct. 6, and Nov. 11, 1927 (National Archives of Ireland S. 4529); *Chicago Tribune,* Oct. 6, 1927.

7. S. P. Breathnach (J. Walsh), Secretary, Dept. of External Affairs, to the Secretary, Executive Council, Dec. 8, 1927, 2 (National Archives of Ireland S. 4529).

8. Ibid., 1.

9. *Chicago Record-Herald,* Jan. 12, 1914; *Chicago Tribune,* Jan. 22, 1928, for his report on Cosgrave's visit; *Milwaukee Sentinel,* Feb. 9, 1929; O'Donnell Bennett, *Gangland;* Inventory of the James O'Donnell Bennett papers, 1896–1936 (Newberry Library, Chicago, online).

10. Smiddy to Minister for External Affairs, Jan. 9 and 13, 1928 (National Archives of Ireland S. 4529).

11. *New York American,* Jan. 21, 1928.

12. *Irish Independent,* Jan. 23, 1928; *New York News,* Feb. 3 1928.

13. *Irish Independent,* Feb. 19, 1929.

14. *New York Evening World,* Jan. 20, 1928; *Chicago News,* Jan. 21, 1928; *Chicago Herald and Examiner,* Jan. 22, 1928.

15. *Chicago Tribune,* Jan. 22, 1928.

16. Smiddy to McGilligan, Jan. 13, 1928 (National Archives of Ireland S. 4529); *Chicago News,* Jan. 21, 1928; *Herald and Examiner,* Jan. 22, 1928; *Chicago Tribune,* Jan. 22, 1928.

17. FitzGerald, *Preface to Statecraft.* A decade later FitzGerald would return to Illinois and deliver at the University of Notre Dame a series of lectures on philosophy and politics.

18. *Chicago Tribune,* Jan. 22, 1928; *Chicago Herald and Examiner,* Jan. 23, 1928; *Irish Independent,* Jan. 24 and 26 (citing *Connacht Sentinel*) 1928; O'Kennedy-Brindley, *With the President in America,* 8, 23, 75–77 (speech); Smiddy to Patrick McGilligan, Jan. 13, 1928 (National Archives of Ireland S. 4529).

19. *Chicago Tribune,* Jan. 22, 1928; Bukowski, *Big Bill Thompsom, passim;* Lewis and Smith, *Chicago,* 392–95.

20. *Washington Star,* Jan. 23, 1928; *Chicago Herald and Examiner,* Jan. 22, 1928.

21. *Washington Star,* Jan. 23, 1928.

22. *Chicago Tribune,* Jan. 22, 1928; *Chicago Herald and Examiner,* Jan. 22, 1928.

23. *Irish Independent,* Jan. 24, 1928.

24. *Chicago News,* Jan. 21, 1928.

25. *Montreal Gazette,* Jan. 30, 1928; *Ottawa Citizen,* Jan. 31, 1928; *Chicago Tribune,* Jan. 31, 1928.

26. *Chicago Tribune,* Jan. 22, 1928; *Chicago Herald and Examiner,* Jan. 22, 1928.

27. *Chicago Herald and Examiner,* Jan. 23, 1928.

28. *Irish Independent,* Feb. 19, 1929.

29. *Chicago Herald and Examiner,* Jan. 22, 1928.

30. *Irish Times,* Feb. 13, 1928; O'Kennedy-Brindley, *With the President in America,* 66–71.

ELEVEN The Best in the Business

1. Columbia University, Catalog 1928–1929, 115, 142, 144; Anon. "People Talked About," 8 (Duke MSS, O'Shaughnessy Papers, Box 2, File 1).

2. Letter of introduction from George R. Anderson, Manager, Hotel Belmont, July 23, 1929 (Duke MSS, O'Shaughnessy Papers, Box 2, File 2, no. 1 of 2).

3. *Irish Independent,* Feb. 19, 1929.

4. Ibid. The report includes a photograph of James.

5. *Liberty,* Mar. 9, 1929, 83; James O'Shaughnessy, "America's Four A's," May 29, 1929, and Letter from M. L. Sitgreaves to James O'Shaughnessy, Nov. 1, 1928 (Duke MSS, O'Shaughnessy Papers, Box 1, File 7).

6. *Time,* July 1 and 29, 1929; Wendt, *Chicago Tribune,* 461, 471.

7. *Irish Independent,* Feb. 19, 1929; *Time,* July 29, 1929; Norton Smith, *The Colonel,* 136–37, 265.

8. Lundberg, *Imperial Hearst,* 164.

9. *Irish Independent,* Feb. 19, 1929.

10. Reports on *Liberty* advertisers and the relationship with agencies, 1926–1928 (Duke MSS, O'Shaughnessy Papers, Box 1, File 2).

11. *Time,* July 29, 1929 ("Specialist Called").

12. *Liberty* Salary Payments to James O'Shaughnessy (Duke MSS, O'Shaughnessy Papers, Box 1, File 3).

13. *Time,* Apr. 13, 1931 ("Sold: Pride and Liberty").

14. *Liberty,* Mar. 9, 1929, 33; *Printers' Ink Monthly,* Aug. 1929, 16; *New York Herald,* Advertising Convention edition, Aug. 13, 1929.

15. Marx Brothers, *The Cocoanuts,* at 4:25; Anon, "People Talked About," 8.

16. James O'Shaughnessy to May Montgomery, Nov. 8, 1929 (Duke MSS, O'Shaughnessy Papers, Box 1, File 3).

17. James O'Shaughnessy to Max Annenberg, Aug. 22, 1930 (Duke MSS, O'Shaughnessy Papers, Box 1, File 3).

18. J. Walter Thompson Company, Newsletter Collection, 1910–2005, and Personnel Files (Duke MSS); Kenny, "Acland"; Smulyan, *Popular Ideologies,* 189, n. 54; Diaries of Mackenzie King, Sept. 8, 1942. (MS Library and Archives Canada); Weil Davis, *Living up to the Ads,* 102.

19. *Time,* Apr. 13, 1931 ("Sold: Pride and Liberty"). For Mayor Thompson's pamphlet see also Lundberg, *Imperial Hearst,* 391; Smith, *The Colonel,* 550.

20. *Time,* Apr. 13, 1931 ("Sold: Pride and Liberty"); Anon, "People Talked About," 8. Various *Liberty* materials in O'Shaughnessy Papers, Duke MSS, Boxes 1–3. In 1931 the ages of his children were Mary (21), Colman (19), Bride (18), and Jane (13).

21. Application of Intensive Methods to Marketing, Oct. 19, 1926, and O'Shaughnessy to Max Annenberg, Jan. 11, 1932 (Duke MSS, O'Shaughnessy Papers, Box 1, Files 3, 7); Mott, *American Journalism,* 672. The *Mirror* was to be closed suddenly the following year, but not before ' "Dick Tracy" — the "most sociohistorically representative comic strip of all time" — appeared for the first time anywhere in its edition of Oct. 4, 1931 (Roberts, *Dick Tracy and American Culture,* 26).

22. *Inland Press Association Bulletin,* no. 195 (Nov. 1, 1931), 40–45 (Duke MSS, O'Shaughnessy Papers, Box 1, File 7).

23. Letters from Charles E. Chambers, President of the Guild of Freelance Artists of the Authors' League of America (Inc) to James O'Shaughnessy, 285 Madison Avenue, NY, Feb. 4, 1929 (Duke MSS, O'Shaughnessy Papers, Box 1, File 7).

24. James O'Shaughnessy, "What Is 'Art for Art's Sake'?" and "Distress Copy" (Duke MSS, O'Shaughnessy Papers, Box 1, File 7, with telegram May 3, 1932).

25. *Printers' Ink*, Dec. 8, 1950, 7.

26. These were Sister Bride of Wilmington, DE, and Sister Jane Francis of Brooklyn, NY.

27. Correspondence of James O'Shaughnessy, U. Notre Dame, UPCO UPWL 16/47; Ward, *Frank Leahy*, 73.

28. Correspondence of James O'Shaughnessy, U. Notre Dame, UPCO UPWL 16/44; McCarthy, "Irish Americans in Sport," 458.

29. Junior Class of Notre Dame, *The Dome*, 373; Correspondence of James O'Shaughnessy, U. Notre Dame UPCO 6/122.

30. *Chicago Tribune* and *New York Times*, Apr. 3, 1931; Knute Rockne clippings, 1931 (Duke MSS, O'Shaughnessy Papers, Box 2, File 3); *Scholastic* 15, 10 (Feb. 12, 1932); *Chicago Daily Tribune*, Aug. 6, 1933. A copy of the editorial rests among his papers at Duke University, along with a bulging file of old press clippings related to Rockne's life and legacy on which is written "See Adv. Age editorial to explain why this is in collection."

31. Entertainment was provided by showman George M. Cohan, the singer of the wartime song *Over There* and other popular numbers.

32. Anon., *Irish Fellowship Club 1902–1953*, preface.

33. O'Gorman, *Irish Fellowship Club*, 99–100.

34. Ibid., 62–65.

TWELVE Missouri to Manhattan

1. Cited by Fanning at Farrell, *Face of Time*, xv.

2. Ibson, *Will the World Break Your Heart?*, 96, 99–100.

3. Thomas O'Shaughnessy to Roger Faherty, 1951, cited at O'Gorman, *Irish Fellowship Club*, 94.

4. *Chicago Tribune*, Feb. 13, 1956; Barton, "Celtic Revived," 85, 100.

5. *Printers' Ink*, Dec. 8, 1950, 58, 72. The remains of James, his wife, and daughter, Mary, with her husband, Thomas Corning Betts, are buried together in Holy Mount Cemetery, Westchester, New York.

6. *Printers' Ink*, Dec. 8, 1950, 58.

APPENDIX ONE Journalism of James O'Shaughnessy

1. In Johnson, "Reminiscences" (Jan. 28, 1934).

2. For an explanation of the baby's remarkable name see above pp. 19, 21, 27.

3. *Chicago Daily Tribune,* June 29-July 1, 1899 ("In Front of Santiago a Year Ago Today").

4. *Chicago Tribune,* Feb. 7, 1912.

APPENDIX TWO A Missouri-Irish Haunting

1. Hogan, *Missouri 1857–1868,* 162–69.

Bibliography

Books, Articles, and Printed Papers

Abel, Richard. *Americanizing the Movies and "Movie-Mad" Audiences 1910–1914*. Berkeley: University of California Press, 2006.

Abbott, Karen. *Sin in the Second City: Madams, Ministers, Playboys, and the Battle for America's Soul*. New York: Random House, 2008.

Adams, James N. "Illinois in 1956." *Journal of the Illinois State Historical Society* 50, no. 1 (Spring 1957): 71–84.

AIHS (American Irish Historical Society). "Biographies of New Members ['furnished by the members' (p. 517)]." *Journal of the American Irish Historical Society* 10 (1910): 546–47.

Amory, Cleveland. *The Proper Bostonians*. New York: Dutton, 1947.

Anon. *History of Howard and Chariton Counties, Missouri, Written and Compiled from the Most Official Authentic and Private Sources; Together with a Condensed History of Missouri; a Reliable and Detailed History of Howard and Chariton Counties — Its Pioneer Record, Resources, Biographical Sketches of Prominent Citizens; General and Local Statistics of Great Value; Incidents and Reminiscences*. St. Louis: National Historical Company, 1883.

———. *History of Linn County, Missouri: An Encyclopedia of Useful Information, and a Compendium of Actual Facts*. Kansas City, MO: Birdsall and Dean, 1882.

———. *Irish Fellowship Club of Chicago 1902–1953: Its History and Objectives*. Chicago: IFC, 1953.

———. Obituary [1] of James O'Shaughnessy Senior. *Brunswicker*, Nov. 1918.

———. Obituary [2] of James O'Shaughnessy Senior. Unidentified in transcript, 1918. http://www.findagrave.com/cgi-bin/fg.cgi?page=grandGRid=58709626.

———. "Paving Men Advertise to Placate Critical Taxpayers." *Printers' Ink*, Apr. 26, 1917: 37–38.

———. "People Talked About: Ad-Man O'Shaughnessy." *The Pathfinder*, no 1,940 (Mar. 7, 1951): 8.

Anon., ed. *Guide to the Irish Industrial Village and Blarney Castle: The Exhibit of the Irish Industries Association*. Chicago: Irish Village Book Store, 1893.

Anthony, Ethan. *The Architecture of Ralph Adams Cram and His Office*. New York: Norton, 2007.

Appel, John J. "From Shanties to Lace Curtains: The Irish Image in *Puck*, 1876–1910." *Comparative Studies in Society and History* 13, no. 4 (Oct. 1971): 365–75.

Arceneaux, Noah. "News on the Air: *The New York Herald*, Newspapers, and Wireless Telegraphy, 1899–1917." *American Journalism* 30, no. 2 (2013): 160–81.

Ayer and Sons. *American Newspaper Annual: Containing a Catalogue of American Newspapers*. Philadelphia: N. W. Ayer, 1888 and 1890.

Baker, Laura E. "Civic Ideals, Mass Culture, and the Public: Reconsidering the 1909 Plan of Chicago." *Journal of Urban History* 36, no. 6 (2010): 747–70.

Ballou's Pictorial Drawing-Room Companion. Boston, MA: Ballou, 1857.

Barton, Timothy. "Celtic Revived: the Artistry of Thomas O'Shaughnessy." In *At the Crossroads*, ed. Skerrett, 85–101.

Baskin, O. L. *The History of Clinton County, Missouri*. St. Joseph, MO: National Historical Co., 1881.

Bayor, Ronald H., and Timothy J. Meagher. *The New York Irish*. Baltimore, MD: Johns Hopkins University Press, 1997.

Beattie, Seán. "Cottage Industries: Arts and Crafts in Donegal 1880–1920." *Donegal Annual* 60 (2008): 59–81.

Benson, John. "How American Association of Advertising Agencies Works for the Good of Advertising." *Printers' Ink*, May 24, 1923.

Bishop, Glenn A., and Paul T. Gilbert, eds. *Chicago's Accomplishments and Leaders*. Chicago: Bishop Publishing, 1932.

Bird, Harry L. *This Fascinating Advertising Business*. Indianapolis: Bobbs-Merrill, 1947.

Blake, Martin J. "Tabular Pedigree of O'Shaughnessy of Gort (1543–1783)." *Journal of the Galway Archaeological and Historical Society* 6 (1909–1910): 53–64 and 7 (1911–1912): 53 (a correction).

Bogart, Michele H. *Artists, Advertising and the Borders of Art*. Chicago: University of Chicago Press, 1995.

Bonner, John. "History of Illustration Among America's Major Newspapers." *San Francisco Chronicle*, Feb. 24, 1897.

Bowe, Nicola Gordon. "Imagining an Irish Past: The Celtic Revival 1840–1940." *Irish Arts Review Yearbook* 10 (1994): 106–70.

——— . "The Irish Arts and Crafts Movements (1886–1925)." *Irish Arts Review Yearbook* (1990/1991): 172–85.

Bradley, Robert L., Jr., *Edison to Enron: Energy Markets and Political Strategies*. Hoboken, NJ: Wiley, and Salem, MA: Scrivener, 2011.

Brown, Charles H. *The Correspondents' War: Journalists in the Spanish-American War*. New York: Scribner, 1967.

Brown, Thomas N. "The Origins and Character of Irish-American Nationalism." *Review of Politics* 18, no. 3 (July 1956): 327–58.

Buckley, Homer J. *The Science of Marketing by Mail.* New York: Forbes, 1924.

Buckley, John P. *The New York Irish: Their View of American Foreign Policy, 1914–21.* New York: Arno, 1976.

Bukowski, Douglas. *Big Bill Thompson, Chicago, and the Politics of Image.* Urbana: University of Illinois Press, 1998.

Burnett, Robyn, and Ken Luebbering. *German Settlement in Missouri: New Land, Old Ways.* Columbia: University of Missouri Press, 1996.

Burns, Robert E. *Being Catholic, Being American: The Notre Dame Story, 1842–1934.* 2 vols. Notre Dame, IN: University of Notre Dame Press, vol. 1, 1999; vol. 2, 2000.

Campbell, W. Joseph. *The Year That Defined American Journalism: 1897 and the Clash of Paradigms.* New York and London: Taylor and Francis, 2006.

——— . *Yellow Journalism: Puncturing the Myths, Defining the Legacies.* Westport, CT: Praeger, 2001.

Carroll, Francis M., ed. *The American Commission on Irish Independence: The Diary, Correspondence, and Report.* Dublin: Irish Manuscript Commission, 1985.

Carroll, Francis M. *American Opinion and the Irish Question 1910–1923.* Dublin: Gill and Macmillan, 1978.

Çelik, Zeynep, Diane Favro, and Richard Ingersoll, eds. *Streets: Critical Perspectives on Public Spaces.* Berkeley: University of California Press, 1994.

Chapman Bros. *Portrait and Biographical Record of Buchanan and Clinton Counties; Containing Biographical Sketches of Prominent and Representative Citizens.* Chapman Bros: Chicago, 1893.

Chicago Blue Book of Selected Names of Chicago and Suburban Towns for the Year ending 1908. Chicago Directory Company, 1908.

Chicago Daily News, ed. *Notable Men of Illinois and Their State. Chicago Daily News,* 1919.

Chicago Historical Society. *Annual Report 1904.* http://www.archive.org/stream /1904a05annualreportoochicuoft#page/204/mode/1up.

——— . *Encyclopedia of Chicago.* 2005. Electronic publication. http://www .encyclopedia.chicagohistory.org/.

Cleveland, Newcomb. *Agency Association Progress in the United States.* New York: American Association of Advertising Agencies, 1927.

Committee on Public Information. *Government War Advertising: Report of the Division of Advertising, Committee on Public Information.* CPI: [Washington], 1918.

Conard, Howard L., ed. *Encyclopedia of the History of Missouri: A Compendium of History and Biography for Ready Reference.* 6 vols. New York, Louisville, and St. Louis: Southern History Company, 1901.

Coogan, Timothey P. *Michael Collins: The Man Who Made Ireland.* New York: Palgrave, 1990.

Coolidge, Calvin. Address before the American Association of Advertising Agencies. 1926. http://www.presidency.ucsb.edu/ws/index.php?pid=412.

Coolsen, Frank G. "Pioneers in the Development of Advertising." *Journal of Marketing* 12, no. 1 (July 1947): 80–86.

Cox, Jim. *Sold on Radio: Advertisers in the Golden Age of Broadcasing.* Jefferson, NC: McFarland and Co., 2008.

Creel, George. *How We Advertised America: The First Telling of the Amazing Story of the Committee on Public Information That Carried the Gospel of Americanism to Every Corner of the Globe.* New York and London: Harper, 1920.

——— . *Ireland's Fight for Freedom: Setting Forth the High Lights of Irish History.* New York and London: Harper, 1919.

Crimmins, John D. *St. Patrick's Day: Its Celebration in New York and Other American Places, 1737–1845.* New York: Crimmins, 1902.

Cronin, Mike, and Daryl Adair. *The Wearing of the Green: A History of St. Patrick's Day.* London: Routledge, 2002.

Curtis-Wilson, Kathleen, Gary McCain, and Nina M. Ray. "The Challenge of Creating And Maintaining Respected Country-Of-Origin Assets: The Irish Linen Story." *Journal of Business Case Studies* 2, no. 3 (2006): 71–84.

Daley, Anna. "Alphonse Mucha in Gilded Age America, 1904–1921." MA thesis, Cooper-Hewitt National Design Museum, Smithsonian Institution, and Parsons, The New School for Design, 2007. http://si-pddr.si.edu/jspui /bitstream/10088/8790/6/AnnaDaleyAlphonseMucha.pdf.

Danckers, Ulrich, and Jane Meredith. *A Compendium of the Early History of Chicago to the Year 1835.* Chicago, IL: Early Chicago Inc., 2000.

Davis, Hartley. "The Journalism of New York." *Munsey's Magazine* 24, 2 (1900): 217–33.

Davitt, Michael. *The Fall of Feudalism in Ireland: or the Story of the Land League Revolution.* London and New York: Harper and Brothers, 1904.

De La Salle Brothers. *Mississippi Vista, the Brothers of the Christian Schools in the Mid-West, 1849 – 1949.* Winona, MN: St. Mary's College Press, 1948.

Dezell, Maureen. *Irish America: Coming into Clover.* New York: Anchor Books, 2000.

Dictionary of Irish Biography: From the Earliest Times until 2002. Ed. J. McGuire and J. Quinn. 9 vols. Cambridge: Cambridge University Press, 2009.

Digby-Junger, Richard. "'The Main Rendezvous for Men of the Press': The Life and Death of the Chicago Press Club, 1880–1987." *Journal of Illinois History* 1, no. 2 (1998): 74–98.

Dolan, Jay P. *The Irish Americans: A History.* New York: Bloomsbury, 2008.

Donnelly, James S. *The Great Irish Potato Famine.* Stroud, UK: Sutton Publishing, 2001.

Doorley, Michael. *Irish-American Diaspora Nationalism: The Friends of Irish Freedom, 1916–1935.* Dublin: Four Courts, 2005.

Dorn, Jacob. "'Not a Substitute for Religion, but a Means of Fulfilling It': The Sacramental Socialism of Irwin St. John Tucker." In *Socialism and Christianity in Early 20th Century America,* ed. Dorn, 137–64. Westport, CT: Greenwood Press, 1998.

Doyle, David N. "The Irish in Chicago." *Irish Historical Studies* 26, no. 103 (May 1989): 293–303.

Draper, Joan E. "Planning Wacker Drive." In Çelik, Favro and Ingersoll, *Streets,* 259–76.

Drudy, P. J., ed. *The Irish in America: Emigrations, Assimilation and Impact.* Cambridge: Cambridge University Press, 1985.

Drury, John. *Chicago in Seven Days.* New York: McBride, 1928.

Dudley Clarke, Ellen, ed. *Lineage Book.* Vol. 49. Washington, D. C: National Society of the Daughters of the American Revolution, 1901.

Duncan-Clark, S. J. "Stained Glass Lore: On the Trail of an Ancient Art." *Chicago Daily News,* June 5, 1931.

Dunne, Finley Peter. "Molly Donohue Who Lives across the Street from Mr. Dooley." *Ladies Home Journal* 17, No. 1 (Dec. 1899): 6.

———. *Mr. Dooley in Peace and War.* Boston: Small, Maynard and Co., 1899.

Edelstein, Teri J., ed. *Imagining An Irish Past: The Celtic Revival 1840–1940.* Chicago: The David and Alfred Smart Museum of Art, The University of Chicago, 1992.

Edwards Bros, ed. *An Illustrated Historical Atlas of Chariton County, MO.* Philadelphia, PA: Edwards, 1876.

Egan, Maurice F., and James B. Kennedy. *The Knights of Columbus in Peace and War.* 2 vols. New Haven, CT: Knights of Columbus, 1920.

Elzey, Wayne. "Jesus the Salesman: A Reassessment of *The Man Nobody Knows.*" *Journal of the American Academy of Religion* 46, no. 2 (June 1978): 151–77.

Emery, Edwin, and Michael Emery. *The Press and America: An Interpretative History of the Mass Media.* 4th ed. New Jersey: Prentice-Hall, 1978.

Emery, Michael, Edwin Emery, and Nancy L. Roberts. *The Press and America: An Interpretative History of the Mass Media.* Needham Heights, MA: Allyn and Bacon, 2000.

Emmons, David M. *Beyond the American Pale: The Irish in the West 1845–1910.* Norman, OK: University of Oklahoma Press, 2010.

Fahey, Jerome. *The History and Antiquities of the Diocese of Kilmacduagh.* Dublin: Gill, 1893.

Fahy, Mary de Lourdes. *Kiltartan: Many Leaves, One Root.* County Galway: Kiltartan Gregory Cultural Society, 2004.

Fanning, Charles. *Finley Peter Dunne and Mr. Dooley: The Chicago Years.* Lexington: University Press of Kentucky, 1978.

———— . "Mr. Dooley Reconsidered: Community Memory, Journalism, and the Oral Tradition." In *At the Crossroads*, ed. Skerrett, 69–83.

Fanning, Charles, ed. *Mr. Dooley and the Chicago Irish: An Anthology*. New York: Arno Press, 1976.

Farnum, Allen L. *Pawnee Bill's Historic Wild West: A Photo Documentary of the 1900– 1905 Show Tours*. West Chester, PA: Schiffer, 1992.

Farrell, James T. *The Face of Time*. With an introduction by Charles Fanning. Urbana: University of Illinois Press, 2008.

Federal Trade Commission. *Annual Report of the Federal Trade Commission for the Fiscal Year Ended June 30, 1930*. Washington, DC: Government Printing Office, 1930.

———— . *Annual Report of the Federal Trade Commission for the Fiscal Year Ended June 30, 1925*. Washington, DC: Government Printing Office, 1925.

Finegold, Kenneth. *Experts and Politicians: Reform Challenges to Machine Politics in New York, Cleveland, and Chicago*. Princeton: Princeton University Press, 1995.

Finnegan, Richard J. "Social Responsibilities of the Newspaper." *Annals of the American Academy of Political and Social Science* 219 (Jan. 1942): 166–68.

FitzGerald, Desmond. *Preface to Statecraft*. New York: Sheed and Ward, 1939.

Fitzpatrick, David. *Irish Emigration 1801–1921*. Dundalk, IRL: Dundalgan Press, 1984.

Fleming, Thomas. *The Illusion of Victory: America in World War I*. New York: Basic Books, 2003.

Forbes, Thomas. "The Early Years [of the American Association of Advertising Agencies]." *Agency* 3, no. 1 (Spring 1991, published by the AAAA): 24–33.

Foster, Roy F. *W. B. Yeats: A Life. I: The Apprentice Mage 1865–1914*. Oxford: Oxford University Press, 1997.

Fox, Stephen. *The Mirror Makers: A History of American Advertising and Its Creators*. Urbana: University of Illinois Press, 1997.

Fratcher, William F. *The Law Barn: A Brief History of the School of Law, University of Missouri-Columbia*. Columbia: School of Law, University of Missouri-Columbia, 1978.

Funchion, Michael F. "Irish Chicago: Church, Homeland, Politics and Class — The Shaping of an Ethnic Group, 1870–1900." In *Ethnic Chicago*, ed. Holli and d'Alroy, 57–92.

Gay, Peter. *Pleasure Wars: The Bourgeois Experience: Victoria to Freud*. New York: Norton, 1999.

Glazier, Michael, ed. *The Encyclopedia of the Irish in America*. Notre Dame, IN: University of Notre Dame Press, 1999.

Gleijeses, Piero. "1898: The Opposition to the Spanish-American War." *Journal of Latin American Studies* 35, 4 (2003): 681–719.

Goldstein, Carolyn M. "From Service to Sales: Home Economics in Light and Power, 1920–1940." *Technology and Culture* 38, no. 1 (Jan. 1997): 121–52.

Greer, Carl L. ("The Buckeye Cover Man"). *Across with the Ad-Men: International Advertising Convention London, 1924*. Hamilton, OH: Beckett Paper Co., 1924.

Gregory, Augusta. *The Kiltartan History Book*. Dublin: Maunsel, 1909.

———. *Our Irish Theatre: A Chapter of Autobiography*. New York and London: Knickerbocker Press, 1913.

———. *Poets and Dreamers: Studies and Translations from the Irish*. Dublin: Hodges Figgis, 1903.

———. "Why the Irish Love Ireland." *Muskogee* [Oklahoma] *Times Democrat*, Mar. 16, 1912, and other newspapers. Copy at National Library of Ireland, MS L.195.

Gregory, Augusta, ed. *Sir William Gregory, K.C.M.G., Formerly Member of Parliament and Sometime Governor of Ceylon*. London: John Murray, 1894.

Hammond, Percy. "First Performance in Chicago of 'The Playboy of the Western World'; No Riots." *Chicago Tribune*, Feb. 7, 1912.

Harper's Pictorial History of the War with Spain. 2 vols. New York and London: Harper, 1899.

Harris, Neil. "Selling National Culture: Ireland at the World's Columbian Exposition." In *Imaging an Irish Past*, ed. Edelstein, 82–105.

Hart, Albert B., ed. *Selected Addresses and Public Papers of Woodrow Wilson*. New York: Boni and Liveright, 1918.

Hassett, Joseph. "What Raftery Built." *Yeats Annual*, 18 (2013): 97–106.

Hearst, William R. *William Randolph Hearst: A Portrait in His Own Words*, ed. Edmond D. Coblentz. New York: Simon and Schuster, 1952.

Heisler, Karen C. *Fighting Irish: Legends, Lists and Lore*. Champaign, IL: Sports Publishing L.L.C., 2006.

Hennessy, M. W. "William from Galway: First Irishman in America." In *America 1776–1976: The Galway Connection*. Galway, IRL: *Galway Advertiser*, 1976.

Henning, Arthur Sears. "Colorful Reporters of 1900." *Chicago Daily Tribune*, Sept. 11, 1953.

———. "New Reporter Is Last Hired, So First Fired." *Chicago Daily Tribune*, May 19, 1953.

Hickey, Michael P. "Father O'Growney." *Irish Ecclesiastical Record*, 4th series, 6 (July-Dec. 1899): 426–43.

Hill, Judith. *Lady Gregory: An Irish Life*. Cork: Collins Press, 2011.

Hillier, Alfred J. "Albert Johnson, Congressman." *Pacific Northwest Quarterly*, 36, no. 3 (July 1945): 193–211.

Hixson, W. W. and Co. *Plat Book of Chariton County, Missouri*. Rockford, IL: Hixson, n.d.

History Committee. *The Four Minute Men of Chicago*. Chicago: History Committee of the Four Minute Men of Chicago, 1919.

Hogan, John J. *On the Mission in Missouri, 1857–1868*. Kansas City, MO: John A. Heilmann, 1892.

——— . *On the Mission in Missouri and Fifty Years Ago: A Memoir*, ed. Crystal Payton. Springfield, MO: Lens and Pens Press, 2009.

Holli, Melvin G., and Peter d'Alroy Jones, eds. *Ethnic Chicago: A Multicultural Portrait*. 4th ed. Grand Rapids, MI: Eerdmans, 1995.

Holtz, Allan. *American Newspaper Comics: An Encyclopedic Reference Guide*. Ann Arbor: University of Michigan Press, 2012.

Hope, Arthur J. *Notre Dame: One Hundred Years*. 2nd ed. Notre Dame, IN: University Press, 1948.

Howard, Timothy E. *A History of St. Joseph County, Indiana*. 2 vols. Chicago and New York: Lewis, 1907.

Hoye City Directory Company. *St. Joseph, Missouri, City Directory and Buchanan County Taxpayers*. Kansas City, MO: Hoye, 1890.

Hunt, Hugh. *The Abbey: Ireland's National Theatre, 1904–1978*. Dublin: Gill and Macmillan, 1979.

Hyde, Douglas. *Abhráin Atá Leagtha ar an Reachtúire, or Songs Ascribed to Raftery*. Dublin: Gill, 1903.

Ibson, John D. *Will the World Break Your Heart? Dimensions and Consequences of Irish-American Assimilation*. New York and London: Garland, 1990.

Illinois War Council. *Final Report of the State Council of Defense of Illinois 1917 — 1918 — 1919*. State of Illinois, 1919.

Jackall, Robert, and Hirota, J.M. *Image Makers: Advertising, Public Relations, and the Ethos of Advocacy*. Chicago: University of Chicago Press, 2000.

Jacobs, Randy D. "Advertising Agencies and the Adoption of Radio: A Diffusion of Innovations Perspective." *CHARM* (Conference on Historical Analysis and Research in Marketing) *Proceedings*, 15 (May 2011): 84–95.

Johnson, Albert. "Some Reminiscences: Ups and Downs in a Life of Twenty Years 'A-growin'; Twenty Years as a Reporter and Editor, and Twenty Years in the National House of Representatives." *Grays Harbor Washingtonian* (Hoquiam, WA), Dec. 31, 1933-May 6, 1934 (every Sunday).

Joyce, William L. *Editors and Ethnicity: A History of the Irish-American Press, 1848–1883*. New York: Arno, 1976.

Junger, Richard. *Becoming the Second City: Chicago's Mass News Media, 1833–1898*. Urbana: University of Illinois Press, 2012.

Junior Class of Notre Dame. *The Dome, xxiv*. South Bend, IN: University of Notre Dame, 1930.

Katzenberger, George A. *Catalog of the Legal Fraternity of Phi Delta Phi*. Ann Arbor, MI: Inland Press, 1898.

Kelly, Mary C. *The Shamrock and the Lily: The New York Irish and the Creation of a Transatlantic Identity, 1845–1921.* New York, NY: Peter Lang, 2005.

Kennedy, David M. *Over Here: The First World War and American Society.* New York: Oxford University Press, 1980.

Kennedy, Joseph C. G., ed. *Population of the United States in 1860; Compiled from the Original Returns of the Eighth Census under the Direction of the Secretary of the Interior.* Washington, DC: Bureau of the Census Library, 1864.

Kenner, Hurnard J. *The Fight for Truth in Advertising: A Story of What Business Has Done and Is Doing to Establish and Maintain Accuracy and Fair Play in Advertising and Selling for the Public's Protection.* New York: Round Table Press, 1936.

Kenny, Colum. "Imaginative Decoration: Peregrine Acland as Author, Adman and Political Aide." *International Journal of Canadian Studies: Revue internationale d'études canadiennes* 50 (Nov. 2014):[forthcoming]

——— . *Irish Patriot, Publisher and Advertising Agent: Kevin J. Kenny, 1881–1954.* Bray, IRL: Ox, 2011.

——— . "Tom Grehan, Advertising Pioneer and Newspaper Man." In *Independent Newspapers,* ed. O'Brien and Rafter.

Kibler, M. Alison. "Pigs, Green Whiskers, and Drunken Widows: Irish Nationalists and the 'Practical Censorship' of McFadden's Row of Flats in 1902 and 1903." *Journal of American Studies* 42 (2008): 489–514.

Kilner, Frederic R. *Battery E in France: 149th Field Artillery Rainbow (42nd) Division.* F. R. Kilner: Chicago, 1919.

Kilroy, James. *The "Playboy" Riots.* Dublin: Dolmen, 1971.

Koenigsberg, Moses. *King News: An Autobiography.* Philadelphia, PA: Stokes, 1941.

Laird, Pamela W. *Advertising Progress: American Business and the Rise of Consumer Marketing.* Baltimore, MD: Johns Hopkins University Press, 1998.

Lears, Jackson. *Fables of Abundance: A Cultural History of Advertising in America.* New York: Basic Books, 1994.

Lee, Alfred M. *The Daily Newspaper in America: The Evolution of a Social Instrument.* New York: Macmillan, 1937.

Lee, Joseph J. *Ireland 1912–1985: Politics and Society.* Cambridge, UK: Cambridge University Press, 1989.

Lee, Joseph J., and Marion R. Casey. *Making the Irish American: History and Heritage of the Irish in the United States.* New York: New York University Press, 2006.

Levin, Gail. *Edward Hopper: An Intimate Biography.* Berkeley: University of California Press, 1998.

Lewis, Lloyd, and Henry J. Smith. *Chicago: The History of Its Reputation.* New York: Harcourt Brace, 1929.

Library of Congress, *Catalog of Copyright Entries, Part 1: Books, Group 2.* Washington, DC: Government Printing Office, 1917.

Lincoln Park. *Report of the Commissioners of Lincoln Park 1913–1916*. Chicago: Fred J. Ringley, undated.

Lockwood Williams, Sara. *Twenty Years of Education for Journalism: A History of the School of Journalism of the University of Missouri Columbia, Missouri, U.S.A.* Columbia, MO: E. W. Stephens Publ. Co., 1929.

Lombardo, Robert M. *Organized Crime in Chicago: Beyond the Mafia*. Urbana: University of Illinois Press, 2012.

Lundberg, Ferdinand. *Imperial Hearst: A Social Biography*. New York: Equinox, 1936.

Lytle, H. W., and John Dillon. *From Dance Hall to White Slavery: The World's Greatest Tragedy*. s.l.: Thompson, 1912.

Massachusetts Historical Commissions, Reconnaissance Survey Town Report: *Milford* (1983). http://www.sec.state.ma.us/mhc/mhcpdf/townreports /Cent-Mass/mil.pdf.

Matsen, William E. "The Battle of Sugar Point: a Reexamination." *Minnesota History* 50, 7 (1987): 269–75.

Matthews, George R. *When the Cubs Won It All: The 1908 Championship Season*. Jefferson, NC: McFarland, 2009.

Maxwell, Kenneth R. "Irish-Americans and the Fight for Treaty Ratification." *Public Opinion Quarterly* 31, no. 4 (Winter 1967–1968): 620–41.

Mackay, Angus. "Selection of the Fittest: Or, How Irish Colleens Were Chosen to Represent Ireland at the World Fair." In *Guide to the Irish Industrial Village and Blarney Castle*, ed. Anon., 31–45.

McCaffrey, James M. *Inside the Spanish-American War: A History Based on First-Person Accounts*. Jefferson, NC: McFarland, 2009.

McCaffrey, Lawrence J. "Irish-American Politics: Power with or without Purpose?" In *Irish in America*, ed. Drudy, 169–90.

———. *The Irish Diaspora in America*. Bloomington: Indiana University Press, 1976.

McCaffrey, Lawrence J., ed. *Irish Nationalism and the American Contribution*. New York: Arno Press, 1976.

McCaffrey, Lawrence J., Ellen Skerrett, Michael F. Funchion, and Charles Fanning, eds. *The Irish in Chicago*. Urbana: University of Illinois Press, 1987.

McCandless, Perry. *A History of Missouri, Volume 2, 1820 to 1860*. Columbia: University of Missouri Press, 2000.

McCarthy, Lawrence J. "Irish Americans in Sports: The Twentieth Century." In *Making the Irish American*, ed. Lee and Casey, 457–71.

McDonald, Forrest. *Insull: The Rise and Fall of a Billionaire Utility Tycoon*. Chicago: University of Chicago Press, 1962.

McLaughlin, John Gerard. *Irish Chicago*. Charleston, SC: Arcadia, 2005.

McNamara, Denis R. *Heavenly City: The Architectural Tradition of Catholic Chicago*. Chicago: Archdiocese of Chicago, 2005.

McNeil, Joanne. "The 'White Slavery' Panic." *Reason,* 39, no. 11 (Apr. 2008), 58–61.

Meagher, Timothy J. *The Columbia Guide to Irish American History.* New York: Columbia University Press, 2005.

———, ed. *From Paddy to Studs: Irish-American Communities in the Turn-of-the-Century Era, 1880–1920.* New York: Greenwood Press, 1986.

———. *Inventing Irish America: Generation, Class, and Ethnic Identity in a New England City, 1880–1928.* Notre Dame, IN: University of Notre Dame, 2001.

Messinger, Gary S. *The Battle for the Mind: War and Peace in the Era of Mass Communication.* Amherst: University of Massachusetts Press, 2011.

Meyer, Christina. "Urban America in the Newspaper Comic Strips of the Nineteenth Century: Introducing the Yellow Kid." *ImageTexT: Interdisciplinary Comic Studies* 6, no. 2 (Spring 2012). http://www.english.ufl.edu/imagetext / archives/v6_2/meyer/.

Miller, Kerby A. "Assimilation and Alienation: Irish Emigrants' Responses to Industrial America, 1871–1921." In *Irish in America,* ed. Drudy, 87–112.

———. *Emigrants and Exiles: Ireland and the Irish Exodus to North America.* New York: Oxford University Press, 1985.

———. *Ireland and Irish America: Culture, Class, and Transatlantic Migration.* Dublin: Field Day, 2008.

Minogue, Anna C. *Loretto Annals of the Century.* New York: The America Press, 1912.

Miscamble, Wilson D. *Go Forth and Do Good: Memorable Notre Dame Commencement Addresses.* Notre Dame, IN: University of Notre Dame Press, 2003.

Moore, Philip S. "Academic Development, University of Notre Dame: Past, Present and Future." Notre Dame, 1960. http://archives.nd.edu/moore/moore.htm

Moran Gerard, ed. *Galway History and Society: Interdisciplinary Essays on the History of an Irish County.* Dublin: Geography Publications, 1996.

Morgan, Hiram, ed. *Information, Media and Power through the Ages.* Dublin, IRL: UCD Press, 2001: 202–21.

Morris, Catherine. "Alice Milligan: Republican Tableaux and the Revival." *Field Day Review* 6 (2010): 133–65.

Morton, Richard A. *Justice and Humanity: Edward F. Dunne, Illinois Progressive.* Carbondale: Southern Illinois University Press, 1997.

Morton, Richard A. "Illinois' Most Progressive Governor." *Journal of the Illinois State Historical Society* 83, no. 4 (Winter 1990): 218–34.

Mott, Frank L. *American Journalism: A History of Newspapers in the United States through 250 Years, 1690 to 1940.* New York: Macmillan, 1947.

Mullaney, Bernard J. *"Public Relations" in the Public Utility Industry.* Urbana: University of Illinois, 1924.

Mulrooney, Margaret, ed. *Fleeing the Famine: North America and Irish Refugees 1845–1851.* Westport, CT: Praeger, 2003.

New, William H., ed. *Encyclopedia of Literature in Canada.* Toronto: University of Toronto Press, 2002.

Nilsen, Kenneth E. "The Irish Language in New York, 1850–1900." In *New York Irish,* ed. Bayor and Meagher, 252–74.

Nofi, Albert A. *The Spanish-American War 1898.* Conshohocken, PA: Combined Books, 1996.

Norris, James D. *Advertising and the Transformation of American Society, 1865–1920.* Westport, CT: Greenwood Press, 1990.

North Missouri Railroad Co. *Facts for Emigrants. Northern Missouri, a New and Important Region!* St. Louis: North Missouri Railroad Co., 1870.

Norton Smith, Richard. *The Colonel: The Life and Legend of Robert E. McCormick, 1880–1955.* Evanston, IL: Northwestern University Press, 1997.

O'Brien, Gillian. "The Chicago Press and Irish Journalists." In *Irish Journalism before Independence,* ed. Rafter, 120–34.

O'Brien, Mark, and Kevin Rafter, eds. *Independent Newspapers: A History.* Dublin: Four Courts, 2012.

O'Day, Alan. "Media and Power: Charles Stewart Parnell's 1880 Mission to North America." In *Information, Media and Power through the Ages,* ed. Morgan, 202–19.

O'Donnell Bennett, J. *Chicago Gang Land: The True Story of Chicago Crime.* Chicago: *Chicago Tribune,* 1929.

O'Donnell, Charles L. *Dawn on Eternal Hills.* New York: Brevier Press, 1930.

O'Donovan, Fred. "Aim of Irish Players." In *The Abbey Theatre: Interviews and Recollections,* ed. E. H. Mikhail, 101–4. London: Macmillan, 1988.

O'Farrrelly, Agnes. *Leabhar an Athar Eoghan: The O'Growney Memorial Volume.* Dublin: Gill and London: Nutt, 1904.

O'Gorman, Thomas J. *The Irish Fellowship Club of Chicago, 1901–2001: One Hundred Years.* Chicago: Irish Fellowship Club, 2001.

O'Kelleher, Andrew, and Gertrude Schoepperle, eds. *Betha Colaim Chille: Life of Columcille. Compiled by Manus O'Donnell in 1532.* Urbana: University of Illinois, 1918.

O'Kennedy-Brindley. *With the President in America: The Authorised Record of the American Tour* [of W.T. Cosgrave]. Dublin: O'Kennedy-Brindley, 1928.

O'Laughlin, Michael C. *Irish Settlers on the American Frontier 1770–1900, vol. 1.* Gateway West through Missouri Specially Commissioned Patrons' Issue. Kansas City, MO: Irish Genealogical Foundation, 1984 (2nd ed. 2007).

Oldham Eagle, Mary K., ed. *The Congress of Women Held in the Woman's Building, World's Columbian Exposition, Chicago, U.S.A.* Chicago and Philadelphia: Monarch, 1893.

Olson, Greg. *Voodoo Priests, Noble Savages, and Ozark Gypsies: The Life of Folklorist Mary Alicia Owen.* Columbia: University of Missouri Press, 2012.

Onahan, William J. "Random Recollections of Sixty Years in Chicago." *Transactions of the Illinois State Historical Society for the Year 1916:* 79–88.

O'Neill, William J., ed. *Catholic Directory of Illinois 1906–1907.* Chicago: O'Neill, 1907.

Organ, Minnie. "History of the County Press of Missouri." *Missouri Historical Review* 4 (1910): 111–33, 149–66, 252–308.

O'Shaughnessy, Francis. "General James Shields of Illinois." *Transactions of the Illinois State Historical Society 1915:* 113–22.

O'Shaughnessy, James. "A.A.A.A. Service to Advertising in Past Rewarded by Prospect of Big Year Ahead. Members of American Association of Advertising Agencies Will Place More Business in 1921 than They Have in 1920." *Advertising and Selling* (Dec. 25, 1920): 14.

——— . "Advertising Agencies and the Farm Press." An address at the annual meeting of the Agricultural Publishers Association, Chicago, Oct. 15, 1925. Special Bulletin No. 96 of the Agricultural Publishers Association, Nov. 4, 1925 (University of Illinois Urbana-Champaign, Agricultural Communications Documentation Center, C24911).

——— . "Constructive Cooperation." In *The Advertising Year Book for 1925,* ed. N. T. Praigg, 84–86. New York: Doubleday, 1925.

——— . "Getting National Advertising for the Country Newspaper." *University of Missouri Bulletin,* 26, no. 26 (1925), 13–16.

——— . "The Meal Ticket of American Art." *Printers' Ink,* Apr. 24, 1924.

——— . "Modern Advertising and Modern Printing." *Advertising and Printing* (Nov. 1912): unpaginated.

——— . "More Money for Advertising." *Advertising and Selling,* Aug. 21, 1929: 28, 66.

——— . *Paving Knowledge.* Chicago, 1917.

O'Shaughnessy, Thomas A. ("Gus"). "250th Anniversary of the Arrival and Sojourn of Father Marquette on the Site of Chicago: an Artist's View." *Illinois Catholic Historical Review* 7, no. 1 (July 1924): 210–11.

——— . "Window Story of the Springfield Cathedral." *Diocesan Diamond Jubilee and Cathedral Dedication, 1853–1928.* Springfield, IL: Diocese of Illinois, 1928, 47–54.

Overland, Orm. *Immigrant Minds, American Identities: Making the United States Home, 1870–1930.* Urbana: University of Illinois Press, 2000.

Parker, James. *Rear-Admirals Schley, Sampson and Cervera: A Review of the Naval Campaign of 1898, in Pursuit and Destruction of the Spanish Fleet Commanded by Rear-Admiral Pascual Cervera.* New York and Washington: Neale, 1910.

Parrish, William E. *A History of Missouri, Volume 3, 1860 to 1875.* Columbia: University of Missouri Press, 2001.

Payton, Leland, and Crystal Payton. *Mystery of the Irish Wilderness: Land and Legend of Fr. John Hogan's Lost Irish Colony in the Ozark Wilderness.* Springfield, MO: Lens and Pen Press, 2008.

Plat Book of Chariton County, Missouri. [Minneapolis, MINN]: North West Publishing Co., 1897.

Presbrey, Frank. *The History and Development of Advertising.* New York: Doubleday, Doran and Co., 1929.

Press Club of Chicago. *Official Reference Book.* Press Club of Chicago, 1922.

Quinn, David B. *Ireland and America: Their Early Associations, 1500–1640.* Liverpool, UK: Liverpool University Press, 1991.

Quinn, Dermot. *The Irish in New Jersey: Four Centuries of American Life.* New Brunswick, NJ: Rutgers University Press, 2006.

Quinn, Peter. *Looking for Jimmy: A Search for Irish America.* New York: Overlook Press, 2007.

Rafter, Kevin, ed. *Irish Journalism before Independence: More a Disease than a Profession.* Manchester, UK: Manchester University Press, 2011.

Rasmussen, R. Kent. *Critical Companion to Mark Twain: A Literary Reference to His Life and Work.* 2 vols. New York: Facts on File Inc., 2007.

Ray, Nina M., and K. Gary McCain. "Taking the 'Sham' out of Shamrock: Legacy Tourists Seek the Real Thing." In *European Advances in Consumer Research* 6, ed. Darach Turley and Stephen Brown, 54–59. Provo, UT: Association for Consumer Research, 2003.

Redmond, John E. *The Chicago Convention.* "The Irish Question" series, no. 3. London: Irish Press Agency, 1886.

Rhodes, Leara D. *The Ethnic Press: Shaping the American Dream.* New York: Peter Lang, 2010.

Richards, Jeffrey H. "Brogue Irish Take the American Stage, 1767–1808." *New Hibernia Review* 3, no. 3 (Autumn 1999): 47–64.

Roberts, Garyn G. *Dick Tracy and American Culture: Morality and Mythology, Text and Context.* Jefferson, NC: McFarland, 2003.

Roberts, Randy, and Carson Cunningham. *Before the Curse: The Chicago Cubs' Glory Years, 1870–1945.* Urbana: University of Illinois Press, 2012.

Rodechko, James P. *Patrick Ford and His Search for America: A Case Study of Irish American Journalism, 1870–1913.* New York: Arno Press, 1976.

Roosevelt, Franklin D. "You Cannot Robotize Advertising: Its Tools Are Human Brains and These Can't Be Monopolized." *Printers' Ink* (June 18, 1931): 44.

Russell, Charles E. *Bare Hands and Stone Walls.* New York: Scribner, 1933.

[Rutt, Christian L.] *The Daily News' History of Buchanan County and St. Joseph, Mo. from the Time of the Platte Purchase to the End of the Year 1898. Preceded by a Short History of Missouri. Supplemented by Biographical Sketches of Noted Citizens, Living and Dead.* St. Joseph, MO: The St. Joseph Publishing Company, 1898.

Saloga, Jean. "Treasure Shines in Stained Glass." *Chicago Daily Herald,* Dec. 21, 1990.

Schmidt, John R. *"The Mayor Who Cleaned Up Chicago": A Political Biography of*

William E. Dever. DeKalb: Northern Illinois University Press, 1989.

Schrier, Arnold. *Ireland and the American Emigration 1850–1890*. Minneapolis: University of Minnesota Press, 1958.

Shanabruch, Charles. *Chicago's Catholics: The Evolution of an American Identity*. Notre Dame, IN: University of Notre Dame Press, 1981.

Shaughnessy, Edward L. *Down the Nights and Down the Days: Eugene O'Neill's Catholic Sensibility*. Notre Dame, IN: University of Notre Dame Press, 1996.

Sheehy, Jeanne. *The Rediscovery of Ireland's Past: The Celtic Revival, 1830–1930*. London: Thames and Hudson, 1980.

Shovlin, Frank. *Journey Westward: Joyce, Dubliners and the Literary Revival*. Liverpool, UK: Liverpool University Press, 2012.

Simpson, Wendell L. "After Action Report, 3rd Brigade, 1st Division, Fifth Army Corps, to Adjutant-General First Division, Fifth Army Corps." (Fort San Juan, July 5, 1898). http://www.history.army.mil/html/documents/wwspain/buffalos_sjh/3bde1div5cps.html.

Skerrett, Ellen. "A Canvas of Light: Tracing the Artistic Vision of Thomas O'Shaughnessy." *American Catholic Studies Newsletter*, 41, no. 1 (Spring 2014): 8-11.

——— . "The Catholic Dimension." In *Irish in Chicago*, ed. McCaffrey et al., 22–60.

——— . "The Development of Catholic Identity among Irish Americans in Chicago, 1880–1920." In *From Paddy to Studs*, ed. Meagher, 117–38.

——— . "Irish." In Chicago Historical Society, *Encyclopedia of Chicago*.

Skerrett, Ellen, ed. *At the Crossroads: Old St Patrick's and the Chicago Irish*. Chicago: Wild Onion Books, 1997.

Skerrett, Ellen, and Mary Lesch, eds. *Chief O'Neill's Sketchy Recollections of an Eventful Life in Chicago*. Evanston, IL: Northwestern University Press, 2008.

Smith, Richard N. *The Colonel: The Life and Legend of Robert R. McCormick, 1880–1955*. Evanston, IL: Northwestern University Press, 2003.

Smythe, Colin, ed. *Robert Gregory 1881–1918: A Centenary Tribute*. Buckinghamshire, UK: Colin Smythe, 1981.

Smulyan, Susan. *Popular Ideologies: Mass Culture at Mid-Century*. Philadelphia: University of Pennsylvania Press, 2007.

Sperber, Murray A. *Shake down the Thunder: The Creation of Notre Dame Football*. Bloomington: Indiana University Press, 2002.

Stoddart, Charles H. "Chicago — Wonder City of Advertising." *Advertising and Selling*, Sept. 25, 1920: 15–18.

Stoltzfus, Duane C. S. *Freedom from Advertising: E. W. Scripps's Chicago Experiment*. Urbana: University of Illinois, 2007.

Stone, Melville E. *Fifty Years a Journalist*. Garden City, NY: Doubleday, 1921.

Sullivan, William L. *Dunne: Judge, Mayor, Governor*. Chicago: Windermere Press, 1916.

Tarbell, Ida M. "How Chicago Is Finding Herself." *Christmas American Magazine*, Nov. 1908.

T[aylor], S[ue]. "Thomas A. O'Shaughnessy." In *Imagining an Irish Past*, ed. Edelstein, 154–55.

Thackeray, W. M. *The Works of William Makepeace Thackery, with Biographical Introductions by His Daughter, Anne Ritchie, in Thirteen Volumes: Volume 5. Sketch Books.* New York: Harper, 1898.

Thompson, Joseph J. *A History of the Knights of Columbus in Illinois.* Chicago: Universal Press, 1921.

Towey, Martin G. "Kerry Patch Revisited: Irish Americans in St. Louis in the Turn-of-the-Century Era." In *From Paddy to Studs*, ed. Meagher, 139–59.

Underwood, Doug. *Chronicling Trauma: Journalists and Writers on Violence and Loss.* Urbana: University of Illinois Press, 2011.

Vaughn, Stephen. *Encyclopedia of American Journalism.* New York and London: Routledge, 2008.

Vaughn, Stephen L. *Holding Fast the Inner Lines: Democracy, Nationalism and the Committee on Public Information.* Chapel Hill: University of North Carolina Press, 1980.

Waller, Alexander H. *History of Randolph County, Missouri.* Topeka, Cleveland, OH; Historical Publishing Co., 1920.

Walsh, James J. *The World's Debt to the Irish.* Boston, MA: Stratford, 1926.

Ward, Alan J. "America and the Irish Problem, 1899–1921." *Irish Historical Studies* 16, no. 61 (Mar. 1968): 64–90.

Ward, Archie. *Frank Leahy and the Fighting Irish: The Story of Notre Dame Football.* New York: Putnam, 1944.

Watt, Stephen. "Irish American Drama of the 1850s: National Identity, 'Otherness' and Assimilation." In *Fleeing the Famine*, ed. Mulrooney, 97–109.

Webb, Jim. *Born Fighting: How the Scots-Irish Shaped America.* New York: Broadway Books, 2004.

Weil Davis, Simone. *Living up to the Ads: Gender Fictions of the 1920s.* Durham, NC: Duke University Press, 2000.

Wendt, Lloyd. *Chicago Tribune: The Rise of a Great American Newspaper.* Chicago: Rand McNally, 1979.

Wendt, Lloyd, and Herman Kogan and Bette Jore. *Lords of the Levee: The Story of Bathhouse John and Hinky Dink.* 2nd ed. Evanston, IL: Northwestern University Press, 2005.

White, Trumbull, and William Igleheart. *The World's Columbian Exposition, Chicago.* Chicago and Philadelphia: International Publishing Co., 1893.

Yeats, William Butler. *Autobiographies.* London: Macmillan, 1955.

———. *The Celtic Twilight.* 2nd ed. London: Bullen, 1902.

———. *A Selection from the Poetry of W. B. Yeats.* Leipzig: Tauchnitz, 1913.

Yeats, William Butler, ed. *Fairy and Folk Tales of the Irish Peasantry.* London and Felling-On-Tyne: Walter Scott, [1888].

Manuscripts/Typescripts

AAAA (4AS), NEW YORK

"Genesis of the American Association of Advertising Agencies." Ed. Richard Turnbull (then a Senior VP of the AAAA), 1969. Typescript with copies of clippings.

"Marshalling the Forces of Advertising in the National Interest 1917–1920 through the Division of Advertising of the U.S. Committee on Public Information and the Advertising Agencies Corporation Subsidiary of the A.A.A.A." Ed. Richard Turnbull, June 1969.

"Decennial Anniversary of the New York Council, American Association of Advertising Agencies, Apr. 13, 1921, Hotel Commodore, New York City." Transcript reproduced in Genesis of AAAA (AAAA MS), Appendix, 51–52. [incl. reference to column headed "Jim" on Editorial Page of New York *Herald* "about two or three days ago."]

"Minutes of the Second Annual Meeting of the American Association of Advertising Agencies, Oct. 1918." Printed.

"Minutes of the Fifth Quarterly Meeting of the Executive Board, AAAA, New York, Oct. 8, 1918." Typescript.

ASSOCIATION FOR DIPLOMATIC STUDIES AND TRAINING

Foreign Affairs Oral History Project. Ambassador William Howard Taft III interviewed by Charles Stuart Kennedy, Apr. 30, 1987. http://memory.loc.gov /service/mss/mssmisc/mfdip/2005%20txt%20files/2004taf02.txt.

CHICAGO CITY COUNCIL

Record relating to Irish Fellowship Club and James O'Shaughnessy. City Council, Chicago, "Journal," Oct. 3, 2001. Online. http://www.chicityclerk.com /journals/2001/oct3/oct3_2001_part3.pdf.

CHICAGO HISTORY MUSEUM

Roger T. Faherty Papers [manuscript], 1910–1965 (formerly "Irish Fellowship Club of Chicago records"). MSS Lot F.

Irish Fellowship Club of Chicago: Its History and Objectives, 1902–1953. Rare pamphlet. [16] p. : ill., map ; 22 cm. Call no. F38JR .I6I6H.

CHICAGO PUBLIC LIBRARY

Order Sons of Italy. Bulletin of the Illinois lodge of the Order Sons of Italy, Apr. 1937. In "Chicago Foreign Language Press Survey [microform]: Italian." Facsimile at http://www.archive.org/details/5425702_1.

DUKE UNIVERSITY

David M. Rubenstein Rare Book and Manuscript Library

American Association of Advertising Agencies, Records, 1918–1998. Administration Files. Boxes AF2, AF3 and AF7.

James O'Shaughnessy Papers, 1888–1936. Boxes 1–3.

J. Walter Thompson [J.W.T.] Company Archives, Newsletter Collection, 1910–2005: Peregrine Acland, "It Takes Too Much Time to Sell Bulk Goods." (Sept. 1925).

J. Walter Thompson Company Archives, Newsletter Collection, 1910–2005: Peregrine Acland, "Make a Sale Every Time You Get an Interview." News Bulletin, June 1926.

J. Walter Thompson [J.W.T.] Company Archives, Personnel Files: Box 1, Folder Acland, Peregrine, 1925.

EPISCOPAL DIOCESE OF CHICAGO

St. Stephen's Episcopal Church. Box A1146.

Catalog of Treasures of Poetry and Art in St. Stephen's, the Little Church at the End of the Road. 3533 North Albany av, Chicago. Typescript.

GALWAY PUBLIC LIBRARY, IRELAND

Ordnance Survey Name Books, sub. "New Hall" and "New Hall House," County Galway. Database at http://places.galwaylibrary.ie/default.html.

US NATIONAL ARCHIVES AND RECORDS ADMINISTRATION

James O'Shaughnessy, Passport Application. National Archives and Records Administration, Washington D.C. *Passport Applications, Jan. 2, 1906 — Mar. 31, 1925;* Collection Number: *ARC Identifier 583830 / MLR Number A1 534;* NARA Series: *M1490;* Roll #: 2532. Accessed via ancestry.com.

NATIONAL ARCHIVES OF IRELAND

USA: Visit by Ministers 1928. Cabinet File. Dept. of the President. (National Archives of Ireland, S. 4529). Mainly correspondence from/to Timothy A. Smiddy, Washington, DC, 1925–1928.

NATIONAL LIBRARY OF IRELAND

Eugene O'Growney to Eoin MacNeill (NLI MS 10,875). These fifteen files include MacNeill's recollections in English of O'Growney (no. 2, ostensibly for a 1942 broadcast in Irish) and a sketch by O'Growney, (no. 4, perhaps of the Aran Islands).

Gregory, A. "Why the Irish Love Ireland." US syndicated article. Copy at NLI MS L.195. Apparently based on a lecture of which New York Public Library has the original typescript, with the author's manuscript corrections, dated Feb. 1912 (NYPL, Lady Gregory collection of papers,1873-[1965] bulk (1873–1932)).

Finerty to Redmond, Mar. 3, 1903, May 10, and June 28, 1924. In Papers of John Redmond (NLI MS 15,236/7). See also Ward, "America and the Irish Problem," 65.

NATIONAL UNIVERSITY OF IRELAND, GALWAY

Moore Institute, NUI Galway, Landed Estates Database sub "Estate: O'Shaughnessy (Gort)" http://www.landedestates.ie/LandedEstates/jsp/estate-show.jsp?id=928.

OLD ST. PAT'S CHURCH, CHICAGO

Letter from Bernard E. Gruenke Jr., Conrad Schmitt Studios, Inc., to George Maher re: restoration work.

UNIVERSITY OF ILLINOIS

"Advertising Agencies and the Farm Press." An address by James O'Shaughnessy at the annual meeting of the Agricultural Publishers Association, Chicago, Oct. 15, 1925. Special Bulletin No. 96 of the Agricultural Publishers Association, 4 Nov. 1925 (University of Illinois Urbana-Champaign, Agricultural Communications Documentation Center, C24911).

Bernard J. Mullaney, "Public Relations in the Public Utility Industry," Lecture Series Publication, May 24, 1924 (University of Illinois, 9/1/809).

Irwin St. John Tucker Papers (Special Collections, Richard J. Daley Library).

UNIVERSITY OF MISSOURI

Plat Books of Missouri. A collection of 114 books showing subdivisions of land in Missouri counties, W.W. Hixson and Co. Although the year of publication is unclear, it is thought to be late 1920s to early 1930s. Copies in Collections Department, Ellis Library, University of Missouri-Columbia and St. Louis Public Library.

UNIVERSITY OF NOTRE DAME

Correspondence from/to James, Francis, Thomas (Gus) and Martin O'Shaughnessy to/from Notre Dame's presidents Andrew Morrissey, Matthew Walsh, Charles O'Donnell, 1897–1934. CJWC 8/02, 8/03; UPCO 6/123–7; UPEL 55/17, 55/26, 55/28, 61/40, 66/16, 74/05, 74/07, 74/11, 74/18, 111/10; UPWL 16/44, 16/47.

Official Site of Notre Dame Athletics: Men's Basketball http://www.und.com /sports/m-baskbl/archive/nd-m-baskbl-a-coaches.html (2013).

Thomas A. O'Shaughnessy papers, 1892–2009. CTAO 1–8.

Websites

Ancestry.com (as a gateway to facsimiles of census returns of various dates, passport applications, passenger lists, Missouri marriage records, etc.)

Findagrave.com. This supplements information available from census records.

O'Shaughnessy, M. "Un mundo viejo," blog archive of "seanmiguel" (Michael O'Shaughnessy) at http://unmundoviejo.blogspot.com/search?updated -min=2007–01–01T00%3A00–08. Michael O'Shaughnessy was a descendant of John (attorney brother of James the journalist and adman). I am grateful to Michael's widow, Marianne, for drawing this blog to my attention.

Paletteandchisel. "Mucha Night, Guest Book 1906." http://paletteandchisel .wordpress.com/2012/05/19/mucha-night-guest-list/.

Index

Hecht, Charles, 30
Henning, Arthur Sears, 38–41, 220
Hering, Frank E., 57
Hibernia Fire Insurance Company,
Illinois, 122
Hickory Branch, Missouri, 7
Hoffman, Aaron, 140–41
Hogan, John J., 1–2, 5–13, 170–72,
227–31
Holland. *See* Netherlands, the
Hopkins, John, 179
Hopper, Edward, 141
Hoover, Herbert, 151, 199
Hoover, J. Edgar, 159
Houston, Herbert, 127
Howard County, Missouri, 14
Hungary, 173
Hurley, Edward, 193, 195
Hyde, Douglas, 168, 169
Hynes, Aimee, 179, 182
Hynes, Mary, 118, 168, 179, 257n20
Hynes, Mary (Máire Ní Eidhin) 167–69,
253n12
Hynes, Tommy, 168

Illinois: state, 15, 26, 29, 53–54, 65, 76–78,
83, 96, 99, 107–8, 117, 155, 160, 179, 190,
219; University of, 176, 254n43
Illinois and Michigan Canal, the, 4, 23,
66, 74
Illinois bishops, 79
Illinois Chamber of Commerce, 111, 113
Illinois Council of Defense, 48
Illinois Foundation for Gaelic Studies,
175–76
Illinois "Irish Brigade," 157
Indiana, 4, 55, 82, 128, 154
Indiana Spring Company, 122
Indians. *See* Native Americans

Inland Press Association, 207
Inland Printer, 103
Insull, Margaret (Gladys Wallis), 48
Insull, Martin, 70
Insull, Samuel, 48, 70, 179
International Congress of Women, 94
Iowa, 15, 118, 233
Ireland's Fight for Freedom, 136
Irish American Heritage Museum,
Chicago, 86
Irish Association of Advertising
Agencies, 185–87
Irish Fellowship Club, Chicago: and
anniversary celebrations, 210–11; and
Cosgrave visit, 188–99; politics of,
70–73, 88, 191; Foundation, 74–80;
and Fairbanks visit, 80–83; and Taft
visit, 83–88
Irish Fellowship Foundation, Illinois,
175–76
Irish Independent, 181, 182, 185, 198, 200
"Irish Wilderness," Missouri, 6
Irish World (New York) 80, 130
Iroquois Theater, Chicago, 96
It Pays To Advertise, 141

J. Walter Thompson Company, 138, 142,
201, 205
Jackson Park, Chicago, 90, 99
Jacob's Biscuits, 181
James, Jesse, 16
Jameson, Annie, 40
Jesus, 148, 208, 229
Johns, William H., 129, 132–35, 142, 200,
250n88, 251n99
Johnson, Albert, 19–22, 23, 26–27, 53, 118,
204, 221
Johnson, Edmond, 90
Johnson immigration law, 22

Lightning Source UK Ltd.
Milton Keynes UK
UKOW04n2115120215

246176UK00002B/22/P